VOYAGE OF THE
SOUTHERN SUN

AN AMAZING SOLO JOURNEY
AROUND THE WORLD

MICHAEL SMITH

with Aaron Patrick

Black Inc.

For Anne, Jack and Tim
Mum and Grandma

Published by Black Inc.,
an imprint of Schwartz Publishing Pty Ltd
Level 1, 221 Drummond Street
Carlton VIC 3053, Australia
enquiries@blackincbooks.com
www.blackincbooks.com

National Library of Australia Cataloguing-in-Publication entry:
Smith, Michael, 1968– author.
Voyage of the Southern Sun: an amazing solo journey around
the world / Michael Smith; Aaron Patrick.
9781863959308 (paperback)
9781925435801 (ebook)
Smith, Michael – Travel.
Voyages around the world.
Travel – Anecdotes.
Patrick, Aaron, author.

Cover design by Peter Long
Text design and typesetting by Tristan Main
Maps and illustrations: Greg Ure

Printed in Great Britain by Clays Ltd, St Ives plc

FSC
www.fsc.org
MIX
Paper from
responsible sources
FSC® C001695

Contents

Foreword   1

Prelude

1. The Descent   5
2. The Founder   15
3. Empire of the Sun   27
4. Inception   33

Act i

5. Thunderbirds Are Go   43
6. Wake in Fright   53
7. The Year of Living Dangerously   63
8. In the Heart of the Sea   73
9. Catch Me If You Can   83
10. A Passage to India   89
11. The Viceroy's House   99
12. The Kingdom   107
13. Rock the Casbah   123
14. Behind the Glass   131
15. Casino Royale   139
16. The Flying Squad   147
17. The Trip   157

Act ii

18. The Year My Voice Broke 163
19. Dumb and Dumber 169
20. A Good Year 175
21. Midnight Sun 183
22. The Village at the End of the World 191
23. Saved by the Sun 201
24. Canadian Bacon 209
25. Sully 219
26. Key Largo 229

Act iii

27. The Adventures of Huckleberry Finn 237
28. Call of the Wild 249
29. The Odyssey 259
30. Castaway 269
31. The Way Back 277
32. The Secret Life of Walter Mitty 285
33. The Right Stuff 293
34. The Terminal 303
35. The Final Countdown 311
36. Australia 319
37. The Wizard of Oz 329
38. The Way 335

Credit Roll 341

Post-credits Scene: Flying High 344

Foreword

Legendary Australian explorer Dick Smith thinks Michael Smith was unusually optimistic to fly around the world in a plane the size of a Mini. 'He's lucky to be alive,' he says.

When Michael set off in early 2015 for London in an experimental amphibian plane, he had around 450 hours of flying experience. There are commercial pilots with more than 10,000 hours in the cockpit who wouldn't have risked the trip, which required long flights over oceans and deserts, the likelihood of tropical monsoons and some of the most crowded airspace on the planet. Michael, an advanced beginner, wasn't even qualified to fly by instruments. His aircraft, a Searey, was designed in Florida twenty years earlier as a cheap weekender for lake-hopping amateur pilots.

An engineer by training and an entrepreneur by temperament, Michael built in long-range fuel tanks and a satellite tracking system so his family and friends could follow him online, although he told almost no one about his plans. Amazingly, he didn't install an autopilot, standard in every commercial aeroplane manufactured today, and most private ones. Probably no one has flown from Melbourne to London entirely manually for decades. Only a handful of modern adventurers have flown the whole way around without these basic technical aids.

In an era when no part of the world is unexplored, and most records seem to have been broken, it's perhaps hard to appreciate Michael's achievement of becoming the first person to fly solo around the world in an amphibious plane. An indication of the difficulty of the circumnavigation is that no one had done it until Michael in 2015, a full 112 years after the birth of powered flight. The challenge is logistical, geographical and bureaucratic, in a craft by design intended for short flights. The long distances require meticulous planning and a significant financial investment. Crucially, Russia is reluctant to give foreign pilots access to its airspace, making it even harder to cross the Pacific Ocean from either direction. Using Google Earth to find an uninhabited island, Michael decided to try a never-before-taken route: from Alaska to Japan. With days to go before the weather shut out his hope of making aviation history, he set out on a flight he knew could cost him his life. Coincidentally, the first pilot to cross the Pacific was another Australian named Smith: Sir Charles Kingsford Smith, in 1928, who later died while flying from England to Australia, aged just thirty-eight.

As a professional writer and fellow pilot, I was eager to help Michael tell his story. He was reluctant at first to describe some of his traumatic experiences, including a near crash off the Canadian coast. Eventually, he acknowledged that a faithful account had to include the good and the bad, no matter how painful or embarrassingly revealing it might be.

This isn't a traditional adventure story. Michael is fascinated by people, food, cinemas, landscapes, history and movies. He learned about each as he travelled around the globe. By the end of the trip he had realised what was most important to him: community. In a world that seems more troubled by the year, Michael's discovery of the generosity of strangers and the universality of human values is inspiring to us all, aviators and others alike.

Aaron Patrick
July 2017

Prelude

'Everything I learned I learned from movies.'
AUDREY HEPBURN, 1929-1993

1.

The Descent

'Every man dies. But not every man really lives.'
WILLIAM WALLACE, *BRAVEHEART* (1995)

Contrails high in the stratosphere above me marked the routes of the regular trans-Atlantic passenger flights. Thousands of men, women and children were travelling in giant sealed tubes, entirely oblivious to me inching along beneath them. I wasn't envious of the A380s, 747s and 777s streaking across the sky, even if their unreachable presence amplified my isolation. Eighty years earlier, only a privileged few would have been flying this route, lower and slower, and in a craft akin to my own, if a tad larger. If my plane and courage held up, I would fly into aviation history as the first person to circumnavigate the earth solo in an amphibious plane – a flying boat, in fact.

I admired the explorers of days past, who pushed the limits of their equipment and themselves. Long before Facebook and Twitter, their triumphs only became known when – or if – they returned home. My journey was personal. I had no sponsors or publicity machine because I felt those came with a heavy price: additional stress and pressure that I wanted to avoid. I was quietly making, and paying, my own way.

I had steered my plane, the *Southern Sun*, west from a long, smooth runway in Greenland's capital city, Nuuk, on a Saturday morning in the middle of the northern summer. A semi-autonomous province of

Denmark, Greenland is a cold and harsh land, effectively a mile-thick block of ice.

Nuuk is beautifully located inside a vast harbour, well protected from the wild Atlantic seas. After arriving on the Friday, I had checked into a hotel in the centre of town, quickly changed my clothes and gone out walking. The Greenlanders were warm and accommodating, and I was fascinated by the old but brightly painted and exquisitely maintained timber buildings, which were dotted among newer concrete structures built to withstand the Arctic weather. The city had one cinema, which doubled as a theatre and public meeting hall.

I'd hoped to spend two nights in Nuuk, which would have given me a day off flying, but all airports in Greenland are closed on Sundays and I felt an inner pressure to keep going. In hindsight, this was absurd. What was the rush?

After taking off, I headed south-west over the Atlantic Ocean. Within several minutes Greenland had disappeared behind me. All I could see was water, sky, scattered clouds and a few contrails. The air was cool and the sky clear. It was perfect weather for flying.

I climbed to 4500 feet, high enough to clear most turbulence but still low enough to make out the white caps on the breaking waves below. It is the highest anyone is allowed to fly westbound across the Atlantic without instrument navigation. I was following what is known as Visual Flight Rules, commonly called VFR, which meant that once clear of an airport, I wasn't being watched or directed by any air-traffic controllers. Legally, I was relying on the same equipment – a map, a watch and a compass – used by Amelia Earhart when in 1932 she became the first woman to fly the Atlantic solo, and by Charles Kingsford Smith, who in 1928 became the first person to fly from the United States to Australia. Of course, I had two huge safety advantages over Earhart and Smith: I always knew where I was, thanks to my global positioning systems (GPS) receiver, and I had a satellite tracking device with an emergency beacon that could summon help, if needed.

Even with this modern safety equipment, though, beginner pilots like me don't normally attempt solo round-the-world flights in planes with one engine. It's like trying to row your way across Europe in a plywood Mirror dinghy. Oh, someone did that … Okay, what about: it's like cycling across Australia on your BMX using Google Maps while wearing an old pair of thongs. You get the idea: it hadn't been done before, because the plane just wasn't intended for such vast distances. But she was the plane I had, and I was rather fond of her.

My radio was a shorter-range VHF model typically used in smaller planes; it could transmit roughly 100 nautical miles, just over an hour's flying distance. Once over the ocean, controllers were out of reach, but sometimes I could hear and make contact with the jets flying above me, depending on our relative positions and the weather. On this day the radio was silent. By mid-morning I was hundreds of nautical miles from land, and I had never felt more alone in the cockpit.

In flying, altitude is time, and time is life. The more time you have, the safer you are. Any extra time you can stay airborne in an emergency can be pivotal. If the engine failed, I would have roughly nine minutes to glide the *Southern Sun* to a suitable landing site. The *Sun* is an amphibian, meaning she can land on the sea or the ground. If the worst happened, I wasn't going to be scouting for empty fields or roads without power lines, the drills that had occupied me in flight school. I would radio a mayday on the emergency frequency, try to judge whether the swell would swamp the tiny plane – if that was likely to happen, I would have to get out as soon as it touched the water – and line up into the wind, so it would serve as a natural brake and cushion the *Sun* just before landing.

Sitting in the cramped cockpit, I was wearing a Gore-Tex drysuit – a wetsuit crossed with wet-weather sailing gear that was designed to keep me dry and warm longer in extremely cold water. The suit's comforting silicone scarf would ensure the icy Atlantic seawater could not get in and freeze me to death straightaway.

Perhaps the long journey had given me a false sense of safety.

Despite the danger, I did not feel any dread. I had chosen to be there. No one had made me do it. My fate was in my own hands. The *Southern Sun* had already carried me halfway around the world, along the edges of bad weather and thunderstorms, through civil wars and fuel shortages. I had flown through the night, exhausted, seen ice form on the wings and threaten to drag me out of the sky, and been intercepted by military aircraft.

Even though I was, by any professional measure, a rookie pilot, I was becoming more and more confident. 'I can do this,' I told myself. Weather is usually calmer and more consistent over ocean than land. There were no mountains or hills. The *Sun*'s Rotax four-cylinder engine consumed twenty litres of fuel an hour, making it terrifically efficient. Even when fully loaded it was lighter than a 1960s Mini Coupé, and much less roomy. If I filled the large gasoline bladder that had replaced the co-pilot's seat, the *Sun* could fly nonstop for twenty-one hours, which is longer than the huge Airbus A380.

Like most small planes, the *Sun* had no weather radar. I relied on the morning weather report each day (today it had indicated good conditions, with some cloud on arrival in Canada) and on looking to the horizon for storms, as sailors have done for centuries. All I had to do was follow a compass heading of 200 degrees and I would reach my destination in around seven hours.

○

Just as I had dared to hope, the flight was near perfect. The notorious North Atlantic weather had stayed away, instead offering glorious skies, little turbulence and tailwinds that propelled the *Southern Sun* towards the safety of North America.

After five uneventful hours I noticed the coast bulging above the horizon. Within ten minutes a thin strip of white sand marking the beach coastline came into view. This was an isolated stretch of Canada.

I could see no towns, houses or harbours. My map showed the land was predominantly flat, with some small hills. But I couldn't see much beyond the beach because of a thick cover of cloud.

The hard part was over. My Atlantic crossing was just over an hour away from completion, the ninety-eighth day of a historic journey that had started half a world away, in Melbourne. All I had to do was make a short flight inland to Goose Bay, a remote but beautiful city known for its mild winters and a popular airport for transatlantic flights. I planned to land, re-provision and sleep.

As I got closer, I realised the cloud was more of a problem than I had hoped. Two bands of cloud hugged the coast and extended inland as far as I could see. One blanketed the ground, making it impossible to navigate using physical landmarks. The other started at around 2000 feet and extended to 4000 feet, just below my current altitude.

Cloud loves land. When flying over water or sailing long distances, often the first indication of land is the cloud that builds over it. As the ground heats each day, soaking up the sun's warmth, it sends moisture towards the heavens to form clouds.

My morning weather report had suggested there would be broken cloud at the airport, meaning fairly heavy but with a few gaps big enough for the *Sun* to find its way through to the ground. But in this part of the world the weather has a habit of doing what it likes.

I had to make an important decision. I could climb higher and fly over the cloud direct to Goose Bay, using my GPS. If there wasn't an opening when I got there, I would have to descend through the cloud to land at the airport, something I was not altogether comfortable with. As a VFR pilot, I wasn't meant to fly through cloud. I had no way of knowing how low it extended.

I tried to radio the airport to ask for help. The staff there would have access to more information about the cloud cover and the safest route in. But I was 200 kilometres away from Goose Bay and no one responded. I had come so far, yet I was still so alone.

I decided to fly between the two cloud banks at 1500 feet. I wouldn't be able to see the ground. My electronic chart indicated I was flying over a peninsula; it would take about twenty minutes to get to Goose Bay. In a flying boat, it is common to drop down and follow a bay or river up to an airport – not only was this a safe way to fly, it also felt to me like a seaplane's natural habitat.

But first I needed to be able to see the land. As I flew on, the band above me seemed to be getting lower, and the cloud below higher. A vice was closing around the *Sun*. A few more minutes and there was no doubt. There was no safe way ahead. The cloud was merging together from above and below.

Not only was I legally not allowed to fly on through cloud, I really didn't want to. Being in cloud is like having sheets of paper taped to the windows: all you can see is white. And if you're not changing speed rapidly, you have no sense of motion. All you can rely on are your instruments. When you're inside a cloud and unable to see the horizon, you can quickly become disoriented. Your sense of up and down deserts you and you can lose control of the plane very quickly. It could be falling out of the sky and you would have no idea.

In my limited training I had been taught how to climb and descend through cloud but not how to fly along inside a cloud. That is for much more experienced instrument pilots. So I had always tried to avoid cloud on the trip, but I had flown up and down through clouds a few times. Even when I'd had time to prepare and focus on the instruments, it had been a huge relief to pop out the other side and into sunlight again.

A statistic drilled into pilots during their training, and in countless magazine articles, is that visual pilots who inadvertently enter cloud have an average life expectancy of just thirty seconds. A cloud could literally kill me, and quickly.

It was time for Plan B. I knew if I followed the coast about 60 kilometres south, I would reach the protected waters where Lake Melville emptied into the sea. I could then follow the shoreline, at tree-top level if necessary, up to Goose Bay Airport, which was located at the water's edge. Taking this route would add about an hour to the trip, but it was for situations exactly like this that I always carried a few hours' worth of spare fuel. I decided to reverse course and head back to the coast. I tipped the *Sun* into a gentle 180-degree turn.

Perhaps I was tired. Maybe it was nerves. Either way, I made a mistake. Pilots sit in the left-hand side of the cockpit, and 180-degree turns should normally be made to the left so you maintain a clear view forwards, sideways and to the rear, in order to watch for other aircraft, clouds or terrain. But rather than follow my training, I did something instinctive for another vehicle. As someone who has been driving on roads in Australia and England all my life, where the driver sits in the right-hand seat, I did a right-hand U-turn straight into a cloud I hadn't seen. All I could see was white. I was blind.

Thirty seconds.

In those first crucial moments I was caught by surprise. I looked out the window again. It was still white. My mind kept telling me: *You have thirty seconds to get out of here.*

'Focus,' I told myself. 'You've trained for this. Get on your instruments, get the plane level, fly due east and you'll reach the coast.'

I looked at the instruments. The plane was almost level but slowly turning. That didn't make sense. I tweaked the controls but couldn't get the plane to fly straight ahead at a constant compass heading, which would give me some breathing space while I worked out how to get out of the cloud.

The *Sun*'s speed was normal but I was still in cloud. Why hadn't I emerged yet? I couldn't see anything. The windows might as well have been painted black. The compass seemed to be turning faster, which suggested I had entered a slow spin to the right, a potential spiral that could end with the aircraft smashing into the ground. I'm still not sure if it was – more likely I was just turning slowly – but my next decision was one of the worst of my life. I kicked hard on the left rudder to counteract what I thought was the spin to the right.

The aircraft jerked. Something was wrong. I could feel the g-forces pulling at my body. I looked up. The windows were still white. I looked down. The artificial horizon, which displays the angle of the aircraft relative to the ground, showed I was banked at 80 degrees – which meant the *Sun* had almost flipped on her side. The *Sun* was accelerating towards the ground. The speedometer hit 129 knots, which was way beyond the maximum speed she was designed to withstand.

I looked out the forward window again. Not only was it still all white, but now the tough plastic windscreen was caving in towards me. The *Sun* was falling so fast she was about to break apart midair.

Thirty seconds.

This was it. I had lost it. I was madly scanning the instruments without reading them. I couldn't take in the information. It was happening too quickly. Images of my wife and sons flashed through my mind, filling me with guilt. I cursed myself. How could an inexperienced pilot from suburban Melbourne fly around the world in a seaplane? It was absurd. I had failed.

I looked out the window and whimpered, to no one other than myself, 'I'm going to die.'

2.

The Founder

'Oh, yes. The past can hurt. But the way I see it, you can either run from it ... or learn from it.'
RAFIKI, *THE LION KING* (1994)

The moment still haunts me.

I was alone at one end of a long table. At the other end were eight lawyers, one a Queen's Council, another hopeful of taking silk. A judge, all-powerful, stared down from a high bench, my life in her hands. I was being sued for $75 million. I could no longer afford to hire legal advisers.

I had no choice but to defend myself in the Federal Court of Australia, the nation's second-highest court. Most people, lawyers included, told me I was out of my mind. I was facing charges that I had abused my position, lied, tried to cheat my partners and exploited people who had trusted me. I accepted that I had made mistakes, errors of judgement. But I wasn't a crook.

I suspect the lawyers opposing me didn't think I would get through the first day, let alone the three weeks reserved for the case. They were almost right. On the first day, while questioning my first witness, the weight of three years of stress crashed over me like a wave. I collapsed to the floor. The judge adjourned the hearing; 'You poor man,' she muttered as she walked out. For me it was the lowest point of what, with many highs and a few lows, had otherwise been a generally successful forty-five years of life.

I grew up east of Melbourne. My father ran a cleaning-chemical business that was successful enough for us to progressively move to better properties every few years. I spent my formative years on an orchard in Seville. From the time I was young, Dad had a strong influence on me. During weekends and holidays I would help him at the chemical factory or on the farm, planting trees, driving tractors and building sheds. Like Dad, I wanted to work for myself, take risks and get my hands dirty.

After three years of a four-year engineering degree at the University of Melbourne, I picked up a summer job as a labourer, erecting cinema screens for Village, a cinema chain which was building new complexes in fast-growing Melbourne suburbs such as Airport West and Dandenong. I was offered four weeks of casual work.

The work was fun and I had always loved films. After four weeks I was offered more work, as there were more cinemas opening across Australia, so I planned a gap year. I would work for six months, then travel for six months, before returning to complete my engineering degree. The six months came and went, and I never quite embarked on my European tour. Instead I took a leave of absence from university and set up a company to design, manufacture and install cinema equipment. Apart from a lot of energy and those few months of erecting screens, my only qualification was running a weekly film night at Ormond College, my university residence.

The movie theatre companies must have liked my enthusiasm and attitude, though, and the business took off. A couple of years later, my girlfriend, Anne, an interior designer, became my business partner. We did it all: screens, sound, projection, curtains, seats. Even projection port windows.

Our timing was perfect. The growing scale of Hollywood blockbusters had helped trigger a boom in multiplexes. We worked for most of the major Australian cinema chains, including Village, Hoyts and Palace, and set up offices in Singapore and London to give us access to the Asian and European markets, which were expanding fast. We helped create hundreds of complexes across thirty countries.

Within three years I was living at our headquarters, an almost-groovy warehouse in the inner-Melbourne suburb of Brunswick. The business was outgrowing the building, and I wanted a more interesting space to work in. I went looking for an old cinema we could use as an office and a large studio space. A retired projectionist I had met at the Nova cinema in central Melbourne, Brian Davis, told me about a theatre for sale near his home. In fact, he had worked there back in the 1960s.

The Sun Theatre had been closed and unloved for eighteen years, and lay forlorn. When it opened in 1938, the Sun was the most luxurious cinema in the area, perhaps an over-ambitious single-screen in Yarraville, a suburb on the 'wrong' side of the river that separates central and eastern Melbourne from the city's western suburbs. Like many of the grand single-screen cinemas of the era, it was able to screen Hollywood's finest fare to a thousand people at one sitting. The introduction of television in the late 1950s dried up the Sun's audiences. She then screened Greek-language movies until the advent of VHS tapes and SBS TV, along with many of the Greeks leaving the neighbourhood, simply left no audience to keep her alive.

A film hadn't graced the Sun's screen for almost two decades when I crawled in through a hole in the back wall. The lead flashing which sealed the edges of the roof had apparently been stolen and sold for scrap, which meant nothing was stopping the rain pouring in, and so the ceilings had collapsed. Squatters had lit fires to keep warm. Hundreds of needles were strewn about the place.

Yet I fell in love. Standing among the debris, I could see only potential. Her art-deco interiors, from a terrazzo-laid foyer to ornate plaster work, even oversized ceramic urinals, were like an architectural time capsule: a physical reminder from another generation that cinema is a grand artform and deserves a worthy home.

Over coffee with Anne, I sketched out a plan on a napkin to restore the Sun to its former glory. Something like $70,000 and a few months should do it, I reckoned. Anne loved my enthusiasm but was sceptical about my budgeting. 'Try five or ten times that,' she laughed, 'just to get started.'

No one lodged a credible offer at an auction organised by the owners, who were desperate to pass on responsibility for the decrepit building. After the auction failed, my modest proposal was quickly accepted. The week after settlement, as we cleaned out the debris, we discovered that the building was riddled with white ants. Every piece of timber would have to be replaced – a huge task. We installed a new roof, using the shed-building skills of my youth, laid a new floor and painted every surface in undercoat so that we could move in and get back to running our business.

○

The Sun was a renovator's dream – or nightmare. Ultimately, restoring it would take many years and millions of dollars. We had to fix the building in stages, only moving onto the next when we had saved up enough money to afford carpenters, labourers and materials.

We never intended the Sun to be a cinema again. The surrounding Yarraville village didn't have any restaurants, and only a single simple cafe. Many shopfronts were closed and empty. Would anyone in this neighbourhood even want a cinema? There didn't appear to be enough affluence to support one.

But film was an important part of my life. After running the film club at Ormond College, I had begun a film society, Cinema Ulysses, which operated first from my warehouse, and then monthly on Sunday nights at 11 p.m. at the Valhalla Cinema in Northcote. A few years after we bought the Sun, we began screening old movies once a month in the upstairs lounge there. The rickety wooden-framed seats were from the 1930s, and we provided blankets made from cinema curtain offcuts because there was no heating. Over the next few years the club became a popular, if quirky, place to see a film. We didn't have a liquor licence, but turned a blind eye to the bottles of wine that patrons snuck in. Soon we were screening several shows every weekend, which we promoted through an amateur-looking yet appealing quarterly calendar, which I took great pride in writing. It became a fixture on the fridges and toilet doors of many homes in the area.

The neighbourhood morphed around us. Like many inner-city working-class suburbs, Yarraville became wealthier as younger professionals took over the last remaining pockets of cheaper housing close to the city. Those young, hip couples wanted entertainment venues. Our weekend screenings were regularly full. On Boxing Day in 2002, Mike Moore's anti-gun documentary *Bowling for Columbine* began screening in Australian cinemas. It was exactly the kind of movie that our neighbourhood wanted: fiercely opinionated but still entertaining. We asked the distributor for a print and scheduled a few sessions over a weekend. When the opening day at the Sun came several weeks later, the queue stretched around the block.

It was at that moment that I knew our once-decrepit warehouse could become a real movie house again. We'd been building cinemas for other people for fifteen years; now it was time to build one for ourselves.

Anne and I had strong opinions about the movie theatre we wanted to build. Having worked on hundreds of cinemas and visited many more, we knew it had to be a community-focused place that was stylish, comfortable and inviting. Local residents needed to think of it as an extension of their lounge rooms – and that included the right to a drink. The local council agreed, and the Sun became the first cinema in the state of Victoria to obtain a liquor licence for the whole building. It was an important victory. Every film is better with a glass of wine.

Our first three screens were opened in 2003 by the Premier of Victoria, Steve Bracks. We took enormous pride in making sure each one had a specific art-deco style. We wanted to offer space and comfort. The smaller cinemas had leather couches. Each auditorium was named after a local theatre icon long since closed.

The first years of operation were tough, but slowly, steadily, the community embraced the Sun. At the same time, our cinema manufacturing business, after fifteen years of steady growth, was struggling. We had work but faced pricing pressures from imported competition, two of our international clients went into liquidation, and I wasn't as focused on it as I should've been.

In 2004, with the newly opened Sun not yet profitable, and with the manufacturing business struggling with dwindling sales, mounting debts and cash-flow issues, things got so tight we had to sell off assets where we could and restructure through administration, which brought great emotional turmoil. Through the grace of people we had worked with for a long time, we were able to come out of administration by finding a buyer for the manufacturing business, with all staff retaining their jobs.

I was proud to have saved the business, but I was unable to meet the demands of a tax burden that became my personal responsibility, and therefore had to declare personal bankruptcy. I have never shared this publicly before. I was and continue to feel ashamed about that time. While I learned a lot and committed to never let that happen again, it would feel deceptive to celebrate the highs of the last few years without being clear about this.

I went back on the tools for a couple of years, erecting screens for other cinemas in order to cover the Sun's losses, and worked hard to ensure that the dream we had for the cinema would come true. We'd come so close to losing everything, and I was determined never to put us in such a position again. As much as we had been thrown some curve balls, I knew it was my seat-of-the-pants management style and lack of long-term planning that had taken us to that point. I had to find a way to balance my sense of fun (and what others would call my entrepreneurial flair) with some sound management techniques. I applied for an MBA program, but at the time couldn't afford the fee so put it off for a few years. In the meantime I read as much as I could. We chipped away at improving the Sun, doing as much of the work ourselves as we could, as the crowds built and funds became available.

A decade after screening *Bowling for Columbine* in the dusty, converted lounge area, the Sun Theatre had eight fully functioning cinema screens, plush leather seating, stylish decor, luscious carpet, a thriving bookshop, Hollywood blockbusters and as many niche movies and documentaries as the best arthouse cinemas in any Australian city. The average patron visited about seventeen times a year – a rate three times better than that of conventional cinemas – making the Sun one of the more popular movie theatres in Australia. We became an integral part of the social and cultural life of Yarraville, which is now one of western Melbourne's most vibrant suburbs. I was proud we had contributed to the social and economic life of our community.

In the mid-2000s, movies started shifting from film to digital. Instead of reels containing thousands of frames of film, movies were now delivered on hard drives containing billions of ones and zeros. Cinemas had to replace their old projectors, technology almost a century old, with high-end computer-driven projectors. To help cover the cost of this expensive transition, the Hollywood movie studios handed over approximately $100 million to the large Australian cinema chains. Independent operators like us were left out.

I was determined to get the same deal for the Sun and other indie cinemas. Without the new technology, our projectors would be limited to showing old movies and the few niche movies still shot on film. We would be out of business in a few years. I could see that the survival of every family-owned cinema in Australia was on the line.

With the support of other independent cinema owners, in 2008 I became the chief negotiator for our sector of the industry. I flew to Los Angeles, Hong Kong and London dozens of times over two years to

negotiate on behalf of the Sun and hundreds of other struggling opera-
tors. Most of the trips lasted one or two days, and I flew economy and
travelled as frugally as possible. I convinced the film studios, which
stood to save hundreds of millions by no longer making film prints, to
contribute $80 million to our independent (mostly family-owned) cin-
emas across Australia for the digital transition. I relished the experience
and the confidence boost it gave me, and I agreed to undertake the
negotiating for no charge other than having my travel costs reimbursed
once the mission was completed.

In 2010, after two years when it looked like a deal was almost
done, arguments broke out over who owned the rights to the money.
Despite my best intentions, it was perceived that I had a conflict of
interest. I owned a cinema and needed the rebate. I was also a director
of a digital projector supply company, with partners and fellow direc-
tors who would benefit from installing the new equipment. A
disagreement arose. I should have stepped back and let someone else
finalise the deal, but I was too proud. I really wanted to finish what I
had started.

A lawsuit unfolded between the two companies claiming to have the
right to the rebate scheme. I got caught in the crossfire and was named
as the third respondent in a $75-million suit because of my dual role
negotiating the deal and also serving as a director of a company installing digital projectors. Ironically, I actually owned part of the company
that was suing me.

The judge found I had acted inappropriately – as a director I had
breached my fiduciary duties to the equipment company – but seemed
to understand what had happened. She observed, during the trial, that 'I
was digging a deeper and deeper hole' I could not climb out of. My situation had almost derailed the entire rebate; frankly, I'd made a real mess
of it. Once I withdrew from the negotiations, two of my fellow independent cinema owners stepped in and completed the deal. Independent
cinemas across Australia now receive the money.

But these were the worst, most stressful years of my life. I was depressed and achieved little in that time. Our cinema business under-performed. My long-term trusted business adviser, John Geilings, said it was the equivalent of a bad divorce – which was ironic, given how steadfastly Anne stood by me, despite the legal mess and my poor emotional state. I was perpetually drained.

The two main companies on either side of the case appeared to have allocated over a million dollars each to the fight. I had much more limited means, and had to be realistic. After having a lawyer and barrister advise me at the beginning of the three years it took to get to court, I could not afford them when I needed them most – at the trial. So I made the tough decision to defend myself in court, an unusual occurrence in such a complex commercial case. I dreaded the beginning of the hearing so much that every delay, although prolonging the agony, quietly pleased me.

The trial was scheduled to run for three weeks. I stayed up most of each night preparing my questions for the next day. I struggled initially to introduce evidence or make convincing arguments that would help my case. But as the third respondent, I really took a minor role and let the two main companies' barristers dominate proceedings.

A few days in, everything changed. The other companies reached a confidential settlement deal, and it looked like the case was over. Relief flooded through me. Then I received awful news: the deal didn't cover me. Now I was personally being sued for the full $75 million – by a company of which I was still a part owner. I felt even more wretched, sitting alone at the far end of a large table, now with two barristers and two solicitors opposing me at the other end. If I lost, I would be ruined financially, professionally and probably emotionally too.

But I'm someone who hates to give up, and now I had no choice but stand up and take control of my situation. Even though the suit and the impersonal legal system had battered my confidence, I had reservoirs of determination and self-belief left. There was no hiding on the sidelines now: it was all on my shoulders.

As the case went on, I started to get the hang of the courtroom. I was learning how to ask the questions that would help prove my arguments. I accepted that I'd had a conflict of interest, but the central legal issue was whether my dual role had hurt anyone financially. I was convinced it hadn't – that the rebate had always been intended for the benefit of the cinemas, not for me or anyone else. Whether I was right was, of course, for the judge to decide.

Even though I had never studied law, or even finished my engineering degree, I could sense that my arguments were working. The judge, Michelle Gordon, who was later promoted to Australia's highest court, seemed to genuinely believe in the right of citizens to represent themselves in court. She was never condescending towards me, and forgave my inadvertent breaches of court etiquette.

By the third week of the trial I believed I had elicited enough evidence through cross-examination that I was making headway. The other side agreed to settle out of court, which meant the judge wasn't required to rule on the case alleged against me.

I hadn't won. But I hadn't lost either. The terms of the settlement do not allow me to disclose any of its details. I came to appreciate and understand that I had made errors while negotiating the deal. Although I didn't agree with the allegations made against me, I accepted that I'd had a conflict of interest and, despite my best intentions, had not handled things correctly. But it was over now.

I woke up the next morning feeling like a new man. The last few days in court had been liberating, and the can-do person I had been before returned.

My passion for work returned too. But I knew things had to change. After the emotional trauma of the court case, I couldn't go on as before. I had to ensure that I would never forget the lessons I'd learned, not just during the awful last three years but through my entire twenty-five years in business. I enrolled full-time in an MBA course, and a month later I began building the Sun Theatre's final cinemas – the seventh and eighth.

The year 2014 was an incredibly challenging but invigorating one. I'd get up at 6 a.m. each day to study, before heading off to work in the late morning for the rest of the day, managing the building works and running our cinemas.

My health, my business and my family had suffered. But despite the turmoil, I felt like a survivor, and I was eager for my next two challenges. One was to complete the Sun Theatre, and that was now well underway. The other was rooted in an idea I'd harboured for years: to re-create one of the most romantic journeys from the dawn of the age of commercial aviation, a solo voyage in a flying boat from Australia to London. There were only two problems: I had little flying experience, and needed an aeroplane.

3.

Empire of the Sun

'*Even the darkest night will end, and the sun will rise.*'
CROWD OF MARCHERS, *LES MISÉRABLES* (2012)

Every amateur historian has their favourite era, and mine was the 1930s. The Sun Theatre's streamlined art-deco architecture reminded me of sleek ocean liners from that decade, when the *Queen Mary*, the flagship of the Cunard-White Star Line, sailed from London to New York City in record time. Settling in at Melbourne's State Library, I researched pre–World War II history for parallels between then and now. When I learned that Qantas began the first passenger flights between Australia and England in 1938, the same year the Sun opened, an obsession began. I spent almost a decade researching what was known as the Qantas Imperial Empire route.

On the eve of a war that would threaten Australia's sovereignty, Qantas was helping advance it by providing the fastest link for people and mail between outposts of the British Empire. It undertook the huge logistical challenge of keeping a small fleet of flying boats – dubbed 'ships that flew' – in service between Sydney and Southampton. This was one of the earliest opportunities for global sightseeing by plane.

The unpressurised aircraft did not fly above 12,000 feet. If they had, the pilots and passengers would have suffered from the lack of oxygen. Flying relatively close to the earth, therefore, clouds and storms posed a constant and unpredictable threat. The Qantas planes traversed Asia,

India, the Middle East and Europe low enough for the passengers to see individual houses. The original pilots – there were three on each aircraft – wore naval uniforms, reflecting the nautical influence of these planes. They relied on compasses, maps and sextants. Knowing their approximate location at all times was the key to staying alive. If they got lost, their chances of getting to safety weren't good.

Ocean liners invested heavily in passenger comforts in the 1920s and 1930s, especially in first class. Qantas had to compete by offering luxury of its own. Only sixteen passengers were accommodated on each flight in its double-decker flying boats, which were similar in size to the modern Boeing 737, which can carry up to 215 people. Tickets from Sydney to London cost the equivalent of the average annual wage at the time. They were more expensive than a first-class passage by sea, a journey that took four times as long. Passengers were assigned lounge chairs that would not have been out of place in my grandmother's house, ate in a dining room and played minigolf on a promenade deck. The flights departed early each morning and flew all day, stopping twice for fuel. Overnight, passengers stayed at some of the world's most luxurious hotels. The flights were more expensive, in relative terms, than flying first-class between Australia and Britain today. It was truly the golden age of air travel.

Yet the service wasn't funded primarily by its rich human cargo. A desire to speed written communications between Great Britain and Australia led both governments to underwrite the development of the planes and the research for the route. Some 1300 kilograms of freight and mail was carried on each flight – more weight than that of the passengers. The Empire Air Mail scheme cut the average turnaround for letters and replies between England and Australia from three to four months to less than a month, an improvement in the late 1930s of equivalent importance to the introduction of public email in the 1990s, not just for individuals but for commerce.

When World War II broke out, the Qantas Flying Boats were requisitioned by the defence department. Soon the route through Indonesia,

Singapore and Malaysia became too dangerous for passenger flights. In the service of the RAAF, the flying boats were deployed to transport mail, dignitaries and military officers from Perth to Ceylon (now Sri Lanka). The secret route, which was conducted in complete radio silence, took an incredible twenty-eight hours. The planes left just before sunrise and landed the following morning, which meant passengers saw the sun come up twice. One of the flight crews decided to create the 'Secret Order of the Double Sunrise', which was awarded to all who flew on these missions.

Overnight, Australians' perception of distance and their connections to the world shifted. Instead of six weeks by steamer, London – the most important city in the world, economically, politically and culturally – was less than a fortnight away. I wished I could have done the trip in 1938, but I was born at least thirty years too late.

Flying boats were for the elite. The Sun Theatre was for the working classes. Both in the 1930s symbolised a new era for Australians: a time when the world became closer, culturally and physically. Anne and I had resurrected the cinema, and next I wanted to find a way to re-create aviation history. Even before I had chosen a plane, I knew what I wanted to call her.

Sir Charles Kingsford Smith famously flew the *Southern Cross* into the history books by crossing the Pacific. I had an idea to modify the symbol of the famous constellation for a highly personalised name. While private planes are rarely named these days, boats almost always are, so I figured a flying boat destined for a grand adventure deserved a name. The sun had by now become a central theme of my professional life. A stylised neon sun rising over the Sun Theatre was our corporate logo. I liked to suggest, half in jest, that the Sun's patrons were worshipping the sun when they gathered as a community to share stories told through film. Thirty kilowatts of rooftop solar panels helped power the building – the sun powering the Sun. We also owned a cinema in the Victorian town of Bairnsdale, and we named it the Sun too. In East Timor we operated a mobile cinema named Loro sa'e, which means 'rising sun' in the indigenous Tetum language. We had invested in a solar farm along the banks of the Murray River, so we could harvest the sun, and even had a small solar-powered electric riverboat, which we christened *Ra*, the name of the ancient Egyptian sun-god. So when I chose a seaplane, it felt appropriate to name her the *Southern Sun*.

Symbolically, the perfect year for the trip would have been 2013, the seventy-fifth anniversary of the opening of the Sun Theatre and of the inaugural Qantas Imperial service. But that was the year of the court case, and my son Tim was in his second-last year of high school. Leaving on an adventure would have been unfair on the family – even if I wasn't embroiled in litigation.

Circumstances were more favourable two years later. The Sun Theatre project was complete. Tim was entering his first year of university. His older brother, my stepson Jack, was studying the final year of his arts degree. For the first time in fifteen years, Anne and I didn't need to get up in time for the school day. As 2014 went on, my aspiration grew into a plan.

Apart from one unavoidable exception and a different starting point, I decided to follow the route of the Qantas pioneers. I would leave from the Royal Yacht Club of Victoria, on the Williamstown foreshore of Port Phillip Bay. I was one of the club's past commodores, and still regularly sailed there on the former America's Cup yacht *Kookaburra*. I planned to fly to London via Rose Bay in Sydney, Longreach and Karumba in Queensland, Groote Eylandt in the Gulf of Carpentaria, Darwin, Dili in East Timor, Indonesia, Singapore, Malaysia, Thailand, Bangladesh, India, Pakistan, UAE, Saudi Arabia, Jordan, Israel, Crete, Italy, France, and Southampton in England.

In Iraq the Empire flying boats had refuelled on Lake Habbaniyah and the Shatt al-Arab river in Basra. Not only did the Iraqi officials deny me permission to land in Iraq, let alone on the lake, I was derided for even asking. Areas around the lake were controlled by the Islamic State movement, which was at war with the Iraqi government and being bombed by Australian, American and British air force pilots. The *Sun*'s engine was the same as those used in Predator drones, which increased the chance of a misidentification.

My plan wasn't simply to fly from airport to airport, or seaport to seaport. I also wanted to visit the same renowned hotels as those adventurous travellers eight decades earlier. Some were the most famous and luxurious in the world, such as Raffles in Singapore. I planned to spend two or three days in each town or city, exploring and soaking up its history.

There was an educational angle too. For my MBA I was required to write a thesis. I had decided to analyse the perceived value of cinema to communities – using a random sample of cinemas that happened to be located along the route of the first passenger flights from Australia to Britain.

It would be a busy trip after a busy year. The Sun's eighth cinema, the Roxy, was ready just in time for the 2014–15 summer holidays, when the theatre was packed with children and teenagers. As well as managing the development, I had spent many evenings for months working out the detail of my route and seeking permission to enter the airspace of each country. As Christmas approached, I made an important decision: I would set off in April 2015.

The Sun Theatre's twenty-year journey to success had prepared me well for the *Southern Sun*'s voyage. I'd always known renovating a run-down cinema was going to be a big project, but initially I hadn't expected to open even one screen. I'd certainly never imagined the cinema could support eight. The development had evolved over time. I have always been willing to see potential and give it a go – but also to change tack when needed, and follow a course that better suited the conditions.

I was confident I could make it – too confident. I believed in my abilities to such an extent that an even grander challenge lurked at the back of my mind – one that I wouldn't express aloud, even to my closest friends. Even to Anne, let alone myself.

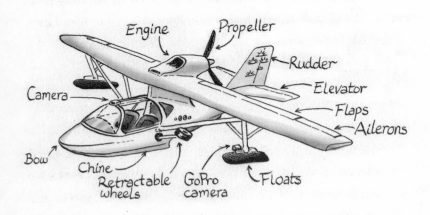

Engine   Propeller

Rudder

Camera   Elevator

Flaps

Ailerons

Bow

Chine

Retractable wheels   GoPro camera   Floats

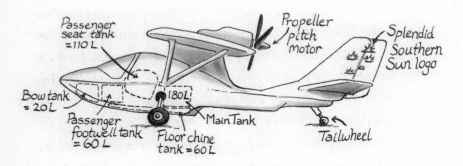

Passenger seat tank = 110 L   Propeller pitch motor   Splendid Southern Sun logo

Bow tank = 20 L

Passenger footwell tank = 60 L   180 L   Main Tank

Floor chine tank = 60 L   Tailwheel

4.

Inception

'What is the most resilient parasite? Bacteria? A virus? An intestinal worm? ... An idea. Resilient, highly contagious. Once an idea has taken hold in the brain, it's almost impossible to eradicate.'
COBB, *INCEPTION* (2010)

I had a plan. I just needed a plane.

Using the internet, I scoured the world for second-hand seaplanes. Even though they carried historical, evocative names – Gooses, Widgeons and Albatrosses, Buccaneers and Renegades – most were decades old. They would require constant maintenance and would be both difficult and expensive for the mission I had in mind. I had to be realistic about my budget, which was not large by aviation standards, and my limited flying experience, which meant I didn't have the skills to fly a sophisticated aircraft, even if that would be safer than the small craft I could afford.

A decade earlier I had owned a second-hand two-seater Searey for a couple of years. It was easy to fly, fairly reliable and could land on water – useful if you were planning to fly over oceans, and lots of fun over lakes and rivers. I contacted Progressive Aerodyne in Tavares, Florida, the company that manufactures Seareys. Progressive's founder, Kerry Richter, had designed the aircraft in 1991. The modestly priced plane wasn't a blockbuster by Cessna standards: about 500 had been built over twenty years. But it was the most successful amphibious aircraft on the market. It could land on water, cruise to the bank, deploy a wheeled undercarriage and drive up onto the land, kind of like James

Bond's underwater Lotus in *The Spy Who Loved Me* (except without the fish smugly dropped out the window).

The Searey's cruising speed is around 80 knots, which is 150 kilometres an hour. In plane terms, that's really slow. The longest single leg on the trip to London would be 800 nautical miles, around 1500 kilometres, which would take ten hours in good weather conditions. For safety's sake, I wanted twelve hours' flying range. The standard Searey's 100-litre tank covers about five hours of flying. Unlike most light aircraft, the fuel is stored in the hull rather than the wings for simplicity and to help keep the plane balanced on water.

Kerry agreed to provide a Searey to my personal specifications. Instead of building a plane from scratch, the company modified an already-assembled prototype for a factory-built version of the kit model. The main change was that the plane needed larger fuel tanks, so it could fly for twelve hours nonstop. Kerry was the only person at the factory who knew I was planning the longest trip ever taken in a Searey. His engineers were told the extended fuel tanks were needed because Australia is such a large country and I wanted one day to fly to New Zealand.

The range could be further extended if you replaced the passenger seat with a large fuel bag, connected by a hose to the fuel system. That seemed an anti-social measure and I didn't expect it would be necessary. Even though this was a solo voyage, I didn't want to give up the extra seat unless it was absolutely necessary. Having a bag of fuel next to you isn't very nice. It is also harder to fill up than a regular tank, and takes up space that can be used to store a bag and your in-flight catering. Having the extra fuel tanks built into the hull would make the cockpit much more pleasant. Kerry and I worked out that a forty-litre fuel tank could be installed on either side of the main tank, which would add four hours' range. The extra tanks would be in the middle of the plane's centre of gravity, which would maintain her finely tuned balance.

But even more fuel would be needed. The Searey's hull is shaped like a boat's, and we worked out that another tank could fit into the bottom of the hull, in the chine between the stringers. A long and slender sixty-litre tank was complicated to build but an elegant solution to my range problem: now I had 5 + 4 + 3 = 12 hours. *Buono!*

The airframe was reinforced to carry extra loads, a strength now standard in every factory-made Searey. I designed the fuel system so it would always feed the engine from the main tank, which would be topped up through hoses from the secondary tanks by an electric pump. Because the fuel tanks that supply an engine can never be allowed to run dry, or else the engine tends to stop, this arrangement extended the aircraft's range a little. Just in case, plumbing was added for a seat-mounted fuel bladder, although one wasn't made at the time because I didn't think I would need it.

We put a lot of thought into the ergonomics and layout of the dashboard. Modern commercial aviation is conducted mainly by autopilot. Because today's airlines are so big and sophisticated, pilots may directly control their aircraft for only a few minutes on a trans-continental voyage. The Searey was low-tech. There would be no autopilot. I would have to control the aircraft for every minute of the trip, which would require me to be mentally alert for hundreds of hours in the semi-reclined seat. I would have to be constantly aware of the aircraft's location, direction and altitude. I would have to think about the weather at my destination, which could be ten hours away, and along the route; I'd also have to communicate with air-traffic control and calculate how much fuel was left. I would have to know what my emergency options were at every moment while airborne. All my body's physical functions would have to be carried out sitting down, often in a sealed drysuit.

Even though the mechanics of piloting the plane would be just like those of the early days of aviation, I would have one big advantage over the pioneers of flight: the GPS information with digital maps would appear on a large electronic screen known as an EFIS. It also showed maps, speed, altitude and an 'artificial horizon' – life-saving information at night or when you're in cloud.

A few back-up instruments would exist in analogue. A little red light would illuminate if the battery stopped charging, which was high on the list of please-god-do-not-happen faults. There would be a built-in radio, of course, and a transponder, which was a legal requirement and would transmit my position to airports and air-traffic controllers. I would keep a spare handheld radio that could be mounted on the dashboard and which I could easily grab if I had to ditch at sea. A satellite tracking device would record my position every fifteen minutes and post it to a website (a device that would have saved much heartache if one had been carried on Malaysia Airlines flight 370, which vanished on 8 March 2014). Like most light aircraft these days, the Searey also had a dash-mounted iPad holder. These tablets are popular with amateur pilots because they are such an efficient way to access information, including maps, flight procedures and airport details.

The *Southern Sun* would be unique in her personalisation. All of Progressive Aerodyne's factory aeroplanes were painted white and dressed up with flashy colour decals. Much to the factory's surprise, I asked for no decals – and the plane was to be painted silver. I wanted her to look like the 1930s Qantas, Imperial and Pan Am planes that inspired the trip. Also, I sourced car-seat leather in Australia and sent it to the factory in Florida, so I would be sitting on not just comfortable but also breathable seats, rather than the vinyl Seareys usually had.

I included one tiny but important piece of equipment that was at the core of my day-to-day living: a universal master key. Progressive Aerodyne normally installed standard aircraft key switches in their planes, but I had another idea.

Years earlier I had started down a path that an observer might say was bordering on obsession of finding 'One Key to Rule Them All'. While restoring the Sun Theatre, it bugged me that so many doors throughout the sprawling building required dozens of keys. At our yacht club, where I was on the committee and Rear Commodore, I had been given a master key, which could open any door or lock. It was magnificent. So I asked the club's security company to visit the Sun Theatre.

We designed a three-level key system, which created different levels of access for me and a few others, depending upon need. There were different keys for different doors, but the master key opened every lock. I loved it so much that a few months later I asked the company to rekey our house too, establishing another chain of keys, but using the same master key as for the Sun. The number of keys I needed was reducing – why stop there? Over the next few years I had our rental properties, our factory and even my mother's house put on the single-key system. Once I had the lock on my bicycle converted, and then finally my car's ignition lock, it was complete. I needed only one key to open or start everything. It was liberating. And so the *Southern Sun* was added to the one-key system too.

I was doing a lot of work in the United States at the time, both in the cinema business and developing solar farms. After a week in Los Angeles, Boston or Knoxville, I would catch a commercial flight to Orlando, drive north to Tavares, and spend the weekend test-flying the Searey. I flew for longer and longer periods, until one day I flew along the coast from Tavares all the way to Key West, at the very southern tip of the state. I circled a few islands and flew back to the airfield, although I didn't land. I still had a few hours' worth of fuel left, and decided to fly an hour north along the beach.

After ten hours of flying, I still had two hours' worth of fuel left. The plane had performed well. When eventually I landed I was physically okay and mentally comfortable. The hours in the seat had not been particularly tiring, and my back was fine. I had emptied my bladder several times into a red bottle with a screw-top lid. (Red as in 'STOP!' – *never drink from the red bottle!*) By the end of 2014 I had a plan, an aircraft and 450 hours' flying experience, which made me an advanced beginner or a fool with a pilot's licence. Experienced commercial pilots have over 10,000 hours.

The factory removed the plane's wings and packed it into a shipping container bound for Australia, where I further tested myself and the aircraft in preparation for departure. From Christmas 2014 through to April 2015, I made small tweaks to the equipment. If I was going to spend hundreds of hours airborne, it was vital that the cockpit was as comfortable and organised as possible.

Some requirements were simple. I had to store three litres of daily drinking water, along with an emergency water supply. A life raft and survival equipment needed to be at hand, but not in the way. I was taking oil, filters, nuts, bolts and other spare parts. In normal operations when flying solo in a Searey (and a number of small aircraft), a small ballast bag of lead shot is placed in the bow to balance the aircraft. This I replaced with bottles of oil and spares. As insurance against headwinds, or in case I had to switch to a longer route on the journey, I designed an extra fuel bladder for the passenger seat's footwell, which kept it well secured and out of the way. That was another sixty litres of fuel, giving me three more hours of range.

One of the great features of the Searey's Rotax engine is that it can use either aviation gasoline (known as avgas) or the same unleaded petrol that is used in cars. I knew the trip might not be feasible without this versatility. Often avgas wasn't available at airports, or was outrageously expensive. Sometimes the quoted price would be over $4 a litre, occasionally even as high as $8, but car fuel was generally less than $1 a litre. I had to buy 180 litres of fuel most days, so the difference for a day's flying could be worth more than $1000. I bought eight twenty-litre fabric collapsible fuel containers, which I could use to pick up fuel from petrol stations. These could be folded up and stored empty on a shelf behind the seat.

There wasn't much room left in the plane, or weight capacity, so I had to scrimp on my personal belongings. I intended to wear flying overalls every day, as I'd been advised you had to wear a uniform to be taken seriously as a pilot at airports through Asia and the Middle East. For streetwear I had a pair of pants with zip-off legs. Every other clothing item was 100 per cent merino wool: five pairs of boxer underwear, two T-shirts, two long-sleeve tops, three pairs of socks and a zip-neck polo jumper. The amazing quality of the merino garments meant they could be worn for a few days before they needed washing, and would provide either coolness in the heat or warmth in the cold. (I'll never understand why we all seemed to spend the last twenty years wearing plastic polar fleeces ...)

A few personal items filled out my small backpack: an iPhone, two iPads and a charger. It was very tough to leave my beloved Leica camera at home. But the latest iPhone had an adequate camera, and I also mounted a Garmin VIRB and a GoPro on the plane to take video. This was to be a personal adventure, not a film shoot, and I knew that if I took too much equipment it would affect how I conducted myself. I wanted the journey to be simple, honest and focused.

One piece of personal equipment was more important than any other: a portable espresso machine. A coffee and a muesli bar early in the morning became an essential part of my daily routine. My days would often start before hotel breakfasts were served, so I travelled with dozens of muesli bars and sixty coffee pods. Why was my morning coffee so important? Well, coffee triggered a morning toilet visit, which meant that when I was flying that day, I only needed a bottle, rather than paper. When you go solo, toilet breaks have to be disciplined.

I'd also been working nonstop on my route, the permissions I needed to enter and land in each country, and where to stay, based on historical records and modern requirements. A lot of the logistical arrangements for the *Sun*'s voyage were carried out by an agent based in York, Mike Gray, of White Rose Aviation. For twenty-five years Mike has been securing flight permits and clearances for private aircraft flying across international borders. Most of this work is for ferry flights – usually for when a plane is bought in one country and needs to be flown to a new owner in another country. Over the years, he has become known as the go-to guy for adventure flights as well. He is very patient and knows whom to contact in governments around the world, and he has a network of ground handlers in each country on call. He was invaluable in the last year of planning, especially for someone who dislikes paperwork as much as I do.

The logistical challenges were daunting. No one had flown a Searey or anything similar from Melbourne to London. I chose not to focus on the difficulties, or even the overall picture. I broke up the task into manageable objectives. I told myself each flight was just another day. That helped me progress, and stopped me focusing on the probability of failing, which was high. The *Southern Sun* and I were ready.

Act i

'The question isn't "What are we going to do?" The question is
"What aren't we going to do?"'
FERRIS, *FERRIS BUELLER'S DAY OFF* (1986)

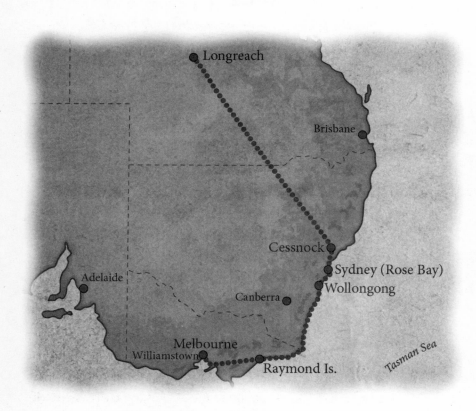

Longreach

Brisbane

Cessnock

Sydney (Rose Bay)

Wollongong

Adelaide

Canberra

Melbourne

Williamstown

Raymond Is.

Tasman Sea

5.

Thunderbirds Are Go

'Roads? Where we're going, we don't need roads.'
EMMETT 'DOC' BROWN, *BACK TO THE FUTURE* (1985)

T he Smith family had a meal together on the morning the *Southern Sun* left for London. After a restless sleep, Anne, Jack, Tim and I sat alone on the deck at the Royal Yacht Club of Victoria, where the *Sun* was waiting inside her yard, fully fuelled and provisioned.

The breakfast was quietly emotional and meant the world to me. It was a Sunday in the middle of autumn. Melbourne was starting to turn cold, although rays of morning light reflected off the clear waters of Hobsons Bay. Boats bobbed back and forth in the foreground, and office towers glinted in the distance. I was leaving a peaceful, familiar world.

Tim, who had just turned eighteen, exuded an understated emotion I had rarely seen in him before. He kept reaching out to touch me across the table. Anne, who had always supported my dreams, no matter how self-focused they were, was affectionate too. She was going to miss me, but wasn't worried for my safety. She didn't even think it was an unusual thing to do; perhaps I hadn't mentioned that no one had done it before. But I was very apprehensive, which I think Tim sensed. Poor Jack had a cold, so his presence meant even more to me. We said goodbye on the boat ramp.

'Have fun, and be safe,' Anne said.

'Please be careful, Dad,' Tim said in his soft voice.

I quietly promised them that I would, hoping it was true. The knot in my stomach told me I was nervous. I felt an overwhelming responsibility to them to return.

They stood back. I climbed into the *Sun* and started the engine, drove down the ramp into the bay and slowly taxied to the end of the marina, all the time worrying over whether I had remembered everything. The manual said the *Sun* had enough power to lift off from the water, even though the plane was carrying more weight than she ever had before. I wasn't certain she would get into the air.

As the last gauge turned green, I looked over to see Anne, Tim and Jack at the end of the marina, waving goodbye. I lined up into the wind and pushed the throttle all the way forward. The *Sun* accelerated smoothly through the water. As she picked up speed, I gently pulled on the stick and she rose into the sky. I circled over my family as I climbed, rocked my wings to bid them farewell, and continued into the sky.

It was the start of a quest ten years in the making, but one that even my closest friends didn't know about. Or my mother. It was time to fess up.

I turned to the east. My first stop was to be Raymond Island, ninety minutes away, in the Gippsland Lakes region of eastern Victoria. My mother had holidayed there as a child, a tradition she passed on to her family. As kids, my brothers and I would get up early on Sunday mornings to watch *Thunderbirds* in bed with our father. Dad passed away much too young many years ago, and Mum retired to Raymond Island with her new partner, Alex. They have six waterfront acres, which they share with kangaroos and koalas. There is no bridge to the mainland. Access is by ferry, boat or – in today's case – aircraft.

I had let Mum know the day before that I might be dropping in. A few minutes into the flight, as I levelled off at 1500 feet, just above the height of the city buildings a few kilometres off to my left, I texted her to say I would be there soon for coffee. I scanned the horizon through the busy airspace over the eastern suburbs of Melbourne. Moorabbin airport was to my south, Essendon airport to my north and Lilydale airport out to the east. But mostly I was still thinking about my family. It occurred to me we hadn't thought to take a family photo with the *Sun* before I left.

After half an hour, the *Sun* settled in at 3500 feet. There was some military airspace near Mum's island, but it wasn't operational on Sundays, which meant I could fly straight to her place. I sent her another message, this time from my iPad. It was a link to the online journal I had set up, which had an entry explaining my plan to fly to London. I suggested she might like to read it before I arrived. I flew over our Sun Cinema in Bairnsdale, and descended towards Raymond Island, following the Mitchell River downstream.

I landed on the waters of Lake Victoria, right in front of Mum's house, lowered the wheels and drove up onto the sandy beach. She was standing on the foreshore, and I saw Alex making his way through the tea-trees. I shut the *Sun* down, climbed out and walked over to Mum. We said hello and I gave her a hug.

'Michael, what are you up to now?' she asked with a worried smile.

Several large kangaroos lay in the sun while we drank coffee on her deck. I explained the dream I'd had for ten years, the planning that had gone into it, and what I was going to do. I expected more questions, but she was subdued. Perhaps it was all a bit overwhelming. As midday approached I needed to keep going, and Mum's farewell was similar to Anne's: 'Have a great trip, but please be careful.'

I later learned that, as I took off from the water, Mum had said to Alex, with a tear in her eye, 'That might be the last time I'll see him.'

~~

The *Southern Sun* followed the stunning yet sparsely populated coast around the south-east corner of mainland Australia at 1500 feet. We passed Gabo Island and some of Victoria's remotest seaside villages.

Whether you're sailing or flying, following the beach from Melbourne to Sydney is not only beautiful, but easy navigation – just keep Australia to your left.

My first night was spent in Wollongong, a small city half an hour's flight from Rose Bay in Sydney Harbour, where the original Qantas flights began. I walked to a local hotel and had a simple and comforting dinner with two Sydney friends, Ian and his partner, Sophie, who'd driven down to meet me. I felt a great relief at finally being on my way. Nonetheless, I was nervous about the landing on Sydney Harbour the following day.

On such a large body of water, strong winds and waves can make landing difficult. To minimise the risk – the winds are usually calmer in the morning – I took off at sunrise, when the air was crisp and a golden light bathed the *Sun*. I followed the coast north, all the way to the harbour. Because of the nearby Sydney airport – named after the first pilot to fly between the United States and Australia, Sir Charles Kingsford Smith – all light aircraft on the coastal route are required to fly along the beaches, at or below 500 feet. The morning was a gorgeous one, so it was like being told to stay up late, watch movies and eat ice cream. If you insist!

The good weather didn't hold, though, and when I was over Port Jackson, the original and little-used name for the water lapping on central Sydney, I saw that the city was enveloped by rain. I flew between the Heads, at the opening to the harbour, and in a gentle arc I passed the Sydney Harbour Bridge and the Opera House on my way back to historic Rose Bay.

The water was choppy but the landing unexceptional. I drove up onto the hard-packed sandy beach. Towering above me were six-storey apartment blocks, populated by people in various states of undress. Some waved. (For the record, the wrong people had little or no clothes on.)

Rose Bay became Sydney's first international airport in the late 1930s. Qantas built a passenger terminal for the London flights, which were undertaken in British-built Short C-class flying boats, better known as Empire Flying Boats. One of Sydney's finer restaurants, Catalina – the name of another famous flying boat – is located right there, over the water. A modern air terminal caters to seaplanes that fly up and down the coast, mostly for tourist sightseers or wealthy Sydneysiders avoiding the beach traffic.

My friend Ian Westlake met me on the beach and gave me a letter to deliver. It was a handmade airmail envelope from his partner, Sophie, addressed to her grandmother in England. Airmail by flying boat had returned. I suddenly wished I'd thought to collect a few more letters to hand-deliver to Old England, in homage to my predecessors.

After a few minutes on land I was back in the *Southern Sun*, taxiing into the water. Apart from several oblivious locals, Ian was the only observer of the official beginning of my attempt to retrace the 1938 Qantas route. He also witnessed my first stupid mistake.

The water was rougher than I had hoped, but not so much that it was dangerous. The *Sun* is designed to lift off at 45 knots; in rough sea, it takes longer to reach that speed because the waves hit the hull and slow her down. If the waves are too big, it can even be impossible to take off, and the aircraft can be swamped.

I taxied out a fair way into the harbour because I wanted ample room to build up speed. Ferries plied their routes in the distance. Just as I was about to line up for take-off, the *Sun* bumped into a sandbar. I felt a shudder go through the plane, but thankfully we passed over it and continued on.

The momentary collision could have been a lot worse. If the water had been just a few inches shallower, the *Sun* might have got stuck. If she'd hit the sandbar while accelerating at full throttle during take-off, the hull could have been damaged, or even holed. It was worrying that, at the symbolic start of my trip, things were already close to going wrong.

Every pilot – amateur, commercial or military – must conduct several basic checks before taking off. In my case they were known by an acronym, GIFFTT, which stood for 'Gear, Instruments, Fuel, Flaps, Trim, Trim' – or, in slightly longer form, landing gear, instruments, fuel pumps, flaps, elevator trim and propeller trim. The wheels had to be up to reduce drag, the instruments had to be working and set correctly, both fuel pumps had to be on, the flaps had to be lowered to make the wings more effective at low speeds, the elevator flaps on the tail had to be trimmed (or adjusted) for climbing, and the propeller had to be angled for maximum thrust. But in a hurry to get started, and flustered by the sandbar bump, I foolishly skipped these essential checks.

The *Sun* ploughed through the harbour into the wind. Everything seemed fine, although she took longer than usual to build enough speed to take off. As she climbed through the sky, I reached for the lever to reduce the amount of flaps, which are used at take-off and landing because they provide more lift, allowing the plane to fly more safely at a slower speed. The lever was already in the upright position. I hadn't extended the flaps, which meant the *Sun* had been forced to go about 10 knots faster than otherwise needed to take off. The higher speed had increased the dangers if she hit a big wave or sandbar. By cutting corners, I had committed one of the ultimate rookie errors in aviation: an inadvertent flapless take-off.

Through gritted teeth, I berated myself. 'I *must* follow procedures and take my time – there really is no rush,' I told myself.

It was an inauspicious beginning.

○

My destination was Longreach, the town where the Queensland and Northern Territory Aerial Services Ltd was founded – the airline that came to be known as Qantas. For me, the day's route would function as a kind of test flight: the 800 miles, nearly 1500 kilometres, was likely to take ten and a half hours. It would be the longest leg of my journey to

London, and the longest of my flying career. I wanted to be on home ground for this physical and mechanical test.

After quickly refuelling at Cessnock, in the Hunter Valley, we climbed easily to 8500 feet, where a tailwind propelled the *Sun* along. We climbed another 2000 feet, where the winds were even more favourable. The original Qantas flying boats generally cruised at around 5000 to 8000 feet. (By contrast, modern airliners operate at around 30,000 feet and above.) It wasn't long before I found that the *Sun's* wings weren't designed to perform in the thinner air. Any lapse in concentration by me at the control stick and she would slip a few hundred feet, which was neither professional nor efficient flying. I found it easier back down at 8500.

To my frustration, I discovered the propeller couldn't be adjusted in flight because of some fault. Altering the angle of the blades at different speeds can make them more efficient, much like changing gears in a car. I was becoming concerned that the *Southern Sun* wouldn't make it to Darwin, let alone to London. (It turned out the problem was easily fixed by re-crimping a loose cable.)

I arrived at Longreach fifteen minutes before dark, and circled a few kilometres from the field while a Qantas passenger flight landed. The *Sun* had three hours of fuel left, which was incredibly reassuring. Fuel exhaustion was one of the biggest killers of early long-range pilots.

A charmless motel was adjacent to the airport. I checked into a basic room that would turn out to be the most expensive of the trip. I spent the evening quietly; in what would become a typical routine for the journey, I prepared my next day's flight plan and dined alone.

The next morning I walked over to the airport before dawn, refuelled and made another stupid mistake. I dragged a small aluminium ladder to the side of the *Sun*, climbed it and checked the oil level in the engine. There was plenty. Reassured, I got into the plane, performed my pre-flight checks and started the engine. Immediately there was a loud *clunk* from outside the cockpit.

I swung my head from side to side, frantically trying to work out what had happened. There was no sign of anyone or anything around the plane. In the dawn light, the airport was completely still. I shut down the engine and got outside. My heart was racing.

The Searey has a single rear-facing 'push' propeller sticking out from the middle of the wings, which form the roof of the cockpit. Suddenly I realised what had happened: I'd left the ladder next to the engine. Normally I checked the engine oil from the left side of the plane, but this time I had put the ladder on the right, closer to where I'd got it from – but that meant I couldn't see it from my seat, which was on the left of the aircraft. When I started the engine, the propeller hit the ladder. This was a serious mistake. It was only day three.

Luckily, there was only a tiny nick in each of the three blades. If the metal ladder had been just a centimetre closer, the propeller could have been destroyed altogether. Fixing it would have required the whole engine to be overhauled. My trip would have ended on the tarmac at Longreach.

I knew that making a quick lap of the plane – which should be a standard check anyway – would have avoided the mistake. I felt sick, and hugely annoyed with myself. *Who the hell did I think I was, planning this trip? How was I going to make it to London if I kept stuffing up like this?* I spent an hour sanding out the nicks and applying a quick-drying epoxy glue to the tip of the propeller blades. But I was still so flustered that I left my BP fuel card in the bowser. I wasn't looking like a guy capable of flying halfway across the world on his own.

All this was really out of character; I'm usually cautious and methodical. I realised that I was deeply apprehensive about the journey ahead. I simply had to calm down and focus. I made a vow. From then on, the ladder would only go on the pilot's side. No matter how small the job, and no matter how much of a hurry I was in, I would always walk a lap around the *Sun* before take-off. Those thirty seconds could save a lot of time, embarrassment and perhaps my life.

While the epoxy glue set I took a photo of the *Southern Sun* in front of the large historical planes at the Qantas museum: a Boeing 707, a 747 and a Catalina. The morning sun cast a delicious golden hue. The *Sun's* metallic silver paint was glowing. She looked beautiful in front of those beasts of the sky.

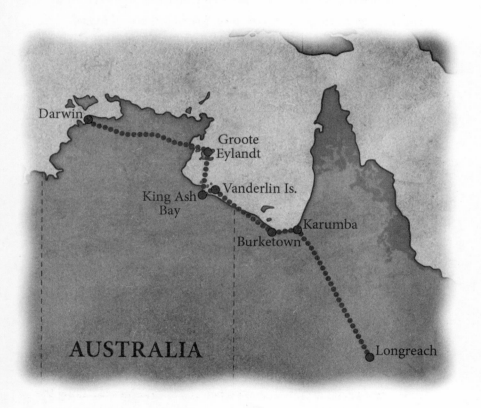

Darwin

Groote
Eylandt

Vanderlin Is.

King Ash
Bay

Karumba

Burketown

AUSTRALIA

Longreach

6.

Wake in Fright

*'To see the world, things dangerous to come to, to see
behind walls, to draw closer, to find each other and to feel.
That is the purpose of life.'*
WALTER MITTY (RECITING *LIFE* MAGAZINE'S MOTTO),
THE SECRET LIFE OF WALTER MITTY (2013)

There's not a lot of water north of Longreach – rather, plenty of red desert. But a trickle brings life. Veins of green vegetation follow the faintest pulse of water through the spectacularly harsh land. As Karumba came closer, those trickles of water became broader and more plentiful. The contrasting desert, saltpan, water and greenery together made the most striking vista.

The Norman River is a gentle giant by the time it empties into the Gulf of Carpentaria at Karumba. The isolated town was once a refuelling stop for the Qantas flying boats: a long, straight section of the river in front of the town was the perfect landing spot. The boat ramp and visitors' building still exist. I landed briefly on the river and took off again, and flew a few circles around the town before continuing west along the remote coastline to Burketown airstrip, where I refuelled briefly. My destination that day was a reunion.

Three families live in their own near-subsistence settlements on Vanderlin Island, in the Gulf of Carpentaria. Somewhere in those 263 square kilometres of scrub, swamp and forest was my brother, Chris, and his wife, Amanda, a descendant of the ancient Aboriginal owners of the land, and their sons, Peter, Casey and Bryson.

There wasn't a street map of the place – in fact, there were no streets – so I was relying on a few photos I'd seen of their beachside property. When some people on the ground waved, I landed on the water in front of the house, but quickly realised it was the wrong place. I waved back and took off again. Ten minutes later I found a pristine crescent-shaped bay which I recognised from a photo. I landed on protected waters and drove up the beach. After just three days of my journey, I was already almost overwhelmed by what I had experienced and seen. I was looking forward to a couple of days with family. It had been too long.

Chris was on his way back from the nearest town, King Ash Bay, which was three hours away by boat. He had a load of gear, including a new water heater. Money was tight and visits to the mainland were limited to one a month. I was astounded by his resourcefulness. The family compound consisted of their home, a teacher's hut, a beach hut for visitors, and storage sheds. Every morning they had to pump water from a spring to a tank positioned on a hill of sand, where gravity would generate water pressure for the house. From before first light until after dark, Chris had to manage a diesel generator, a battery bank and solar panels to maintain power for the refrigerators storing their food.

Chris had assembled or built everything. All the building materials had been brought out piece by piece in his tiny tin boat over several years: steel beams and sheets of corrugated roofing iron, beds, fridges, an oven. Many of the items were bigger than the boat itself. A utility vehicle and quad bikes had been delivered by barge, and when the tractor he needed was too heavy for the local barge, he brought it out in pieces and reassembled it. Did I mention he was resourceful?

The children were educated by the School of the Air, which formerly broadcast lessons over a UHF radio channel, but these days taught classes over sketchy satellite-delivered internet. Visitors coming for a few months would be given free accommodation in return for helping the kids study each day.

The children's lives illustrated the rich potential of an Indigenous upbringing. Outside of school, they spent their days fishing for barramundi from tidal creeks, catching wallabies for the barbecue or shooting bulls with their father. They travelled around the island on quad motorbikes. Their upbringing reminded me of growing up on my parents' farm.

Once a wild animal was shot and caught, the children would light the dead fronds of a nut tree. The fronds would burn intensely for a minute and smoke in a distinctive tall plume – a signal to Amanda to come and skin the animal, at which she was expert. *Who needs mobile phones*, I couldn't help but think as I witnessed this ancient yet efficient method of communication.

I took Chris, Peter and Casey for joy flights in the rough tropical air. It was the first time they had seen their home from above, and Chris spotted a new waterhole. I was chuffed to have helped out my younger brother.

We also drove around the north of the island in an old, beat-up 4WD ute. Peter showed what an incredible storyteller he was, taking me through his 'backyard', exploring multiple landscapes and vegetation types. Witnessing the skill and joy of a ten-year-old catching a barramundi with his spear was wonderful – a world for kids beyond iPad games.

Dinnertime comes earlier in remote Australia than in the cities. The days start earlier, too. Chris had smoked a type of a winged fish that I had never seen before, in a smoker he built himself. It was one of the most delicious dishes of my life, and was followed by some tough bull steaks, which were memorable for a different reason. I'd read about early settlers who got lost in the desert and became so hungry they ate their boots ... Now I know what that would be like.

After dinner, Chris and I reminisced about growing up and talked a lot about our father. Although he'd died in his fifties, he'd clearly imbued both of us with a strong work ethic, and a sense of the broad scope of life's possibilities.

Chris wished me well before I left at 7 a.m. the next morning. He spoke casually, as if I'd be returning soon, but we both knew it would probably be a long time before we next met. It had been great to see him and learn more about his life, even if I felt remiss for taking so long to get there. I hoped I'd be back more often. Chris and I have taken different paths in life, but he is my brother and we have a strong bond. Each of us admires the other's lifestyle, while knowing we've each found the path in life that suits us best.

My enjoyment of Arnhem Land and Kakadu National Park from the air was disrupted by a violent vibration from the engine. An engine failure is the second-worst thing that can happen in a light aircraft – the worst is probably a fire – and my immediate concern was that there had been a catastrophic failure, perhaps a small explosion.

I throttled back. After a few seconds the vibrating eased, and I began to prepare myself for an emergency landing. Within a minute, though, the engine seemed better, even if I could still detect a slight vibration. I reduced the power to 65 per cent and scanned the map for an airfield. The closest was behind me, and extremely remote. My current tailwind would increase the time it would take to get there. I found an airfield on the map ahead of me, and closer to my route.

My training kicked in. I constantly scanned the land below and the horizon for a place to land if the engine cut out. The options weren't great. There were no large bodies of water, and the ground in the national park was irregular and covered with rocks, trees and scrub. Operating at reduced power, the *Sun* could just maintain altitude, which was concerning because she would have to glide to a landing site if the engine quit. The lower I was, the shorter her range would be.

As the minutes passed, I became more confident the *Sun* would make it. But I was still desperate to get on the ground and work out what had gone wrong. I assumed the damage to the propeller from the ladder strike two days earlier was the cause. When I landed, I expected to see a big chunk missing, which would explain the vibration.

After seventy minutes of nervous flying I arrived over the airfield I'd seen on the map – but it was completely grown over and could no longer function as an airstrip. There was no sign of civilisation at all. 'This can't be happening,' I groaned.

The *Sun*'s engine hadn't got worse for the past hour. I seriously considered making a precautionary landing anyway, as it was possible the propeller had suffered a major failure. But a bush landing could have caused even more damage, and forced me to wait for rescue. 'It's better to keep going,' I told myself. 'Whatever it was, it seems to have stabilised now.'

I continued directly towards Darwin on a heading past several airstrips and small towns, taking it slowly the whole way, but sensing that, as the issue seemed to have gone away, I'd be better off landing somewhere I would have the resources to fix whatever the problem was. At Emkaytee, a small airfield on Darwin's outskirts, I was relieved to park and shut down. I climbed out and apprehensively walked to the back of the plane, expecting to see a ruined propeller. In fact it was a minor problem. The protective tape on the leading edge of a propeller blade had been thrown off. Nothing else was wrong, and it would be easy to replace. I breathed a sigh of relief.

Searey propeller blades have a thin stainless-steel adhesive tape along the leading edge to protect them from water and debris. This was not the first time some tape had been thrown off by centrifugal force. But it was the first time it had caused the propeller to vibrate so violently – which I'd mistaken for an engine vibration. The metal tape must have partially unstuck, disrupting the airflow, before detaching altogether. There had been no need for me to slow down; if I'd resumed normal power the *Sun* would have been fine.

I had several spare tapes in the plane, and replaced the missing one immediately. I borrowed a ute from a guy who lived at the airport and drove to the Boomerang Hotel, where I spent the evening planning my next flight, reading procedures and watching a video produced by the Civil Aviation Safety Authority on how to land at Darwin airport.

Darwin was only fifteen minutes away. But it would be my first arrival at an international airport. I would have to lodge an international flight plan, clear customs and immigration, and head off for my longest flight over water ever. Then I would be landing in Dili, the capital of East Timor. Anxiety was tingling in my stomach.

I woke up at 4 a.m., adrenaline having replaced fear. Over my espresso and muesli bar I reread for a fourth and fifth time the procedures for landing in Darwin, and then I drove to the airfield and dropped off the loaned ute – leaving a few beers on the passenger seat, the international currency for a loaned car thankyou. I was quickly ready, climbed in and started up the *Sun*. I pressed the button on the radio to advise our taxi to the runway.

Silence. The radio transmission button on my control stick wasn't working. I tried the button on the passenger-side controls, and it didn't work either. *Seriously? I've never had a problem with this radio, and here I am about to fly into Darwin International Airport, and it's gone out on me!* I shut down the aircraft completely and restarted – a bit like rebooting a computer – and disconnected and reconnected the lead from the radio to the control stick. Hey presto – the radio was back in action.

I suspected the morning dew was responsible. The *Sun* had been parked in long grass, which was wet from the moist tropical air. The only other time she had experienced intermittent electrical faults was at the Point Cook airfield, between Melbourne and Geelong, when she also was parked on longish wet grass. It was a minor electrical fault, but potentially dangerous and definitely disconcerting, given what was ahead.

○

Many people look forward to their first overseas trip with a mixture of excitement and trepidation. Try making your first landing at an international airport amid massive passenger jets and military aircraft.

I started by breaking the first rule of air-traffic control communication. 'Darwin approach, Searey amphibian, November Four Seven Three X-ray Papa, with delta, VFR aircraft request inbound,' I broadcast.

'November Four Seven Three X-ray Papa, Darwin approach,' came the reply. 'Please contact Darwin delivery on one two six decimal eight.'

Oops – I was getting ahead of myself and was on the wrong frequency.

I radioed delivery, and they cleared the *Sun* to enter Darwin's airspace. They gave me a 'squawk code' for my transponder, a device that sends information about the plane to the flight controller when scanned by radar. The code was a four-digit number allocated to a plane for the duration of a flight; it told the air-traffic controller who I was, as well as my altitude, direction and speed. It's a fantastic system that has worked for decades and makes for safer flying.

I was on my way in. I muddled my calls a little and had to ask, 'Say again?' a few times. My lack of experience was showing; I was going to have to get better at this. Every flight from Darwin to Britain would likely be controlled this way.

Eventually I realised my problem: I was so worried that I would make mistakes on my calls that I was being overly cautious, rather than just relaxing and responding. Once on the ground, I requested taxi assistance and was guided to a parking bay with instructions at each intersection. The air-traffic controllers at Darwin, who are military personnel, were very friendly and forgiving.

Clearing customs could not have been easier. I was met at the plane by a ground handler, who escorted me into the terminal. From his office we printed and submitted my flight plan for the next leg (or so I thought). We then went to see customs and immigration. They asked for my passport, where I was going, and my 'Gen Dec'.

'Huh?' I muttered. I had never heard of the document before. It turns out that if you're flying your own plane overseas, you don't fill out a customs form but rather a General Declaration, or 'Gen Dec'. This is used by flight crews on commercial airlines all around the world. When I said I didn't know what a Gen Dec was, the official said, 'Don't worry – have a good trip.'

As I was escorted back to the plane, I was thinking, 'Well, that was pretty easy.' I got into the *Sun*, turned on my radio and contacted the control tower, only to be told there was a problem with my international flight plan. The plan I had filed was the same one I was carrying in the plane with me. It was a domestic flight plan, showing the headings, distances, times and fuel consumption that I would use while navigating throughout the flight. It had never occurred to me there might be a standard format for international flight plans. But there was, and I sat there for nearly an hour while it was sorted out.

The time was precious, as I wanted to arrive in East Timor before the tropical afternoon showers hit Dili airport. The air-traffic controller was sympathetic, and helped me file a flight plan over the radio so that I could eventually get going. The learning curve was steep! Once the paperwork was sorted, the flying itself seemed easy.

I was starting to clue in to one of the great secrets of aviation: it is much easier being told where to fly by air-traffic control rather than navigating by GPS and a map, especially when going solo. Instead of fearing air-traffic control, I had begun to recognise that they were a great resource. It was just a matter of doing as I was told. Commercial pilots did this as a matter of course, but like many amateur pilots I had always nervously avoided air-traffic control.

As the Australian continent faded into the distance behind me, I felt an eerie chill mixed with exhilaration. The seemingly vast Timor Sea was all I could see, and after half an hour I could no longer raise Darwin on the radio. I was very much alone. But the weather was glorious, and my adventure was now truly underway. It felt great to be alive.

7.

The Year of Living Dangerously

'There are things we know we know. We also know there are known unknowns; that is to say, we know there are some things we do not know. But there are also unknown unknowns – the ones we don't know we don't know.'
DONALD RUMSFELD, *THE UNKNOWN KNOWNS* (2013)

Billowing cumulonimbus were building over Timor as the *Southern Sun* approached. In the world of clouds, these are the most dangerous. Vicious updrafts could flip the craft upside down or rip a wing off. Lightning could fry her electrics. Even professional pilots – who, unlike me, were permitted to fly through clouds as a matter of course – wouldn't risk a cumulonimbus.

East Timor is still a nation rebuilding, and there was no radar at Dili airport. That meant its air-traffic controllers were unable to see my position or direct me around the mountains and clouds along the island's spine. I could communicate with them but I was navigating on my own.

I pushed the *Sun* up to 10,500 feet, which was as high as she had ever been. Much higher and I would have to break out an oxygen tank to avoid succumbing to the thin air. 'I'm lucky this damn cloud isn't any higher,' I muttered. 'I'm not ready for this.'

The *Sun*'s GPS map showed our position, and nearby landmarks and airports. Using the GPS, I was able to let the tower know my location relative to the airport. The calm and professional staff in the control

63

tower used this information to track me as I approached from the east, past Cristo Rei, a tall statue of Jesus that overlooks the bay towards the capital. The landing was uneventful. Having completed my first international leg, I instantly felt better.

Angelo Alves greeted me at the airport. He manages Cinema Loro sa'e, a charity Anne and I established to show movies to rural Timorese in their native language, Tetum. Angelo and his assistant, Lou (pronounced Loh), had heard about foreigners arriving in private aircraft before. They were usually twin-engine propeller-driven planes or private jets. They gasped at the size of the *Southern Sun*, and then started laughing. Lou wanted her photograph taken in the plane, and I was happy to oblige. She sat in the pilot's seat, the controls at her fingertips, while I pointed the camera and encouraged her to pretend she was flying – so she flapped her arms!

Alex, my airport ground handler, asked for my Gen Dec. There was that term again – argh! We went to his office and he showed me a blank one, which would have been useful to have got from my handling agent in Darwin. Alex also gave me a copy of an international format flight plan, another form I'd never seen before. I really did have a lot to learn.

For me, these documents weren't what Donald Rumsfeld would have called 'known unknowns'. They were used by pilots all over the world, but I simply had no idea about them – they were definitely 'unknown unknowns'. In my basic hotel I used a spreadsheet on my iPad to re-create both forms from scratch, adding the *Southern Sun* logo at the top. I printed twenty-five copies, with all of the fixed attributes filled out to save time along the way.

An email arrived from Mike Gray of White Rose Aviation in the UK. He advised that I would have to resubmit my planned arrival dates at every airport through to London. Instead of calculating them in Greenwich Mean Time, the reference time of international aviation, I had given the local time in each place. Two more hours wasted because of not knowing what I didn't know.

The first stop on my MBA cinema tour was the Platinum Cineplex in Dili, which was built in a shopping centre by a company from Indonesia. It was designed in a standard cheap style, with tip-up seats. It wasn't very busy and there didn't seem to have been a lot of thought put into the movies shown. The owners had been forced to cut their ticket prices from $10 to just $3. Even that was a lot for the average Timorese family, which earned just $150 a month. The cinema business is a tough one, especially in Dili, where you have to appeal both to cashed-up expatriates and to the masses, and all the while pirated DVDs are readily available for next to nothing on many street corners.

I'd been visiting cinemas around the world for years, and knew that the best way to look around was to simply buy a ticket. The movie showing was *Furious 7*, the latest instalment in the *Fast and the Furious* franchise. After thirty minutes I couldn't handle the script any longer and walked out. Kurt Russell's character, a special forces officer called Mr Nobody, should have been called Mr Ridiculous.

My day off was fairly busy. I had offered to take Angelo and Lou for a flight around Dili, but they declined with a smile. It seemed the *Sun* was too small to be taken seriously. I offered a flight to Alex, my handler, who had been so helpful in explaining and arranging my paperwork. He excitedly agreed. We flew down the beach at 1000 feet towards the Cristo Rei monument, before returning to the airfield. Alex squealed with delight and snapped lots of photos.

The afternoon was spent on Cinema Loro sa'e business with Angelo and Lou, and meeting Matt Wilkinson from the Australian Embassy, a new sponsor. Each year we dubbed a new film into Tetum. For 2015 we had chosen beloved Australian film *Red Dog*, and Matt proved to be a dynamo, helping us develop the program, raise our online presence and connect us with local businesses.

The airport in Dili did not have avgas, so Angelo spent a couple of hours assisting me ferry containers of fuel from a petrol station to refill the plane. After a few drinks with some expats and locals we've worked with over the years, I had a quiet night back at the hotel, writing in my journal and preparing for my second international leg – complete with a new flight plan and Gen Dec forms.

○

Dili airport's control tower took a long time to find my flight plan the next morning, which was surprising given they only had two flights a day. After departing and heading west, I spent a couple of hours trying to raise Indonesian air-traffic control on the radio. Eventually connecting, I informed them I was flying to Lombok, a large island immediately east of Bali. The scenery on the route was incredible, and such a contrast to the flat north of Australia: huge mountains plunging into azure seas, and thousands of farmers' fields covering all but the steepest terrain.

It would have been splendid to land at the city of Bima, on the adjacent island of Sumbawa, one of the refuelling stops on the original Qantas route. Indeed, I would have liked to land near a beach and go for a swim. But Bima didn't have an international airport where I could clear customs, and the Indonesian air force has a reputation for sending MIGs to intercept wayward aircraft in its vast airspace.

Lombok was covered in a grimy soup; at first I thought it was fog but soon realised it was the pollution that seems to lie over the whole of Indonesia. The visibility for the last hour of the flight was just a few nautical miles. As I was a VFR pilot, this was almost the minimum legal visibility. It was too late to go back, though, and I could see the ground just ahead. I was keen to make my way down to land as soon as I could.

The flight controller, who had identified the *Southern Sun* on radar, asked several times if I could see the runway, which only came into sight about two miles out. In the *Sun*, two miles was just ninety seconds of flying time, and I almost flew right past when it came into view. The airport was big, and I found it hard to believe I hadn't been able to see it just minutes earlier. The air-traffic controller kept three Airbuses waiting on the taxiway while I landed. I think he knew he needed to get me down on the ground quickly, given the poor conditions. I was handed over from Lombok Approach to the control tower for the final minute of the flight.

'Lombok Tower, this is a Searey, November Four Seven Three X-ray Papa, two miles east,' I radioed, realising later I was on radar and he knew exactly where I was.

'November Four Seven Three X-ray Papa, you are number two for runway one three after the Airbus,' he replied, meaning the *Sun* would be the second plane to land.

It's hard to describe the thrill I felt at those words, which would become familiar over the following weeks. For someone with so little experience at big airports, to be among these giant jets was surreal. Being told to land behind a jetliner stirred a boy-like pride in me, a sense that the *Southern Sun* and I were achieving great things together. I felt I was becoming a real pilot, even though I was only about to double my successful international flights to two.

It was important that I didn't follow the jet too closely, because the turbulence from its huge engines and the wake from its wings could flip the *Sun* like a leaf. The controllers understood that and kept a fair distance between us.

My nervousness over a number of years about communicating with air-traffic controllers was ill-placed. It was a shame I hadn't realised it earlier. Once you're identified by an airport's radar, it's like having a co-pilot to navigate, allowing you to just fly the plane. Discovering this emphasised for me the importance of mental framing: how we approach a problem directly affects how we handle it, and the results that eventuate. A positive mind leads to positive outcomes.

My local handler had booked me into a nearby resort for the night. I sat outside to enjoy a late-afternoon drink, do some writing and check my email. There was one from Anne, who had been researching the local food speciality of Lombok ayam taliwang, a sweet and spicy chicken dish, and was recommending I try for dinner. I showed the server at the restaurant I went to; it wasn't on the menu, but they obliged and made it nonetheless. It made me smile.

This was the first of many such emails I received from Anne along the way, who vicariously helped me taste the exotic ingredients of my journey. It was a wonderful link that made me feel closer to her as I travelled ever further away.

With my next stop, Surabaya, on the Indonesian island of East Java, I was following in the footsteps of the Qantas passengers of the 1930s. But the city had defied my research attempts: there seemed to be no records of its history as a stopover for flying boats. I was determined to find out something about what I thought was a unique part of the city's past. Surely, once I was there, what I couldn't find on the internet would reveal itself in living colour?

I bought a map and located the city's museum, where I hoped to find a local history expert who could tell me about the experiences of the early Qantas crews and passengers. Dirty, crowded and noisy, Surabaya wasn't the most pleasant city. The taxi drivers didn't seem to know where they were going, and my taxi actually broke down. Eventually the driver, having made repairs with what I suspected was a regularly accessed tool kit, delivered me to the museum, which boasted a proud sign declaring it was a prize-winning institution.

Deflation ensued as soon as I walked inside: the museum celebrated the Javanese tobacco industry, and in particular a family dynasty that had gone from rags to riches picking, rolling, packing and selling the stuff. The founder's first bicycle was displayed, along with some glorious stained-glass windows depicting smokers, and the original costumes of the company's very own marching band.

It was bizarre, but still a dead end – in more ways than one, I suppose. At least the port wasn't far away. I walked for a while, taking in the street life. There were rickshaws everywhere and I accepted the offer of a ride from one, got aboard and pointed to the port on a map. After fifteen minutes of hard pedalling, the rider pulled up at a shop and went in to speak to someone, who came out and asked me to show him the location on the map. He then pointed us back in the direction we'd come from.

That was okay. I'd arrived early, so still had half the afternoon to enjoy. Sadly, when I got to the port I saw no sign of an old seaport at all. Over the years it had been turned into a busy industrial dock featuring a predominance of concrete wharfs. It was a hive of activity, and I watched ships being loaded with old-fashioned cranes and cargo nets rather than containers.

As I walked back, I spotted a gate leading to a Middle Eastern–style bazaar. I bought a bag of pistachios and kept heading deeper into the enclave. A few minutes later I was prevented from going any further by men standing at the entrance to what I then realised was a mosque. At that moment my phone rang. The number started with the digits 972 – Israel. It was a security officer asking about my planned flight to Tel Aviv, and wanting to know more about the countries I would be visiting en route. *That's spooky timing*, I thought.

My next stop was to be in Jakarta, the bustling capital of Indonesia. But an international diplomatic meeting called the Asian-African Conference was being held in the city, and they had run out of aircraft parking space, so I was told to find an alternative. Didn't they realise I could park under another plane? Arrangements were quickly made for me to land in Palembang, on the island of Sumatra; I'd never heard of the city, but apparently I could clear outgoing customs there. Palembang had no direct link to the Qantas route, but it would get me within a couple of hundred kilometres of somewhere I had been searching for.

The next morning I was forced to wait at an airport office for half an hour because no one had the key. Eventually the manager turned up, but by this time I was really annoyed. 'How could you keep me waiting?' I complained, receiving only blank stares in response.

Within a few minutes, I was even angrier at myself for being so terse. But it was good that the incident had happened early in the trip, because it completely reset my thinking. I had read so many books and seen so many documentary films about people who had driven, sailed or flown on long trips, and who complained bitterly about the inefficiency of customs and immigration services around the world. I knew the same would happen to me, and getting annoyed wasn't going to fix anything. It would just leave me unhappy and frustrated, plus it wouldn't actually speed anything up. Worst of all, it would inject an unwelcome sense of negativity into my travels. I decided that I had to accept that this was simply part of visiting other cultures, and it was better to revel in the differences than be frustrated by them.

In Palembang I found a hardware store and bought a small plastic kitchen sink for an important mission the following day. Then I polished up on the procedures for entering the busy airspace over Singapore, which I expected would be the most demanding of the entire trip. On the way there I would pass over the equator, an exciting and romantic prospect for an old sailor like me. I desperately wanted to be looking at my GPS latitude readout when the S became an N. As it turned out, my equatorial obsession would almost trigger a disaster.

8.

In the Heart of the Sea

'Fasten your seatbelts. It's going to be a bumpy night.'
MARGO CHANNING, *ALL ABOUT EVE* (1950)

ometimes you get lucky, sometimes you don't. From the Qantas flying boat itinerary I had tracked down, I knew the last stop in Indonesia was a place called Klabat Bay. Of course, place names in Indonesia had changed since 1938. While some, such as Djakarta, were easy to decipher, others seemed to have disappeared. After a year of research I still hadn't located Klabat.

Studying the charts in my Palembang hotel room, I noticed a bay on the island of Bangka, about halfway between Jakarta and Singapore. I compared the bay with the old Qantas route map. It looked the same. Google Maps listed the waterway as Selat Melaka – or, as most people know it, the Strait of Malacca. I switched to Google Earth, where the bay was named Teluk Kelabat. A local map called it Kelebat Baai. I compared the shape of Kelebat Baai with the Qantas diagram of Klabat Bay. They were a perfect match. I was thrilled at the discovery and started reworking my flight plan straightaway.

It took a couple of hours to get to Kelabat from Palembang. As soon as I arrived, I understood why Qantas had chosen this remote location to refuel. The large body of water was protected from any wind direction. Several big fuel tanks that looked like they had been there since the 1930s still sat on the waterfront. The scene highlighted the logistical

73

difficulties of the journey in the 1930s. It was a remote bay on a remote island, and ships must have delivered high-octane aviation fuel just for Qantas. Staff, fuel and spares would have been needed at every point along the route, and some other points were just as remote as Kelabat.

I circled the bay in the *Sun* and identified the stretch of water the Qantas planes likely used. I briefly landed among a few small fishing boats and then took off without stopping – a procedure known as a 'touch-and-go' for land planes, and commonly nicknamed a 'splash-and-go' for seaplanes. As pleased as I was to have found Klabat Bay, I was also keen to get to the reporting point for Singapore air-traffic control.

One of my ambitions was to land the *Southern Sun* on the equator and conduct an experiment. I grew up sailing, and therefore crossing the equator was a pretty big deal for me. If I weren't flying solo, a traditional seafarers' King Neptune equator-crossing ceremony would definitely have been on the cards. After crossing in the air, I planned to land just south of the equator and cruise across, like a boat. But landing on the open ocean would be much riskier than my usual touchdowns in protected bays or on lakes and rivers.

When I got to the equator I was so excited that I videoed the GPS position indicator shifting from south to north. I then turned the *Sun* around and nudged her into a spiral descent over zero degrees of latitude. What could go wrong? Even though I was hundreds of kilometres from land, there wasn't much wind at sea level. As I looked down from hundreds of feet, there seemed to be no waves. A ship on the horizon gave me a sense of security. It wasn't like I was completely alone.

I pulled the *Sun* out of her descent a few metres above the water. As I looked out the windscreen I realised there was a swell, but, excited about my plan, I decided to land anyway. The *Sun* hit a wave, bounced into the air, hit the water again, bounced a few more times and finally stopped. Ouch.

The poor landing left me feeling frazzled. I was not used to landing in swells and was caught off-guard. All seaplane pilots experience a rough water landing at some stage, but still they are fraught with danger. In a split-second they can go very wrong if the controls aren't managed properly. I'd hit pretty hard on that last bounce, and I was annoyed at myself. But the *Sun* was down and seemed undamaged.

I taxied across the equator and got on with what I thought was a pretty clever experiment. Water in the Southern Hemisphere goes down drains anti-clockwise, and vice versa in the Northern Hemisphere. But what happens on the equator?

As a child I had enthusiastically devoured a television science show hosted by Professor Julius Sumner Miller, who used to ask: 'Why is it so?' I wanted to make a tribute video. Surely no one had ever landed a seaplane on the equator to discover which direction the vortex takes in an emptying sink, if one occurs at all?

My dashboard-mounted navigation iPad was changed into video selfie mode. I opened the window, leaned out into the Natuna Sea, scooped up a bucketful of water and watched it drain through the sink from Palembang. 'The water flows straight out,' I told millions of future YouTube fans. It was slower than usual, and there was some bubbling and gulping, but no vortex swirl. *Wacko*, I thought. *I probably could have found that out on Wikipedia. But hey, I am living it!*

With my experiment completed, it was time to take off, and it began to dawn on me that I had an issue brewing. When I pushed the throttle forward and increased speed, I saw that the size of the swell would make taking off problematic: it was rough, wet and bouncy.

In my rush to get airborne, I pulled the control stick back too early. The *Sun* tried to lift into the sky and then smacked back down on the water several times, probably the hardest she had ever hit. As she finally climbed away from the water, I realised something was terribly wrong: the control stick wouldn't move forward. The craft was stuck in a perpetual climb.

My initial instinct, apart from panic, was to land again before I got too much higher. But given the waves and my distance from land, I decided that wasn't a good idea. First, I had to work out how much control I had over the *Sun*.

I couldn't lower the nose with the stick, but I found that by adjusting the throttle I could get her to fly level. The nose was still pointing higher than normal, which was slowing her down to a car-like 60 knots, but at least we weren't in a permanent climb. At 1000 feet I slowly raised the wing flaps, increasing our speed to 65 knots. It was an improvement, but how was I ever going to land in Singapore? I needed to test the *Sun*'s capabilities further. I climbed a little higher, and then tried easing back on the throttle. The *Sun* began to sink, with her nose still slightly higher than her tail, but I was comfortably in control.

In all facets of flying, and especially in emergencies, pilots are taught to recall a simple hierarchy of priorities: aviate, navigate, communicate. The first and primary step is to keep the plane flying. Then you must focus on where you are going. Finally, maintain contact through the radio; if you're in a life-threatening situation, issue a mayday.

Over the next few minutes I established that the *Sun* could fly and land. The rear of her three wheels may touch down first, which wasn't normal but was survivable. I climbed to 4500 feet and turned towards the location where I would have to report to Singapore air-traffic control. Should I declare an emergency? Or at least a pan-pan, which is a distress call that does not require immediate assistance? Not just yet, I decided. *Let's try some more flying and see how this turns out.*

Of course, I was also trying desperately to work out why the stick wouldn't move forward. I looked around the seat, where the control linkages were, but couldn't find anything amiss. It seemed likely that the hard sea landing had bent the tail, jamming the controls to the elevators, the horizontal edges on the empennage that make the plane ascend or descend by moving up and down. I began to fret. Was this going to be the end of the trip? Were some external parts damaged or had the *Sun*'s main structure bent? The thought of hiring a shipping container to take the damaged *Sun* home was a depressing one.

○

As I approached the first navigational waypoint inside Singaporean airspace, I called air-traffic control. 'Singapore radar, Searey amphibian, November Four Seven Three X-ray Papa, at REPOV on Golf five seven nine, for Seletar.'

'November Four Seven Three X-ray Papa, we've been waiting for your call. Please advise ETA Seletar.'

On my flight plan I'd allowed an extra hour for my diversions, but the *Sun*'s painfully slow speed, combined with a stronger headwind than expected, had put me a further hour back. It was a long delay, and the Singaporean controllers were probably considering raising the alarm for a missing aircraft. I realised I should have communicated my predicament earlier. It was shaping up as a day of tough lessons.

Tiny Singapore has one of the world's busier airspaces. The Singapore Air Force has a base adjacent to the giant Changi International Airport. A few miles away is Seletar airport, which caters to private jets and amateur pilots like me. The crowded skies required a lot of radio calls to controllers and switching of frequencies. It was busy but I managed, helped by the staff's professionalism.

I was directed to fly over Changi Airport at 5000 feet. It was bizarre seeing Boeing and Airbus passenger jets passing beneath the tiny *Sun* on their way to landing. I snapped a single photo, which was perhaps a bit cheeky, given the extra work it was taking to fly the *Sun*, not to mention the importance of maintaining a straight course when there were a lot of other planes around.

The tower at Seletar didn't know about my problem. I felt I had enough control that emergency services wouldn't be needed when I landed. I experimented a little with the throttle, and the *Sun* responded as expected. Push, and she rose. Pull, and she descended. I just used one stage of the flaps, because I had good control of the plane and didn't want to drastically change the pitch or anything else on my final approach. This meant the landing would be a little faster than usual, but there were a couple of kilometres of runway to use up.

I took my time, concentrated, and landed smoothly on all three wheels at once. *Phew*, I thought. *Seriously, phew.*

A ground controller gave me directions over the radio about where to park, and we were guided into our final position by a marshal with his red ping-pong bats. I was relieved to turn off the engine and shut down the electrics. But I was also very anxious to inspect the damage.

I sheepishly climbed out and studied the tail. All looked normal. I used a torch to look inside the tube between the tail and the cockpit, but still I couldn't see anything wrong. I tried the stick again – it was definitely jammed. What was going on?

I removed my bags from the passenger seat and rummaged about in the footwell and under the seat. At last, there was the problem: a small spare part was jammed into the base of the control stick mechanism, in a spot I was unable to see or reach from the pilot's seat. During the rough take-off, many of the spare parts stored in the bow had dislodged. They had slid around the bottom of the plane, where I couldn't see them but where they could interfere with the linkages from the control stick to the wings and tail. I had been very, very lucky.

My poor decisions made me feel physically ill. I had limped through one of the busiest airspaces in the world in a malfunctioning aircraft. I should have advised the authorities of my limited control, and really I should have thought twice about landing on the equator at all. But I was in love with the idea and had convinced myself everything would be okay. I'd studied this psychological phenomenon in my MBA studies: often we tend to see only the information that supports the result we seek. But the 'she'll be right' attitude has no place in aviation or boating, especially when the two are combined.

It was a classic example of being overcommitted to a goal. When I was just above the water, I should have rationally assessed the wave heights and either pulled out completely or at least gone around and approached at slower speed, which would have allowed a smoother landing. Had I done that, I would not have become so anxious about the take-off. It wasn't that the waves were too big: it was that my mental framing was out of whack. Having been landing on enormous two- or three-kilometre passenger jet runways all week, I had become used to the approach speed suited to those conditions. When faced with different terrain, I had to mentally reset.

I felt shaken, and I needed to talk. I called Anne and described what had happened. I had promised her I'd be careful, and this was the first time I had broken that pledge.

In a cab to the Singapore Yacht Club, where I was staying, I swiped through my iPad to watch my equatorial *Why Is It So?* sink video. I had fluffed it. The recording began not when I started the experiment, but when I intended it to stop, and just the rough take-off unfolded.

Over the previous few years I had been pretty critical of the selfie movement, which I regarded as a tad narcissistic. Now, for my first ever video selfie, the god of taking one's own image – Selfpictus? – was perhaps exacting revenge. The video showed my grimacing and scared face as the *Sun* smashed from the tip of one wave to another. Then the craft hit the water so hard that the iPad was thrown from its mount to the bottom of the cockpit, still recording, which made it look like the *Sun* had flipped over onto its back. It was a sickening sight that could have been real. *Serves me right*, I thought.

The episode taught me a painful lesson, but it's an incident I've avoided talking about. Landing on the equator was such a great story, but it could have ended in disaster. The good news was that the plane was fine. I would secure everything in the front compartment much more carefully from now on. In truth, the *Southern Sun* was a lot stronger than I was that day. She really looked after me.

9.

Catch Me If You Can

'You know ... I'll bet those Golden Tickets make the chocolate taste terrible.'
CHARLIE BUCKET, *WILLY WONKA & THE CHOCOLATE FACTORY* (1971)

Qantas's first international passengers flew in luxury but sometimes slept a little rough. Karumba, Timor and Surabaya weren't at the forefront of tourist hospitality before World War II. (Nor are they now, truth be told.) It was when the travellers arrived at Singapore that the pampering kicked off. I imagined that as soon as the paying guests stepped off the giant Empire flying boats, they were whisked away by rickshaw to the Raffles Hotel, which was then on the waterfront and one of the grandest in the British Empire.

Land reclamation has since moved Raffles inland, but the hotel still epitomises the grandeur of the British Empire, and there remains an aloof calmness about its marble hallways and staircases. The rooms start at $800 a night but that wasn't in my budget; I would never part with that kind of cash unless Anne was there to enjoy it too. Instead, I decided to try a Singapore Sling in the Long Bar and write a postcard to my grandmother, who has been a faithful correspondent of mine since I was a young teenager. Glory be to handwritten communication; it was not lost on me that it was the demand for airmail, not passenger travel, that provided the financial impetus to the flying boat service in 1938.

I perched myself at the corner of the bar. After a while I calmed down about my near-miss over the equator, and I began feeling better about having made it this far. It was such a great spot for writing that I decided to eat as well. That would prove a mistake.

Given that Singapore is a cultural melting pot, Anne recommended I try some 'fusion' food. Alas, I was boring and just had a chicken satay at the bar. Diarrhoea hit the next morning. On my first full day off in twelve I was suffering from a 'rather loose stool', which kept me in my room for several hours. I worked, booking some films for the cinemas back home; wrote my journal and arranged photos in the digital realm in between running to the bathroom.

Around midday some medicine allowed me to get out and visit a few cinemas. Anne and I had done a lot of work for Golden Village in the 1990s in Singapore, so we knew how vibrant the city's film scene was. At the Lido Art House I watched *Child 44*, a French-produced movie based on a great, if disturbing, book I'd read about a Soviet serial killer; the film never made it to Australian cinemas. At the Cathay cinema on the famous Orchard Road I also watched the second quarter of *Furious 7* but was again forced out by my intolerance for the story's ludocracy (which is not a real word … *but it could be*).

○

Leaving Singapore was a lot easier than arriving. By flying north, I avoided the crowded airspace over Changi International. Oh, and I had full control of the plane. I asked air-traffic control for clearance to 6500 feet. When they asked if the *Sun* could reach 10,000 feet, I reluctantly replied that she could. They assigned me that altitude the whole way over the Malay Peninsula.

Getting that high was a hassle and used a lot of fuel. The *Sun* takes about fifteen minutes to climb to 5000 feet, and another twenty-five to thirty minutes to get to 10,000, where the air is thinner and the rate of climb decreases. It was high for a small plane, even if only a quarter of the height that most commercial airliners fly at, and so cold I had to wear gloves – not what I'd been expecting in the tropics. The ground was a musky haze, making it difficult to navigate by map.

My arrival in Penang, a smaller international airport on the island off the north-west coast of Malaysia, was straightforward. George Town, the capital of Malaysia's Penang state, was listed as a world heritage site in 2008. I checked into a cheap hotel in the heart of the old city, where many of the colonial buildings and structures are intact and still in use. At Fort Cornwallis, fabulously named after the British general who surrendered to the Americans and French in 1781 at Yorktown, I found a yardarm and an ancient cannon. That made my day. Simple things can be very satisfying.

It was my day off, but I wanted to fill the *Sun* with more affordable petrol from a service station outside the airport. It took a while to get the fuel and return, but I was making progress when a police car raced up behind me with its blue lights flashing. The police wanted to know what I was doing on the airfield with eight bags of fuel in a wheelbarrow. When I explained and revealed I'd flown from Australia, they drove me the rest of the way, and took turns having their photo taken sitting in the *Southern Sun*.

The best way to avoid suspicion at airports is to not wear street clothes. Even if you are a private pilot in your own plane, if you are not wearing a uniform, security and airport staff throughout Asia, India and the Middle East may not believe you are a pilot. I usually wore the overalls common among flight crews the world over. Today was the first time I'd been at the airport in civilian clothes, and the airport staff were immediately suspicious. It made me realise how easily I had accessed some secure airport areas in my flying suit, and brought up memories of the movie *Catch Me If You Can*, about Frank Abagnale Jr, a conman who, among other misdeeds, impersonated pilots. His story, deliciously portrayed by Leonardo DiCaprio, started to seem very plausible.

It wasn't mandatory to hire a ground handler in Penang, and I decided to save the fees and do it myself. But everything probably took twice or thrice as long. Picking up the fuel consumed hours. To file my flight plan, I was directed to the control tower, which was accessed through a security door into the smallest, skinniest lift I'd ever seen. When the doors opened I stepped out to see a wonderful panoramic view of the airport. There were a few staff, and the manager was very helpful, but that was another couple of hours. After she helped me with the charts and suggested a route to Bangkok, she then told me where to find the Penang laksa that Anne had recommended I try for dinner.

The next morning, when I got back to the airport, I found the world's largest commercial aircraft – the famous Antonov freighter – parked next to the *Sun*. These awesome planes are used worldwide to transport what are now known as 'RBTNQ' – or 'really big things needed quickly'. This one was carrying petroleum-industry equipment. Others have transported heavy machinery, rock band equipment and even yachts. All I had to deliver was an airmail letter. I tried not to feel inadequate.

After a tiring and stressful eight-hour flight over the Gulf of Thailand, dodging rain, low cloud and storms, I landed at Bangkok and got to my hotel by 4 p.m. Keen to explore, I scrubbed up, changed and asked the concierge for a taxi to the Mandarin Oriental, a layover hotel on the original Qantas route.

After forty-five minutes the cab pulled up at a swanky hotel, but something didn't seem right. The building was modern, and the letter-head on the front desk boasted 'since 1965'. This was the Mandarin, not the Mandarin Oriental. Another cab soon deposited me at the glorious old hotel, where my kangaroo-leather boots made a lovely squeaking sound on the marble floor of the foyer. The colonial-style building in which the Qantas guests slept is now overshadowed by a modern hotel tower, but the original section has been beautifully preserved and compared favourably with Raffles. A writers' room still exists, and high tea is served every afternoon.

Under Anne's guidance I had been enjoying eating local delicacies. But once I read the words 'duck liver pâté', the rest of the menu became a blur. The dish went well with the vibrant orchid martini on the sneakily accessed 'house guests only' terrace, and I watched the sun set while traditional boats and ferries plied the river. What a fabulous evening.

Bangkok held one more challenge. The SF Cinema City complex was at a nearby mall. The seats were quite good, wider and longer than expected, and the foyer was stylish. I was collecting good data for my thesis. I was only buying tickets in order to have a look around the cinemas, so it didn't really matter which film I chose, but this turned out to be the fifth ticket admission on the trip thus far for *Furious 7*. I had lasted just fifteen to twenty minutes at each screening, sometimes seeing the same part over, so at this rate I might manage to see the whole film by the time I got to the Middle East. It felt like eating brussels sprouts as a child – much more palatable to consume in small nibbles than in one go.

10.

A Passage to India

'It's not a lie, it's a gift for fiction.'
WALT PRICE, *STATE AND MAIN* (2000)

Myanmar was a military dictatorship nervously transforming itself into a parliamentary democracy. Highly suspicious of outsiders, the government had not exactly refused me permission to land, but they had made the paperwork and getting fuel too difficult. They did at least provide airspace clearance for the *Southern Sun* from Chiang Mai, our last stop in Thailand, to Chittagong, Bangladesh.

Having crossed the heavily forested, mountainous region west of Chiang Mai, the *Sun* entered Myanmar's airspace. I tried to make contact with an air-traffic controller, standard procedure when crossing an international border. My call was met by silence, so I flew on unannounced for a few hours. There was a huge area of prohibited airspace in the middle of the route. I didn't know what it was used for, but the military had controlled Myanmar for fifty-three years, so it was easy to guess. The restricted zone started at 3000 feet and extended above the *Sun*'s maximum altitude.

I decided to fly along the bottom of the zone at 3000 feet. An airport would be my sole waypoint across the desolate countryside, which looked more like the red earth of outback Australia than the lush fields and jungle of Thailand. Thirty miles, or roughly 50 kilometres, from the airport,

I tried to raise the tower on the radio. I tried again at twenty miles, fifteen miles, ten miles and five miles. Perhaps they were having a day off.

A minute later a light-blue fighter jet sped past about a thousand feet below me, at a right angle to the direction I was heading. Stunned and fearful, I frantically scanned the sky behind me. The jet, which seemed to be alone, looked like a MiG-29, a large twin-engine Soviet jet designed to counter the F-16 Fighting Falcon deployed by the US Air Force in the late 1970s.

The radio silence was finally broken when a voice came over the radio: 'November Four Seven Three X-ray Papa, please advise position.' The man sounded excited to hear from me.

'Overhead the field, I have been calling for a while,' I replied.

'Yes, November Four Seven Three X-ray Papa, you must remain in contact.'

Hmm ... The jet landed at the airfield below me and deployed a parachute from its tail to slow down. The control tower, which in most countries helped aircraft avoid each other, didn't mention the encounter. Perhaps I was target practice, or maybe the MiG had just spotted me and asked what a little flying boat was doing out there. I never found out.

Chittagong is one of the bigger military bases in Bangladesh. The city of 4.5 million lies at the mouth of the Karnaphuli River, which drains into the Bay of Bengal, and has been an important trading hub between India and South-East Asia for hundreds of years. To get there, the *Southern Sun* flew over a vast delta of muddy waterways winding towards the ocean. I was booked to stay at the Chittagong Boat Club, which is part of the city's large naval base and sits directly under the final stage of the runway flight path.

Paradoxically, the countries that can least afford large bureaucracies often have the biggest. When I landed at Chittagong, fifteen people walked over to the *Sun* and offered to sell me fuel, arrange my landing fees or book me a hotel. It took eight officials an hour to clear me through immigration, even though there were no other flights leaving or arriving at the time. Each one personally inspected my passport and read every visa stamp – and there were many. They even read the middle pages – the ones explaining that there was a microchip embedded in the passport. I could tell who the more important officials were because they got to read it twice. There were a lot of serious phone calls. Then came the question that had apparently caused the delays, concern and consternation: 'What is your flight number?'

Wow, that's a new one! I thought. I decided it was an opportunity to stake a claim in the world of international flight numbers. 'SS1,' I declared. There was a collective 'ahh' from the officials. As they repeated that official-sounding designation, SS1, I perceived a distinct shift in attitude. I was cleared to leave. They didn't even bother to issue me with a visa or stamp my passport.

On checking in at the Boat Club, I asked for a taxi into the city. That was not possible, the staff said: it was election day. For my own safety I had to stay within the club grounds. When I suggested the poll was a great reason to go into town, I was told it was forbidden. I walked around the club, which was located next to the river, but the Boat Club had no boats that I could use to escape. I felt deflated, but later read on the news that at least seventy-five people had died in election-related violence that year. Understandably, the staff were being protective of their foreign guest.

The next day I was advised it was okay for me to visit the town. I said I wanted to visit a cinema but was told: 'No, there are no cinemas for you in Chittagong.'

'Oh, there must be some cinemas here?' I said, knowing the Subcontinental love of the movies.

'There are no cinemas suitable for you.'

I explained that my family ran cinemas, and that I was visiting cinemas in every country I went to. In particular, I was researching how locals enjoy cinema. The staff were impressed and sent me to their favourite. It was a cracker.

The Almas Cinema Hall's brutal Bauhaus-style concrete exterior looked like a pre-war telephone exchange. The ticket booths in the dusty foyer were small slits in a stone wall which the Terminator would have had trouble breaching. The candy bar was empty – not just of people but of products – and the seats had seen better centuries. If there had been floor lighting it would have shown that the floors were worn to the concrete. It was like a grand home run down by generations of neglectful owners. I loved it.

Bureaucracy's dead hand kept me longer in Chittagong than planned. I had tried to file a flight plan for Kolkata the day before, and was assured several times that one wouldn't be necessary. When I was ready to leave, the Bangladeshi flight controllers wouldn't let me go without clearance to land in India. The Indian authorities, who were stalling, only relented after I photographed my handwritten flight plan and emailed it to my Indian flight handler. The Indians had decided that I wasn't welcome in Kolkata, even to overfly; it was 'too busy', they said, which seemed a little harsh. They directed me to Patna, in northeast India, which was way off my route.

I wonder what's there? I thought.

○

Northern India was brimming with life, activity and kindness. I had worked in India many times over the years, and was eager to return. For me, the Subcontinent reinforced a powerful lesson about societies: sometimes those who have the least to give are the most generous.

I asked Prakash Ranjan, my ground handler at Patna airport, where I could find some of the local delicacies, showing him Anne's emailed suggestions.

'You won't find those at the hotel,' he said. 'It is street food – I will take you.'

A few hours later he picked me up from my hotel. On his small motorbike. With one helmet. *Hey, live life*, I thought. *Let's go!*

Initially I was worried about the notorious Indian traffic, but I placed my trust in Prakash. We spent three glorious hours crisscrossing the city and visiting street stalls. Prakash, in his late twenties, was very proud to be showing off his beloved city and its best food. The most sublime dish was one of the simplest: a sprout salad served on a large leaf; you used a quarter of another leaf as a spoon. We finished with a soothing *lassi*, a milk yogurt drink clearly designed to settle any fire in the roof of one's mouth.

As we neared my hotel, we were engulfed by an Indian wedding ceremony. The guests were all marching down the street – it seemed the reception was to be held at the hotel. It was loud, raucous, colourful and magnificent. They really knew how to celebrate. For a few hours I sat up and enjoyed the visual and aural feast; I couldn't help laughing when someone decided that firecrackers were just what the party needed, but they exploded with such ferocity that the bridal party ran like Olympic champions, backwards.

My next stop was Gwalior, a quiet air force base near nowhere – other than the lake that was once a refuelling stop for the Qantas Imperial flying boats. The tower directed me to land with a ten-knot tailwind, which is not altogether safe, especially in a plane like the *Sun*, which has two wheels at the front and one in the rear. My annoyance was tempered, however, when I found out the airport was closed on Saturdays and had been opened just for me.

The biggest event in Gwalior that week was the opening of the action film *Gabbar Is Back*. The main actor, Akshay Kumar, looked like an Indian version of Dirty Harry. He turned out to be more complex: Chuck Norris crossed with Charles Bronson, and Robin Williams in *Dead Poets Society*. A beloved professor by day and an exposer of corruption by night. Even though I don't speak Hindi, I enjoyed the movie so much that I returned after intermission (yes, intermission) to watch the second half. I have even put the trailer on my website just so you can watch it (www.southernsun.voyage/gabbar).

I took a three-day break in Gwalior, and was thoroughly enamoured by it. I even found time to catch up on work back home. Part of the reason I had not told many people about my trip was so I could continue to do this – I was able to answer emails most nights, so many of the people I worked with outside our office didn't realise I was away. When I had a little more time, and reasonable internet, I was able to watch trailers and book upcoming films. Glory be to the interweb!

Gwalior was more interesting than I'd expected. The most common billboards, and they were prolific, promoted education: tutors to get students into high school and university, as well as the institutions themselves. This focus on education I hadn't seen elsewhere. I was meeting many locals on the streets and in the parks; often whole families walked up to say hello.

Then it occurred to me that I hadn't been asked for money in the streets at all during the trip – with the exception of an older man at the fuel station in Indonesia, who opened his dressing gown and showed me his weeping stomach wounds and a colostomy bag, a memory I had tried to erase. It was wonderful meeting so many people who wanted to talk and be hospitable, and who had no other agenda than being sociable.

The ancient temples, palaces and forts were magnificent. It was incredible to find buildings ranging from 800 to 2500 years old in a part of India the rest of the world seemed unaware of. I didn't see a single other foreigner the whole time I was there.

Then there was the Jai Vilas Palace, the most extravagant nineteenth- -century building I had ever seen. The maharaja who built it had perhaps somewhat questionable taste: a lot of the building was out- right hilarious, either for its attempt at grandeur or for its outright weirdness. A solid-silver model train set had been built to transport

94

food and condiments around a dining table that could seat over 100 people. A later maharaja proudly displayed photos with third-world dictators and despots, and a collection of unusual vehicles, including a swan-inspired baby carriage. Perhaps that had had a long-term effect on him, as later in life he commissioned a rather unusual marble statue of a woman in a somewhat intimate encounter with a swan (see the first photo section). This brought back a distant memory...

A decade or so earlier, when I was Commodore of the Royal Yacht Club of Victoria, one of my duties was to host an annual Christmas lunch. I had thus been asked to comment on the menu.

'Can we have swan?' I asked. It seemed a reasonable request.

'No, you can't,' I was told a few hours later. 'The wholesaler doesn't stock swan.'

I wasn't entirely surprised. The folklore I had heard – yet never checked its veracity, for I loved the story too much – was that swans were protected throughout the Commonwealth, being considered the property of the Queen. Only she was allowed to eat them. And not wanting to seem extravagant, she only ate swan for lunch on Christmas Day. I could picture the swan being brought out to the table, and the Windsors digging in to the most impressive of many courses. The leftovers would go back to the kitchen, and perhaps the next day Lizzie and Phil would enjoy cold swan and watercress sandwiches for lunch...

What would be closest to swan? 'Probably goose,' I was told, but was assured it was a greasy and not altogether pleasant bird, while turkey was much nicer and readily available.

'Okay, turkey it is,' I said. 'But don't tell anyone else what we are having, and leave the menus to me.'

A close ally in the club office and I designed a classically styled menu inside a neatly folded card:

Entree: Grain-fed prawns

Main: Roast free-range swan ...

I've forgotten what we had for dessert.

The big day came around, and before I stood to welcome the members to the sold-out lunch, I could already hear the murmurings. 'Swan?' people were saying. 'Have you had swan before? And how do you get prawns to eat grain? Don't they have really small mouths?'

I formally welcomed the members, and went on to explain that we had prepared something special for lunch. To start with, we had secured prawns that, after being raised on sea grass, had been fed grain for the last few months of their lives to fatten them up. 'When I first became a flag officer and knew that one day I'd likely be Commodore,' I continued, 'I knew this would be a great opportunity to serve swan for Christmas lunch. They can't be bought, but I discovered a loophole: if the swans are raised on your own property, they can be eaten. So, four years ago, I acquired some swan eggs, hatched and raised the swans, and eventually a dozen swans roamed our backyard. The lawn and the pool have been an awful mess for all that time. Today, you will enjoy these birds, and Anne gets her yard back. Here's to a great lunch.'

Some members realised I couldn't be serious, but my delivery was so heartfelt and straight that others were excited. A few were offended: how on Earth could we eat beautiful swans? To this day, a number of members still believe that they ate swan for lunch that day, and that it tasted a bit like turkey, but better.

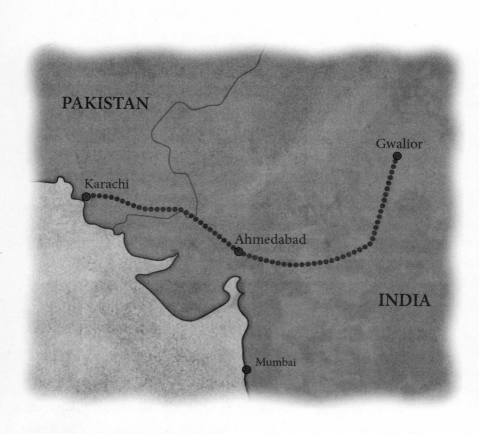

11.

The Viceroy's House

'I have found it is the small everyday deeds of ordinary folk
that keep the darkness at bay.'
GANDALF, *THE HOBBIT* (2012)

There was a problem departing Gwalior: the tower advised me that a visual take-off was prohibited because visibility was only 4000 metres. I was sitting in the cockpit and ready to go, but unable to see the problem. Just as I thought, *What the hell do I do now?* the controller offered a helpful suggestion: 'Would you like to request special VFR?'

That was exactly what I wanted to do!

'Affirm,' I radioed back. 'November Four Seven Three X-ray Papa requesting special VFR departure for Ahmedabad.'

'Stand by,' he replied. About ten minutes later the call came through: 'November Four Seven Three X-ray Papa cleared for special VFR, cleared for start-up, report when ready.'

A special visual flight rules clearance is like official permission to break the normal rules of visual flight when conditions are marginal. The guys in the Gwalior tower weren't so bad, I decided, although up in the air the visibility was more like 10 kilometres, which was well within the rules.

It was a long journey, in increasingly hot desert conditions. I had to track a long way south via Bhopal, which added over an hour to the flight. There was not a lot to see, but the heat caused turbulence, which made it difficult to maintain the altitude I'd been allocated. The air-traffic controller didn't seem to appreciate how much a small plane can be thrown up and down.

At Ahmedabad I was directed to park on the edge of the airfield, where my team of handlers were waiting, among dozens of parking bays, mostly empty. No sooner had I shut down and climbed out than a large helicopter landed right next to the *Sun*. The wash from its huge rotor would have thrown the plane around like a dandelion if four of us weren't there to hold it down. I looked around at all the other empty parking spots and thought, *Really?* The helicopter pilot thought it was hilarious. To me, his moustache was the joke. Grrr.

I had been looking forward to Ahmedabad because it was the site of Mahatma Gandhi's Sabarmati Ashram. It was a sprawling yet incredibly humble abode. What most caught my attention was a display of the loosely addressed mail sent to Gandhi over the years – the envelopes bore addresses such as 'Gandhi, India', but had nevertheless been faithfully delivered. Mail was not only part of the backstory of my trip, but I have been an enthusiastic 'postcarder' all my life. One of my favourite things is sending them with pictorial addresses and seeing if they arrive; thus far they always have.

After some wandering, I stumbled across what would be one of the cinematic highlights of my whole journey. Ahmedabad has an amazing drive-in cinema. Who knew? Indian indoor cinemas still use the pricing structure of cheap seats down the front, and the drive-in took the same approach. There was a grass area in the front for the cheapest tickets, then rows of concrete seating, car spaces, and several hundred seats on either side of the projection box, which was framed by a huge balcony with more seating – the most expensive tickets. A full house would probably be 10,000 people.

And the place was pumping. With prices starting at forty rupees, the equivalent of eighty cents, I was not surprised. The cheapest movie ticket elsewhere in India was 140 rupees, and the average was 180 rupees. With the evening temperature in the mid-thirties, it was the perfect way to see a film, and hundreds of families clearly loved it. Cheap, open-air cinemas could have much broader potential, I realised, and are a wonderful communal place for shared storytelling.

The border with Pakistan really worried me. With the *Southern Sun's* engine being the same as those in Predator drones – a Rotax 914, in the same backwards-facing configuration – I was very conscious that the India–Pakistan border is highly militarised, and therefore I was concerned about the *Sun's* sound signature. The two sides have fought four wars over seventy years. More than once during that lonely flight I wondered what radio call I should make if someone started shooting at me. Friends were concerned for my safety, too, which added to my anxiety. But in the event everything was fine.

The arid landscape in the border region was spectacular. Comprising vast stretches of sandy land, it was even more desolate than anything I'd seen in the Australian outback. There really was nothing out there.

On the ground at Karachi, Pakistan's largest coastal city, I was approached by a group of men who had a small truck carrying a 44-gallon drum of avgas. They insisted I had to refuel there and then. I always preferred to refuel just before departure, and something about their attitude made me uncomfortable. So I asked a question

I'd never thought to put before: 'How much is the fuel?'

The answer came back: US$6 a litre, an outrageous four times the standard price, and eight times the cost of local petrol. I asked to buy regular petrol, which they said was not possible. We politely argued a little. I was starting to lose hope when I asked how they could justify such a high price. They answered simply: 'We have a monopoly.'

Part of me admired their frankness, but there was no way I was going to agree.

In a moment of inspiration, I remembered that the Rotax engine manual referred, somewhere, to petrol being its preferred fuel. All the *Sun*'s manuals were stored on my iPad, and I quickly searched for 'petrol' and found the paragraph.

Shown written proof of my need for petrol rather than avgas, Karachi airport's monopolists folded. The Subcontinental respect for paperwork had saved me. I was relieved but weary: it was going to take me another four hours to get into town and buy petrol. To my huge relief, though, and for the first time on the trip, there was a petrol bowser at the airport. Not only was it one of the quickest refuels of the trip, the price was only US$1 a litre. Bravo!

This was not the first fuel fight I'd had along the way. At Chittagong a petrol station sold me low-grade fuel that could have damaged the *Sun*'s engine. It took an hour to return it and instead fill my eight canteens with premium petrol. At the airport, security guards insisted the containers be X-rayed with my regular luggage. One of the lids wasn't screwed on tightly enough and some fuel leaked into the machine, which was nerve-racking. Surely leaking fuel in an X-ray machine was a fire hazard ...

Before I got to Ahmedabad, the airport staff there informed me that petrol from the town was prohibited on the airfield, and I would have to buy their expensive avgas. After arriving, I asked a local agent to help. They arranged the petrol in a very helpful way: it was both much better for the *Sun*'s engine and a fraction of the price. Often, despite the supposedly rigid rules, people on the ground were simply happy to help their fellow man.

○

Karachi's Nueplex cinema was hailed as the best in Pakistan. Its reputation lured me to make a dicey trip to the city's new outer suburbs. It took about fifty minutes in an auto rickshaw, which broke down twice on the way.

In Pakistani and Indian cinemas, much like we once did back home, the audience is expected to stand when the national anthems are played at the start of films. Both governments had created wondrously nationalistic and chintzy video clips to go with their scratchy mono recordings. I loved them. They brought back childhood memories of 'Advance Australia Fair' at the local town hall.

For such firm enemies, Pakistan and India have remarkably similar taste in film. The Nueplex was showing *Gabbar Is Back*. As much as I was a fan, after fifteen minutes looking around I was ready to leave. I wanted to get to the Capri cinema in town by 10.30 p.m. to see the last thirty minutes of *Furious 7*. I couldn't imagine that seeing it dubbed in another language would make it hard to follow.

Out on the street, my rickshaw taxi driver was lying on the ground, trying to fix his vehicle. I waited for a taxi. And waited. It dawned on me that there were only private cars on the road. It was a new suburb with great facilities, but had been built, I later learned, mainly for senior members of the military, who all had cars and drivers. Someone advised me to wait at a petrol station up the road, where a cab might stop to refuel. There was no way of calling for one, he said.

By now I was starting to feel stranded. Pakistan has a serious terrorism problem, and Westerners have been targeted in the past, although Pakistanis are overwhelmingly the victims. After an hour of fretting, and wondering which shrub I might have to sleep under, a well-dressed man in a new BMW approached me. 'What on Earth are you doing out here at this time of night?' he asked.

I gave him a thirty-second explanation.

'You're taking a huge risk,' he said. 'Please get in. I'll give you a lift to your hotel.'

I got into his BMW, all the time wondering if I was doing the right thing. *Why didn't he ask where my hotel was until I was in the car?*

But I soon relaxed, and my visions of sleeping behind the petrol station quickly dissipated. The man was the Karachi manager of SC Johnson, a manufacturer of household cleaning supplies – Mr Muscle and the like. He had worked with many Australians throughout Asia, and he insisted on giving me a tour while we chatted. When I mentioned the ruins I had seen in Ahmedabad, he helped design me a tour of sites for the next day.

After forty-five minutes, as we approached my hotel, I thanked him and asked his destination – it turned out he lived just two minutes from the petrol station we'd started at. Now that I was safe, he would go home to his family.

The generosity of strangers, which I had already experienced a number of times – being lent a car in outback Australia, taken on a motorcycle food tour in Patna, and rescued in Karachi – had a powerful impact on me. I saw similar kindnesses all along my journey. And it was so often the people with the least, or in the places that the evening news would have us nervous to visit, where I was met with the greatest good-will. Our governments may argue at the highest level, but on the ground we are all just trying to care for our families – and, from time to time, a solo traveller.

Thank you, Ahmed Naazer Minhaj.

12.

The Kingdom

'Do. Or do not. There is no try.'
YODA, *STAR WARS EPISODE V: THE EMPIRE STRIKES BACK* (1980)

Pakistani air-traffic control seemed determined to end my trip. From Karachi, I needed to fly due west, over the Arabian Sea, skirting south of Iranian airspace over the Gulf of Oman to Dubai.

It wasn't uncommon for flight controllers to reject the first route I filed. Usually they wanted me to fly higher than the 4500 feet I requested, or to follow the IFR airway routes used by commercial aircraft. Often, after I'd agreed to these longer routes, and was well away from the airport, they would allow me to switch to a more direct route.

The officials in Karachi didn't object to my flight plan, which I estimated would take eight hours, seven of which would be over the waters of the Gulf of Oman. But after taking off I was directed to fly south-west. At first this didn't raise any alarm bells. I was used to being directed out of the way of commercial flights near airports. But as I neared the edge of the *Sun*'s radio range, my protests were ignored. The controller insisted I follow the heading for 70 nautical miles, or about 130 kilometres, away from land and towards the middle of the ocean and, ultimately, war-torn Somalia. Then, after I was handed from one control zone to another, a very agitated controller came on the radio.

'November Four Seven Three X-ray Papa, confirm you are VFR.'

'Affirm, VFR, November Four Seven Three X-ray Papa.'

'November Four Seven Three X-ray Papa, that is not possible – VFR flights over water are not allowed. You must follow the coast; turn heading 350.'

I couldn't believe it. They seriously wanted me to head north, towards Iran, when I was trying to get to Dubai, on the south side of the Persian Gulf? Given that the *Sun* was a seaplane, this was ludicrous. It was also dangerous, and triggered a deep sense of dread in me. Presumably, they wanted the *Sun* to fly west along the Pakistani coastline to Iran, when I would no longer be their responsibility. I did not have clearance for Iranian airspace; I hadn't even sought it, assuming it wouldn't be granted.

A quick calculation on my iPad navigation software indicated that, as a result of flying south-west for 70 miles, it would be 80 miles north to the coast – an hour of flying, which would take me further away from Dubai. When I reached the edge of Pakistani airspace, I would have to fly due south for half an hour to get around the Iranian airspace, before resuming my route towards Dubai. And all for no sound reason!

There were headwinds in the area, and even with three hours' worth of spare fuel loaded, this would add a couple of hours. The *Sun* might not make it to Dubai.

I asked the controller to confirm his instructions. He was adamant I should not be over water. I explained that the *Sun* was an amphibian aircraft but he didn't care. I told him I didn't have Iranian airspace clearance – again he didn't care. Then I played my big card.

'Karachi, Three X-ray Papa, proposed course may cause fuel shortage; request direct TAPDO.' This was the waypoint at the airspace boundary between Pakistan and UAE airspace.

The fuel warning should have sealed it, as safety is the top priority of every person working in civil aviation. Air-traffic controllers, who have thousands of lives in their hands every day, carry this responsibility more directly than anyone else in the industry.

He didn't care. 'Three X-ray Papa, you must not be over water; turn right, heading 350.'

I asked to speak to his supervisor.

There was silence. A few minutes later, another voice came over the radio: 'Three X-ray Papa, track direct TAPDO.'

Sanity had prevailed: I had been cleared to fly direct to the international boundary. Phew.

Several dull hours over water ensued, but I was pleased by the sense of routine I was now feeling about longer flights. Just a couple of years back, a three-hour flight seemed almost unbearable; now, seven to eight hours passed by quite comfortably. I had worked out that it was better to attend to the plane and myself regularly. On the hour, every hour, I would check the fuel status and transfer fuel as needed, and then fuel my body. Rather than having lunch, I ate a small amount every hour. Perhaps a handful of nuts, a piece of fresh fruit (or dried fruit if it wasn't available), maybe half a muesli bar. I also kept up my liquids, drinking two to three litres of water each day. This made my energy levels very even, I found, and I never suffered the mid-afternoon nods so many of us get each day, particularly at work! In fact, I think this practice helped me physically and mentally. Especially on the long flights over water or desert, it gave me something to look forward to each hour. I could take one hour at a time, breaking the journey into bite-size pieces, so to speak, and staving off boredom. I was also losing weight along the way, and had taken in my belt a couple of notches. Maybe it'll become a new fad – the Circumnavigation Diet!

Eventually we crossed the Arabian coast at Muscat and continued over the desert to Dubai. The contrast in air-traffic control was as vast as the sands below. An Australian voice welcomed me and said I could fly to the runway without delay. As the airport came into view, I saw a multitude of circling roads below. It looked more like the sprawling freeway network of Los Angeles than how I imagined the Middle East. One minute out from landing, I took a deep breath as I absorbed the sheer size of the place, and started counting how many planes the controller had waiting while I landed.

There were nine queued up to take off when the *Sun* finally touched down at Dubai International Airport, including a huge Airbus 380. Given the size difference between us, I imagined that the controllers, the other pilots and perhaps even thousands of passengers were smiling as they watched me arrive. After clearing customs and immigration, I was met by long-time Dubai resident and Emirates pilot Pete Forbes.

Contrary to the common perception, Dubai doesn't have as much oil as some of its neighbours. The city's wealth was primarily built over the past century from its position as a trading and travel hub between Asia and Europe. The massive airport is the physical embodiment of that longstanding function. The city's international reputation is shaped by its seven-star hotels, property developments, busy container port and indoor ski field. Beyond the reinforced concrete, though, Dubai has a rich history that should have been experienced by the Qantas Imperial passengers and crew who stayed there from 1938.

That history is why, although tired after the long flight from Karachi, I agreed to Pete's suggestion that we explore a boat yard on the bank of Dubai Creek. Old-style cargo still thrives in the Persian Gulf. There wasn't a shipping container in sight, and I imagined the place looked similar in 1938. Today, traditional timber ships are still hand-loaded (often with a few cars on top), and ply their trade from Kuwait and Oman to Pakistan and India. Several ships were being built at the yard. Pakistani and Indian labourers worked by hand on timber milled on-site from trees delivered by boat. It was incredible to see traditional craftsmanship being deployed on such a large scale.

I was determined to find out where the Qantas passengers stayed. Pete knew that Dubai's original airport was in neighbouring Sharjah, and had heard something about a museum. We decided to head there. The airport was built in the early 1930s, when Britain's Imperial Airways first started an airmail plane service to the outposts of the British Empire.

The original Sharjah airport terminal is now an aviation museum, though it resembled an Arabian fort. The flying boats had landed on Dubai Creek, 15 kilometres away, but the Qantas Imperial passengers and crew stayed in Sharjah, where there were basic motel-style rooms. The museum suggested that there had been nowhere suitable for the passengers in Dubai, and that the security of the fort-like grounds was needed at the time. It was a shame to learn that the pampered passengers had missed out on experiencing a unique part of the world.

My next departure brought a mixture of excitement and terror. I planned to leave Dubai at 5 p.m., when the worst of the desert heat had dissipated, and arrive at Abu Dhabi thirty minutes before sunset. Dubai's terminal for private aircraft is a glorious building, befitting the wealth of those who see the world from private jets. Then, for contrast, there was me in my overalls. In these splendid surroundings, I was handed the bill for storing the *Sun* at the field, and I nearly collapsed to the floor: it was almost US$3000. I'd only been there one night!

I remained as calm as I could; in that environment I didn't want to seem like some complaining Western pauper. But the fee was ridiculous. I asked if it wouldn't be too much trouble to get a breakdown of the charge.

'Certainly, sir,' they answered ever so politely.

The crux of the problem was that parking wasn't $100 per night – even that would have been very expensive by world standards – but $100 per hour. And to think I'd almost decided to stay two nights.

I asked if they could reconsider the parking fees, given the size of my plane. After all, it wasn't as big as the $30-million Gulfstream jets parked either side of the *Sun*. It took a few minutes on the phone before the fee was halved – but the good news was presented to me in a way that made it clear I should never think of asking this again. With gritted teeth, but still smiling, I paid the fee and went on my way. There was nothing I could do, but I did decide to warn other pilots away from stopping there. And, all in all, it had been pretty cool to land at that runway and explore Dubai's docks. In life, some experiences just cost more than others.

I was given permission to taxi towards the runway among several large passenger jets. Just as I reached the final holding point, where I was to wait before taking off, the ground controller told me to switch to the control tower's radio frequency. After a few minutes I realised that, while I could hear all of the jets around me talking on the radio, I couldn't hear the tower and it couldn't hear me. Jets behind me were starting to ask to go around me 'if he's not going to respond to the tower's directions'.

The embarrassment of holding up professional pilots was excruciating. I asked the pilot of the Airbus at the adjacent holding point to explain over the radio that I could hear everyone except the tower. A message was relayed back that I would have to wait for an airport official in a marshal's car. He arrived quickly and said that I could not operate the *Sun* at the airport without a working radio. She was being grounded.

The *Sun* was sitting in a small dip in the ground next to a large radio tower, which I believed was used for navigating instrument landings. *Could that be blocking the radio signal?* I thought. *Or am I just too low to the ground?* I asked the marshal to advise that my radio was working fine, and I believed I was just being blocked somehow. Could I try moving to another spot? I pictured the controllers in the tower shaking their heads and wondering why they let these little planes in here.

After forty-five agonising minutes, I was directed to follow the marshal car. It led me towards a second runway. As soon as we'd taxied about fifty metres the tower came back on the radio perfectly.

'Dubai Tower, Three X-ray Papa reading you, five out of five,' I said.

'Three X-ray Papa, also reading you,' the controller replied. 'Continue following the marshal car.'

What a relief, I thought.

I taxied for ten minutes and lined up at the second runway. The tower cleared me for take-off and granted permission for a touch-and-go on Dubai Creek, an opportunity I wasn't going to pass up. An early-evening golden sun painted the river, which was smooth and filled with timber boats plying their trade. It was a fabulous feeling to land on the water seventy-seven years after the first Qantas Imperial Empire flying boats.

An air-traffic controller directed me to 'follow the coastline not above 1500 feet'. Sweeter words had never been heard by this pilot. With the Dubai city skyline to my left glowing in the setting sun, I flew over The World, a series of artificial islands shaped like a map of the Earth, and The Palm, which deployed the same concept in the shape of a tree. They were incredible sights, although I remember thinking both projects were ridiculous when they were proposed. The Palm had sold out; a second version is now under construction. The World, though, was a disaster. There just weren't many people prepared to pay millions for a patch of sand in the shape of a country off the coast of Dubai, where it is so hot and salty. The World's islands were already eroding away, looking more like sandy blobs than discernible countries. *Oops,* I thought, my mood lifting after the radio embarrassment.

The night landing at Abu Dhabi was glorious. The quiet, private airport had no other planes landing or taking off, which made it stress-free after the busy Dubai International. The majestic Sheikh Zayed Grand Mosque glowed a spectacular blue beside the runway.

I had booked a room at the Armed Forces Officers Club Hotel. There were two reasons I wanted to stay there: it was next to the airport, and it was called the Armed Forces Officers Club, surely some throw-back to the world of Empire I was seeking. The place proudly advised it had a shooting range; while I didn't have a go at this extra-curricular activity, I thought it was a bizarre attribute to promote.

If Dubai was like Sydney or Hong Kong, Abu Dhabi was Adelaide or Singapore. The city is pleasant, clean and polite. There are fewer high-rises than in Dubai, and most are elegant. The city's Al Mariah cinema had three seating prices, the same system I'd seen in India. But in the sexually repressed Middle East, the rear seating was in private booths, every one of which had a box of tissues and a blanket. I bought my fifth and (I hoped) final ticket, over several thousand kilometres and eight time zones, to *Furious 7*. What better place to finish watching the movie than the city where the grand finale was set and filmed?

○

For a country that spends US$50 billion a year on defence, it was surprisingly hard to let the Saudi Arabian authorities know that I had crossed their border. No one answered my radio calls until I was about 150 kilometres from Riyadh, the capital.

When we did speak, the Saudi air-traffic controller seemed perplexed. 'November Four Seven Three X-ray Papa, please confirm you are a helicopter,' he said.

'Riyadh Approach, negative – I am a fixed-wing amphibian. November Four Seven Three X-ray Papa.'

Ten minutes later he was back on the radio. 'November Four Seven Three X-ray Papa, please confirm radial [the heading from the airport] and distance, and that you are a helicopter?'

'Negative, Riyadh Approach. I am a fixed-wing amphibian. ICAO identifier Sierra Romeo Echo Yankee, on zero seven zero radial at two zero miles.'

Five minutes later he was back again: 'November Four Seven Three X-ray Papa, you are identified, please confirm helicopter.'

It wasn't the first time on the trip the *Sun* had been mistaken for a helicopter; the Saudi controllers had probably never seen a plane flying that slowly before.

As I approached the airport, the air became hotter and more turbulent. It was 53 degrees Celsius inside the cockpit, and I was feeling it.

Riyadh has two parallel runways. The airport had posted a note to pilots, known as a NOTAM, which I'd read that morning before leaving, stating that the left runway was closed. Despite this, the controller directed me to land on the left runway. I wondered if they were instructing me to use it to keep me away from the bigger, faster planes. When I was just 100 feet above the ground, and only seconds before I touched down, a panicked call came from the tower: 'Three X-ray Papa, you are not a helicopter. The runway is closed. Go around; repeat, go around.'

I applied full power and sent the *Sun* back into the sky.

Hot air is less dense than cold air. In the extreme heat the *Sun* struggled to gain altitude. After two minutes the engine began to overheat, even though the fuel levels by now were relatively low, reducing the weight. The tower told me to wait for an Air India Boeing 777 to land, and then the *Sun* was cleared for the right runway.

On the ground, I was directed to a private jet terminal. I was then told to wait with the engine running, until instructed where to park. The engine's temperature gauge started climbing towards red again. Eventually, a ground marshal arrived and walked me the last couple of hundred metres. *What a day*, I thought, the sweat pouring off my body.

Sadly, it wasn't over. Officially, no avgas was sold at the airfield, but a ground handler I had hired in advance had arranged for a fuel truck to come from another airport. I appreciated the consideration, but had been advised that the avgas in the truck was priced at US$6 a litre. The prospect of paying over a thousand dollars to fill the *Sun*'s tanks was sickening, but I had no choice.

As the refuelling was finishing, another small plane landed and parked, flown by two Frenchmen on an expedition. Their handler came out to greet them and, to my dismay, handed them plastic jerry cans filled with fuel, which upon enquiry I discovered was car petrol costing only twenty-five US cents a litre. I asked my handler what was going on. He shrugged – he really didn't care. I asked the other handler how he had arranged the petrol. 'You have the wrong handler,' he replied. I wasn't feeling the generosity I'd experienced in every other city thus far.

Saudi Arabia's austere form of Islam disapproves of alcohol, although apparently not of the exploitation of foreigners. In response to a question on the customs form for private pilots – 'Has bar been locked?' – I wrote: 'Not applicable.' The customs agents didn't believe me and insisted on inspecting the *Southern Sun*. We all got into a minibus and drove across the tarmac, passing many impressive private jets. As we turned the corner and my plane came into sight, they started muttering to each other. There was much head-shaking and gesticulations, and then the minibus did a U-turn before we even reached the plane. *Hah!* I thought. *Take that, Saudi customs service.*

I was looking forward to getting to my hotel and showering. There are no cinemas in Riyadh, party town that it isn't, and anyway I just wanted to rest, write and get an early night. That might have happened if the taxi driver had known where my hotel was. We drove around for over an hour, passing some landmarks three times. He eventually dropped me at the wrong hotel. I got to the right one in the end.

Despite my exhaustion, I felt excited about the next day's adventure. I had a day of discovery in Riyadh, before flying out the following day to follow in Lawrence of Arabia's footsteps, figuratively, by entering Aqaba from Wadi Rum.

T.E. Lawrence didn't change history sleeping in. My planned Riyadh hotel checkout time was 2 a.m. and I reached the airport at 3 a.m. If I could depart in the relatively cool pre-dawn, the *Southern Sun* would have a chance of climbing into the sky with full tanks without overheating, and we would get to Aqaba, in southern Jordan, by the early afternoon.

Flying across the desert during the day is hard work. The intense heat creates thermal columns of air, and these buffeted the tiny *Sun* like a boat on a stormy sea. The near-constant turbulence can cause nausea even in experienced pilots, and makes flying in a straight line at one altitude a physically and mentally draining wrestle with the control stick.

My plan to beat the heat was defeated by the wind. Even if it hadn't been blowing at 50 knots from the direction I wanted to travel – making the flight impossibly slow – the wind was whipping up a dust storm that closed my options down. It was my first weather delay in the thirty-three days since I had left Melbourne. I had been lucky, and I knew it. But of all the cities to be delayed in ... Riyadh is a bustling city, but its lack of tourism and activities for Western visitors meant that it didn't make my list of the top 999 cities to visit before you die. It was only when Anne asked me if the Saudi women seemed repressed that I realised I hadn't seen any.

I waited at the airport all day for the weather to improve. I got a few hours' sleep in a crew room on a vinyl recliner seat that looked like my father's suburban throne back in the 1970s. I was concerned about my onward plans, as while I had permission to land in Jordan, clearance for my next destination had still not come through. I had been working on my Israeli clearance for months, with so many people involved in helping – from a friend, Joel Pearlman, who worked at Village Roadshow in Melbourne, to officials from AOPA, the Aircraft Owners and Pilots Association in Sydney, to local pilots in Israel keen for me to visit – but still we were waiting. I tried calling Israel to confirm the details of my hoped-for arrival in two days, but each time I dialled, the phone disconnected from the network. When I tried ringing Australia, it connected perfectly; only calls to Israel were blocked. *Seriously,* I thought. *At least talk to each other.*

The bad weather would persist for another couple of weeks, according to the air-traffic controllers, but my forecast said the wind would dissipate that night, and the temperature would drop twenty degrees. It seemed my best option was to leave at 10 p.m. and fly ten long hours through the cooler darkness. I was pleased to be a night-rated pilot.

Night flying, clouds and engine failure can be the unfortunate killers of amateur fliers. VFR-rated pilots like me are required to navigate by map and compass. Of course, that's much harder at night when you can't see what is on the ground. In these situations, the GPS becomes an invaluable tool, but it's not infallible. GPS systems can fail, pilots can fall asleep, and it's much easier to lose the horizon at night and hit the ground or a mountain.

I would have preferred to fly during the day, but my choice was either being stuck in the middle of the desert for a few weeks or flying overnight, so I decided it was time to grunt up and take it on. I had done night training but had flown no longer than an hour at a time, and that had mostly been before sunrise or after sunset, and to a familiar airport. I trusted that the sky would be clear, and that the stars would be bright in the desert.

The first two hours were uncomfortable. There was a lot of turbulence; the wind was so strong at one stage that the *Sun* was travelling over the ground at just 45 knots, which was about half my actual airspeed. It rained part of the way, which took me by surprise; during the day, a raincloud could easily be seen and avoided. At night the first I knew of the rain was when the drops hit the windscreen. Night flying was indeed much more demanding.

After a few hours, Riyadh air-traffic control passed me off to a new controller in a different sector. That was when things got interesting – or, as I found myself thinking of VFR, *very friggin' real.*

'November X-ray Papa, confirm your altitude?' the controller requested.

'Eight thousand, five hundred feet, November X-ray Papa,' I replied.

'Why are you at 8500 feet?'

'Eight thousand, five hundred feet was the altitude filed on my flight plan.'

There was silence, then: 'November X-ray Papa, are you VFR?'

'Affirm, VFR.'

'But VFR is not allowed at night. Did you get permission?'

'Yes, I lodged my flight plan. It was approved when I was given departure clearance.'

'But you cannot fly VFR at night.'

'I have been, for three and a half hours. I am night-rated. My flight plan was approved.'

'November X-ray Papa, you cannot fly VFR at night.'

What next? Was he going to make me land? There was silence for what seemed like an age, although it was probably only twenty seconds.

'November X-ray Papa, you must fly IFR. Please climb to 9000 feet.'

'Affirm, climbing to 9000 feet.'

I pulled the stick back and gained an extra 500 feet. The temperature inside the cabin was already cold, and now dropped to just nine degrees. My fingers and toes weren't expecting to be so cold in this part of the world.

But there was silence. *That's all?* I thought. *How bizarre.*

I had tried to sound calm and confident during the conversation, but the thoughts running through my mind were depressing. Would he make me turn around and land at the nearest airport – which I had just flown over? That would have left the *Southern Sun* stuck when the heat and winds returned in the morning, and me potentially stranded in Saudi Arabia for a week or more.

A while later I was delighted to see the sunrise, which revealed a vast array of crop circles in the north-west corner of Saudi Arabia.

What I had imagined was arid desert was in fact a vast food bowl that extended for miles. The landscape changed as I crossed the Jordanian border and the sea came into view, across some brutally harsh vegetation-free mountains that ran right down to the water.

The *Sun* and I landed safely at Aqaba, Jordan's only port. The resort city had no link to the flying boats, but its connection to Lawrence of Arabia was strong. I am a bit of a tragic for seventy-millimetre film, especially David Lean epics and men who dress in uniforms of their own design.

13.

Rock the Casbah

'All men dream, but not equally.'
T.E. LAWRENCE, *LAWRENCE OF ARABIA* (1962)

A password would get me across one of the most bitterly contested borders on Earth. Finally, my permission to fly to Israel had come through, complete with some very specific procedures. The Jordanian and Israeli aviation authorities first had to approve my flight plan. Then I was to call a phone number for Israeli security and provide them with a secret word I had been given to activate approval for my departure. Once that was done, the Aqaba control tower cleared the *Southern Sun* to take off.

With a three-hour flight planned I had much less fuel on board than usual. After successfully passing the first test – telling them the secret word – the tower cleared me for take-off; with its light load, the *Sun* soared into the sky, taking my heart with it. It was amazing to be passing so effortlessly over the desert that took T.E. Lawrence and his Arabian troops two months to cross. I planned to fly north on the Jordanian side of the border to Amman, and from there to the only entry point into Israel by air from the east.

The slightly long way round brought one big advantage: sightseeing. My route was directly over Petra, the famed archaeological site that appeared in *Indiana Jones and the Last Crusade*. Anne and I, on a holiday years earlier, had been enchanted by the historical ruins of this vast city. The main temple, carved into the pink sandstone cliffs, is impressive and familiar because its image appears so often in popular culture. What was stunning was how such an important ancient site reveals itself when you emerge from a large rock-crevice walkway. Beyond the main building, a whole ancient village remains in remarkably good condition.

So thrilled was I to fly over Petra that I did a few circles to get a really good look and take a few photos. Then a call came from an air-traffic controller: 'November X-ray Papa, please confirm your heading.'

'Ah, affirm tracking north for Amman, November X-ray Papa.'

Oops. Given the security concerns and procedures in this part of the world, the *Sun* had better just stick to the flight plan and follow the agreed course. Flying a few circles was probably not what they wanted to see an aircraft doing!

After a while the radio seemed suspiciously quiet, and I realised I had accidentally switched back to the Aqaba control tower's frequency, now long out of range. I toggled back to the Amman controllers, only to hear them calling other aircraft, trying to locate me on the radio. *Oops again*, I thought. Although ever pilot has done this at some point, it wasn't a great part of the world to drop out of radio contact.

Not surprisingly, the procedures for entering Israeli airspace are strict. Pilots, once airborne, need a specific clearance on an Israeli security frequency. If they don't get it, they will likely be intercepted and potentially even shot down. After the problems I'd had with air-traffic control in the Middle East and Pakistan, I was nervous. Amman radar handed me over to the Israeli security frequency. But there was no need to worry: my first call was immediately returned, and I was soon handed over to a Tel Aviv controller who could not have been friendlier.

As the *Sun* crossed the border, the weirdest thing happened. The GPS indicated 'no signal', which meant it couldn't find any satellites. *That's why pilots still need written flight plans*, I thought. The signal returned after several minutes. *Curious.*

About to leave for London from the Royal Yacht Club of Victoria. The flying suit helped me get

The *Southern Sun* lifts off from Williamstown on the first day of her trip. With limited flying experience, I had underestimated how dangerous it would be.

At Lakes Entrance in eastern Victoria, silt from rivers meets the clear ocean. I dropped in on my mother and told her I would be away for a while.

Sydney Harbour on approach to Rose Bay looks beautiful. Qantas departed from these waters in 1938 for a ten-day flight to London.

Picking up an airmail letter at Rose Bay for delivery to London. I drove the *Sun* up onto the beach in front of some apartment buildings.

A river in the Gulf of Carpentaria turns the soil green. This is my favourite photo through to London – I call it 'The Tree of Life'.

The *Southern Sun* makes an appearance at the Qantas Museum of Flight in Longreach, where the company began.

Flying over Vanderlin Island, trying to find my brother's home.

Who needs mobile phones when you have smoke to signal that dinner's been caught?

Lou, who helps run our mobile cinema in East Timor, flaps her arms when I ask her to pretend she's flying.

Looking for local history, I found a museum in Surabaya, Indonesia, that celebrates a Javanese tobacco dynasty.

A rickshaw driver struggles to find the port where the Qantas flying boats landed.

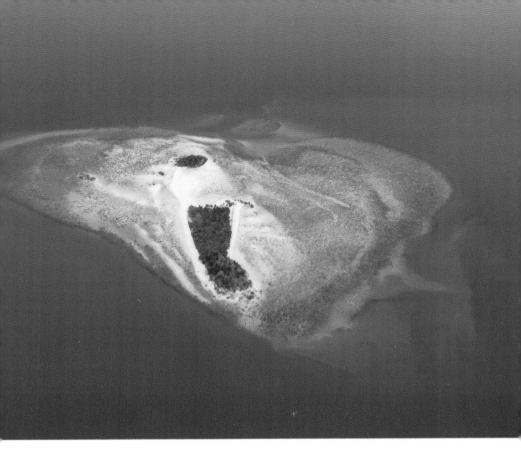

One of three heart-shaped islands I found and always texted to Anne. This one is near the equator.

Writing postcards at Raffles' Long Bar in Singapore. The next morning I couldn't leave my room.

At Penang airport in Malaysia, a famous Antonov freighter parks near the *Sun*. I try not to feel inferior.

Going to a petrol station and filling eight fuel bags often took hours, but was frequently necessary and usually cheaper.

A swan-inspired baby carriage in the Jai Vilas Palace in Gwalior, India.

A rather unusual statue, also in the Jai Vilas Palace.

One of my hobbies is sending postcards from around the world addressed only with the Sun Theatre's logo. They always arrive!

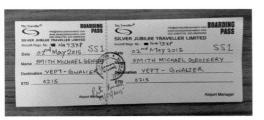

Sometimes bureaucracy even demanded I have a boarding pass to get onto my own plane. I christened my flight SS1.

Gandhi's ashram displays postcards delivered with the flimsiest of addresses.

A day on the beach in Karachi, Pakistan, with a carpet. And a camel. And …

Dubai Creek has developed since the Qantas flying boats landed there in the 1930s.

Approaching Abu Dhabi's
Al Bateen airfield with
the spectacularly lit
Sheikh Zayed Grand Mosque
under the flight path.

The customs and immigration staff at Lake Como in Italy are chiselled from the same mould and as stylish as any in the world.

The Aero Club Como's flying boat museum has a letter from the inaugural Qantas flying boat trip.

The *Southern Sun* arrives at Lake Como, a confluence of fantastic flying and famous movie locations.

Anne greets me at Damyns Hall Aerodrome in London, which was meant to be my final destination.

The airspace over the Thames River is one of the most crowded on the planet. I was nervous and thrilled.

"MY MOST BRILLIANT ACHIEVEMENT WAS TO PERSUADE MY WIFE TO MARRY ME."

Anne at Winston Churchill's birthplace, Blenheim Palace, outside of London. She encouraged me to keep going.

The *Southern Sun* being greeted by her first aerial plane spotters in Sligo, Ireland.

In Iceland's Reykjavik, the *Sun* nestles under the wing of a PBY Catalina, the world's most awesome flying boat.

The icefloes between Iceland and Greenland stretch so far I initially thought they were cloud.

The fjords and glaciers on the southern Greenland coast are some of the most spectacular terrain I've seen. The weather was perfect too.

Flying over Greenland, I'm no longer a short, balding, middle-aged businessman but a daring and resourceful pilot skirting the Arctic Circle.

An iceberg between Nuuk and Goose Bay. It's so big it generates concentric circles through the water.

Botwood honouring me with an old Newfoundland initiation known as the 'Screech In' ceremony.

The *Sun* is the first flying boat to fly from Foynes in Ireland to Canada's Botwood in thirty-seven years.

Flying around southern Manhattan. It was one of the thrills of my life, but I was still recovering emotionally from the incident at Goose Bay.

While I would be spending a few days in Tel Aviv and Jerusalem, today my destination was Haifa, a city 90 kilometres north of Tel Aviv, which had been suggested by the Israeli Association of General Aviation, where landing and plane storage was much more easily organised. A Haifa controller directed me to the airport at 1500 feet along the Mediterranean coast. Soon he came back with a new instruction: I was to head 101 degrees, an unusually precise heading, which are normally in increments of five or ten degrees.

'Confirming one zero one heading?' I asked.

'Affirm one zero one,' he replied.

Haifa was north, yet 101 degrees was a heading just south of east. *That's strange*, I thought, *but I'll do as I'm told*. I was conditioned to following controllers' orders. But as soon as I turned, I saw a clear problem. In about ten minutes – no, probably five minutes – I would fly into a mountain.

It felt like a communication issue. Most of the radio conversations on the airwaves were in Hebrew. When I spoke, they responded in English, which is the international language for aviation. Within a country, though, the government decides what language can be used for local flights.

I queried the heading again, but it was confirmed a second time. I told the controller the direction would result in a 'charlie foxtrot indigo tango', or CFIT, which is the acronym for a very dry aviation term, given the enormity of what it describes: 'controlled flight into terrain'. In other words: *You're going to make me crash!*

Another pilot piped up in a mix of English and Hebrew. By the time the controller got back to me, they had worked out what was going wrong. 'November X-ray Papa, heading zero one zero,' was his new instruction. This translated into a heading of 10 degrees, which is indeed all but north. Not only was this away from the mountain, but I was to return to flying along the beach – a much better outcome.

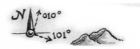

I was so happy to have made it to Israel. The Qantas Imperial flying boats landed on the Sea of Galilee in 1938, when Palestine was a British mandate. Also, some friends from the film industry – Barry, Reparata, John, Brett and Tobi – were in Tel Aviv, fresh from the Cannes Film Festival.

Arriving in Israel in a private plane involved a long and arduous security clearance, which I obtained only with the support of friends and pilots in Israel and Australia, who pleaded my case to the Israeli government. The standout fine chap was Yigal Merav, a pilot and Haifa Flying Club member and the owner of a local pest-control business. Yigal met me on the ground, helped me park and secure the *Sun*, and shepherded me through customs. That was after he'd spent weeks lobbying the Israeli security service to grant me permission to land, going to countless meetings on my behalf. I had never met him before, but he seemed inspired by my quest. Would I have done the same for someone struggling to visit Australia? I'd like to think so, but I couldn't help wondering if I was receiving more support than I deserved.

While Israel is in the Middle East, it has a European atmosphere, and when I looked out at the Mediterranean Sea, London seemed close. I felt like I was almost on the home stretch. The *Southern Sun* had made it this far admirably. With more relaxed European airways ahead, I expected the flying to be a lot easier.

○

People say Tel Aviv is like New York. It isn't. The city has a buzz of its own and was much more pleasant, especially with the Mediterranean weather. There were wonderful Bauhaus buildings and other art-deco designs. My favourite public architecture was the exquisitely detailed manhole covers – a certain sign of civilisation and culture.

The authorities wouldn't allow me to land the *Sun* on the Sea of Galilee, which forms part of the border with Syria. I took a taxi instead. There are good photographic records of flying boats on the lake in the

1930s, including the huge Empire flying boats on their way to and from London.

That evening I headed back to Haifa and gave a presentation to the Israeli branch of AOPA, IAGA, the Israeli Association of General Aviation. It was the first time I had talked about the trip in any kind of forum, and I'd spent several hours over the previous two days thinking about the journey's highlights and broader significance, and assembling a slide show of photos.

During stopovers I had been writing an online journal (which my kids tell me is really called a blog). I hadn't sought attention or sponsors for my retracing of the airmail route, nor had I done anything to promote it online, but I did want to share my story with other pilots and adventurers. A satellite tracking device on the dash of the *Sun* had been automatically sending her location to the website every fifteen minutes, allowing my family, friends and anyone else who was interested to follow me in real time. At every city I tried to include something a little colourful about the day's flying and the places I had visited, and I thanked people for their generosity.

I used the blog as the basis for my presentation to the Israelis. It was an honest account, but not a fulsome one. I mentioned my equatorial sink experiment but not the jammed control stick. With the audience I laughed about Riyadh air-traffic control but I skipped over my radio stuff-up near Amman. The ladder-damaged propeller certainly didn't make an appearance.

To be frank, I was having mixed feelings about what I was doing. I was not only an amateur pilot, but an inexperienced one. By virtue of my passport and my business success, I was fortunate to be able to undertake this incredible experience. Through my own mistakes I had put myself at risk, and potentially caused pain to others. I had benefited hugely from the generosity of strangers, but worried that I had given little back.

I made a big effort to make my presentation engaging and interesting, and the room seemed captivated. As I talked, I knew I was very lucky to be here, on the adventure of my life. I was very conscious that it had partly been made possible by my Israeli friends' tireless efforts, and they received me with warmth, generosity and enthusiasm.

14.

Behind the Glass

'You'll have bad times, but that'll always wake you up to the good
stuff you weren't paying attention to.'
SEAN MAGUIRE, *GOOD WILL HUNTING* (1997)

Even though the flight from Haifa to Crete was to be my longest over water to that point, I wasn't worried. Perhaps I had a false sense of security about the Mediterranean Sea. It was hardly the Gulf of Thailand, where monsoons regularly sweep through, or even the Timor Sea, where the afternoon rains fall so hard that planes aquaplane down the runway when they land.

After departing Palestine, the Empire flying boats would stop for fuel in Crete, the largest island in Greece. They then quickly left for a night in Athens, which at that time was ruled by a pro-British government led by a fascist dictator, Ioannis Metaxas. To recover from the long flight, I decided I would spend a night in Crete, avoid busy Athens and fly over another 1930s refuelling stop, Brindisi in southern Italy, and snap a photo from above.

There was nothing of note to see while crossing the Med, so I worked on the journal that eventually evolved into this book. I wrote by hand, with the control stick wedged between my knees. As long as the shadow cast over the page by the windscreen frame didn't move, I knew the *Sun* was flying straight at a constant altitude. I thought of it as an old-school form of autopilot.

131

Arriving over Crete was spectacular. Steep mountains rose from the water, some virginal, others intricately manicured into farms. When I saw how beautiful it was, I regretted planning only one night there. With no time to look around, I decided on a quick dinner at the port, followed by cinema research.

There were two cinemas in the capital, Heraklion. The one I visited was part of the British Odeon chain, which was owned by a British private-equity firm, in a fairly new shopping mall. It was uninviting and uncomfortable, and – go figure – all but empty. The floors were vinyl and the cheap tip-up seats were similar to those in the cinemas of my childhood. I understood why cinemas were built that way twenty years ago, but doing so today was just disrespectful of your audience.

○

The *Sun* had now flown almost 20,000 kilometres in forty days. She had landed at twenty-four runways, eight waterways and passed through fourteen countries. Her pilot had suffered diarrhoea, nausea and anxiety. But mainly he'd felt delight. He had at times been ripped off, messed around and ignored by people paid to look after him, yet he was having a ball. Even so, I needed a break. All I had to do was get to Croatia, where several friends were waiting for me with another boat – one with sails – for a blissful week exploring the Adriatic coast.

The flight would be fairly simple. The *Sun* would track along the north coast of Crete, turn right and fly to the south-west tip of Greece, go straight to the 'heel' of Italy, and then veer right again to the Croatian port city of Split, where I planned to store the *Sun* for ten days. Split is the nation's second-largest city, and was a summer palace for the court of Roman emperor Diocletian. Roman buildings dominate the centre of the city, and draw hundreds of thousands of visitors a year.

This was how I described the approach and landing at Split in my online journal:

There were good openings in the clouds but lots of islands around, so for peace of mind I did a spiral descent over water, as some of the islands were very steep and tall. The descent confused my satellite tracking, as it saw my ground speed go below 35 knots and it thought I had landed! But no, not at that level ... There was a fair bit of weather around and it kindly started lightly raining just on the way in but the tower were legends and turned on the runway lights, which made it heaps easier.

The reality was much more serious. A blanket of cloud at 2000 feet over the Italian coast killed my chances of taking an aerial photo of Brindisi to capture the Empire route landing spot. Because the clouds were worse a little north of the city, I requested and was granted permission to fly at 8500 feet. A couple of hours later I needed more altitude to get over the cloud, and climbed to 10,500 feet.

When there are a lot of clouds it can be hard to determine from looking towards the horizon what altitude to fly at. The difficulty is establishing a horizontal reference point, which allows you to see which clouds are above or below your level.

It was comforting to be able to see the Adriatic Sea. As long as it was below me, I wasn't going to hit a mountain. It was rare that cloud completely covered the water, which is so common over land. The fact that the *Sun* was a seaplane made it feel safer than a regular aircraft.

The weather worsened as I flew north. I got clearance for 12,500 feet, which was the highest the *Sun* had ever gone. Then the Italian air-traffic controllers allowed me to climb another 1000 feet. Because the tailwinds were stronger up there, the higher the *Sun* was, the faster she went. The air was so thin that I had to breathe from an oxygen canister to make sure I didn't lose concentration or black out. My oxygen supply was limited to several cans, but I didn't believe I would need anywhere near that much.

While climbing, the *Sun* passed through the tops of a few wispy clouds. I could still see blue sky above, and at one point became aware of a change in the sound of the flowing air – it was almost like a flapping. I looked out to see if something was loose. Ice from the moisture in the cloud was forming on the forward edge of the wings and the struts that connected the wings to the fuselage. It was possible ice was forming on the stainless-steel edges of the propeller blades too, although they were moving too fast behind me for me to tell.

Ice is extremely dangerous on aircraft. By altering the asymmetrical shape of the wings – which is what gets planes off the ground – it can literally pull them out of the sky. Ice on the propeller reduces forward thrust, adding to the danger. I had never seen ice on the *Sun* before so I was very surprised. But, then, I had never flown so high before, and I hadn't planned to that day, so I hadn't taken note of the 'freezing level', the altitude at which the temperature, moisture and conditions would likely create ice on metal. I always carefully check the freezing level when flying near mountains, but now that I'd been flying over desert and ocean, I had fallen into the trap of not doing so.

Rather than descend into the cloud, which could have made the problem worse, I climbed towards the blue sky, which was not so far above me. The clear air wouldn't have enough moisture to generate ice, I reasoned. A minute later the *Sun* was in sunshine and the ice melted away.

The incident made me paranoid about going back through cloud again. But I had 13,500 feet to lose on a very cloudy day. Normally, if I had to, I would descend partially through a few clouds to get to the ground. I had been trained to do this. This time, I looked for a hole in the cloud cover big enough to descend in a tall, continuous spiral.

After I found one, the air-traffic controller in Split gave me permission to descend to 2000 feet. The *Sun* was out of the cloud, but now beneath it, in a rainstorm that made it almost impossible to see what was in front. I still had a good view out sideways. The heavy cloud had made it dark around the airport. The controller, instead of directing my approach, let me find my own way in. I wished he had taken the lead to help me home. I was flustered and still didn't have the confidence to do what I should have, which was to 'request vectors', a series of compass headings that would take me to the runway.

Split airport is right alongside the coast. There is an island close to the shore on the approach route to the runway I was assigned. As I neared the airport, the controller directed me to descend further. I was distracted, trying to follow the directions from my GPS, and I didn't realise the island was there. Instead, I discovered the island when it was just 500 feet beneath me. Although the controller, using his radar, knew the *Sun*'s altitude above the island, the sight of land emerging out of the rain freaked me out. It wasn't exactly a near miss, but not having seen it gave me a big shock. If I'd been flying any lower, the consequences could have been disastrous.

According to my GPS, the runway was two nautical miles away (3.7 kilometres). But I couldn't see it through the rain pelting on the windscreen. VFR pilots like me are used to being able to see where they are going to land from at least 10 kilometres out – it gives them time to prepare for landing. In this case, I felt like I was going in blind.

Suddenly, the airport appeared from the gloom like a welcome Christmas tree. The control tower had switched the runway lights on so it was now easily visible. I landed safely and thanked the tower. Their reply was telling: 'We're just happy to have you on the ground safely.'

I never told anyone how difficult my landing at Split really was. I sat in the airport's cafe for over an hour, digesting the last stage of the flight, and wrote frankly in my diary – my leather-bound confessional. When I met my friends that night, they could tell I wasn't myself. One friend, Nick, said I was white as a sheet and seemed to be in shock. He had just arrived on a commercial flight that was diverted away from Split because a storm had made it too dangerous to land – the same storm the *Sun* had flown under and around.

Even though I was eating and drinking with my friends, I was full of guilt and fear, and so I clammed up. But my diary reveals my true state of mind: 'You promised Anne you'd be safe, and today you broke that promise a few times. Today wasn't so marginal but if you push things further when the conditions are worse, you will go too far.'

Over the following year, I mentally blocked out what had happened. On reflection, though, it taught me a couple of important lessons. Firstly, just wait. The *Sun* had three and a half hours' worth of fuel on board, so I could have easily circled for twenty minutes until the storm passed. Secondly, if you aren't sure, be sure. At least ask. I could have asked air-traffic control for a weather update rather than being so determined to land as soon as possible. I should have requested specific directions to the runway, or flown entirely over the water. The *Sun* could have flown to the west of the island to be 100 per cent safe.

They say that once you get your pilot's licence, it is really a licence to keep learning. For me, Split brought that home.

15.

Casino Royale

'The unknown future rolls towards us.'
SARAH CONNOR, *TERMINATOR 2: JUDGEMENT DAY*
(1991)

After a week with some of my fellow cinema owner friends – Valhalla founder Barry, John from Nova, Ingrid of Luna, Nick de Dendy and Rachel of Orpheum – sailing the Dalmatian coast from Split to Dubrovnik – which included a day trip to Montenegro, an experience I highly recommend everyone have at least once in their life – it was time to fly again.

With a lot of competition across Europe for tourists, Split's airport is a well-oiled machine. Staff from its General Aviation division had looked after all my arrangements: filing my next flight plan, nine days' parking at the airport, tie-downs to make sure the *Sun* didn't blow away, a transfer from the terminal, refuelling and other organisational details. All for just €80, when ground handlers at other airports had charged hundreds of dollars. And they couldn't have been nicer or more efficient.

After a week of sailing under sunny skies, I was looking forward to seeing Croatia from above. At the same time, the *Sun's* difficult arrival in Split had left me feeling apprehensive and had shaken my confidence somewhat. Luckily, it was a perfectly clear day.

Croatia from the air didn't disappoint. The first couple of hours were along the western edge of Croatian airspace, and the Adriatic Sea glowed a glorious blue. There was not a single cloud. My destination was Lake Como, in northern Italy. One of the most romantic locales on this wee planet held an extra allure for me: Anne, rather than meeting me in London, was now coming to Como, where we'd be reunited after nearly seven weeks apart. It was the perfect place for a rendezvous.

The wishbone-shaped body of water was not on the Qantas Imperial flying boat route, but it does have the oldest continuously operated seaplane base and school in the world. It looks rather exquisite too, which is why it has been the backdrop for so many movies, including *Star Wars: Episode II – Attack of the Clones, Ocean's Twelve* and James Bond's *Casino Royale*. Famously, at the Lake Como village of Laglio is the holiday home of George Clooney, whose film *Tomorrowland* was playing in cinemas as I landed. I had hoped to meet with the actor and receive a personal apology for the two hours of my life spent watching it which I can now never get back. But the lights weren't on at his home.

As I got closer to the famous lake, the snow-peaked Dolomites mountain range came into view, overlooking flat and intricate farmland. *Down there is some of the most wondrous scenery and food the world doth know*, I mused admiringly, feeling confident in my flying again.

The standard seaplane approach route to Lake Como is at 2000 feet, which means the nearby mountains tower a few thousand feet above the planes. My destination was the town of Como, at the lake's southwestern tip. I had been under the directions of an air-traffic controller since leaving Split. As the lake came into sight, he closed my flight plan, which meant I was free to fly where I wanted to make my way onto the lake. It was time for some old-fashioned water flying. There were still radio calls to be made, but with no tower at Como, like at most small airfields, the calls are made simply to let other planes in the area know where you are and your intentions. Often these calls go unanswered, as you may be the only one there, but Lake Como was a hive of activity.

'Como traffic, Searey November Four Seven Three X-ray Papa, 10 miles south, leaving 2500 feet for 2000 feet, inbound,' I broadcast.

'Searey X-ray Papa, welcome to Lake Como. I think is your first time?' a pilot in a Cessna called back. The imperfect English spoken with an Italian accent was as romantic as the villas along the lake's edge.

'Si, um, affirm, first time,' I replied.

'Okay, you see I am doing circuit – follow me downwind when arrive and I show you the runway.'

A runway on a lake? This was interesting. A few minutes later I was over the historic town of Como, behind a Cessna that had floats instead of wheels.

'Searey X-ray Papa, overhead Como, 2000 feet, joining downwind, following Cessna, for water operations,' I said.

'Ah, Searey, hello – just follow me and you will see the pattern and runway,' he replied.

'Searey following.'

As I descended, I aimed the *Sun* towards a sea of terracotta roofs. The Cessna seemed to hug the mountain to our right, the eastern side of the lake. While concentrating on flying was important, it was hard not to be distracted by the scenery. *Bellissimo!*

Ahead of me, the Cessna turned towards the landing zone. When I reached the same position a minute later, the 'runway' became clear. Large yellow buoys marked the perimeter of the landing area. The Cessna in front touched down briefly on the water, skimmed for a few seconds and then climbed over the shoreline and back into the sky.

Waves and slop caused by ferries crisscrossing between towns were churning up the landing zone. Having learned from the *Sun*'s bumpy equatorial landing, I levelled out just above the water, took my time and slowed to just 40 knots before planting her firmly on the water.

'Searey X-ray Papa, clear of the runway. Taxiing for Aero Club Como,' I broadcast as I turned right and began making my way to the shore.

Arriving at the Aero Club Como was one of the great moments of my life. I taxied the *Sun* up a wide concrete ramp. Swans swam past.

Sure, I hadn't exactly summitted Mount Everest, but I had wanted to visit this place for many years, and I felt proud that I had flown a flying boat all the way there from Melbourne. Many pilots and their friends at the club seemed surprised at the size of the *Southern Sun* and the Australian flag on her tail. I don't speak Italian but overheard them mention Australia while shaking their heads many times.

I was even complimented by the club's chief flying instructor. He told me he thought a small plane like the *Sun* might struggle to land in the relatively rough water, but from the air he saw my landing and was impressed.

A past president of the club, Cesare Baj, who now serves as its librarian and historian, had arranged space for the *Sun* in the crowded hangar, and for three immigration and customs officers to meet me shore-side to check my British passport. They all seemed to come from the one gene pool, having the same lean physique, olive skin, two-day growth and cleanly shaven head.

Cesare, wearing a chic linen summer jacket, showed me round. The art-deco building and cavernous hangar were built in the 1930s, when Italy was industrialising under Benito Mussolini. The club allowed me to use an apartment in the building that had once been the manager's residence.

Cesare is a world-renowned historian in seaplane circles and has amassed what must be the most thorough collection of books, magazine articles, newspaper cuttings, paraphernalia and original airmail letters relating to flying boats and seaplanes. He proudly showed off some of his prize possessions, including one I think he knew would have special meaning for me: a letter sent on the inaugural Sydney to Southampton Flying Boat Air Mail service in 1938. The specially made envelope was exquisite and exciting to hold. Covered in postage stamps and inked rubber stamps and with a typed address, it was a unique if esoteric part of aviation history. All of a sudden, Lake Como felt connected to my flying boat journey.

After a walk around the gorgeous town it was time for dinner, my last solo meal before Anne arrived the next day. I decided there was no better place to eat than the Yacht Club di Como, which was on the waterfront next to the Aero Club. They accepted my Royal Yacht Club of Victoria membership card and welcomed me as a guest. I sat for a couple of hours, writing some postcards and in my diary, while enjoying the vista of boats under the long twilight after the sun dipped behind a tall mountain.

The next morning, with Anne not due until late afternoon, it was time for a joy flight. I flew the length of the lake and back, including some brief landings and take-offs on water. I was most excited to stop on the waters at Bellagio, a medieval town that juts out into the lake. Villages along the bank were packed with old Italian villas, separated by surprisingly large stretches of woodland.

There were plenty of other pilots out, and they filled the radio with business-like chatter. Some were seaplanes on charters. Others were pilots training from the base at Como. I broadcast my position at key points so the other pilots would know where I was. It was the busiest seaplane activity I'd ever seen, in the most spectacular of settings.

The Aero Club could only accommodate the *Sun* for one night, but club officials had made arrangements for me to store her at a private airfield in the nearby town of Lecco while Anne and I enjoyed a lakefront holiday. The airfield, which was so small it was actually tricky to spot, was owned by the factory that manufactured Kong outdoor equipment, such as abseiling harnesses and rigging fittings.

The Kong runway was 430 metres long. According to the *Sun*'s manual, she needed only 200 to 300 metres to land or take off. But as I'd been using runways that were as long as 3 kilometres for most of the trip, the grass-surrounded concrete field looked very, very short.

I decided to do a complete lap and have a really good look from the air before making a cautious approach. After I did so, the *Sun* touched down right at the runway threshold – known in pilot-speak as landing 'on the numbers' – and pulled up with a quarter of the runway spare. *That felt good*, I thought. But I knew landing was one thing; how would I go taking off with more fuel on board?

Adding to my concern, the *Sun's* pitch motor – the device that adjusts the angle of the propeller to make take-offs easier – wasn't working; it was like driving a car without first gear. I knew I was going to spend the next week worrying if the airfield was long enough. So I got on the radio and advised whoever was listening – no one seemed to be – that I was taking off again for a 'circuit'. I followed the textbook procedures for short runways, which is basically to deploy full flaps, lock the brakes on, push the throttle all the way forward and let her rip.

There was nothing to worry about. The *Sun* was in the air about two-thirds of the way along the runway, in still conditions. A headwind would make the take-off even easier.

○

My experience getting to the town of Pognana Lario, which is halfway between Como and Bellagio, felt like an Italian version of *Planes, Trains and Automobiles*. It was just fifteen minutes directly by plane yet four hours by foot, taxi, bus, train and another taxi. Exhausted, I got to the rented villa just before Anne arrived by taxi from Milan. It was wonderful, if a tad surreal, to meet her on the steep driveway leading down to the lake. The small villa Anne had booked, right by the water's edge, was perfect. We had a quiet night catching up, with a small dinner and champagne in our front yard, which looked across the lake to – of all places – George Clooney's house, and planned some activities for the week ahead.

We decided to spend our first day in Bellagio. There was a ferry stop close by, and we ventured off mid-morning. It took ninety minutes to cover just 13 kilometres. *There are two ways to view this form of travel*, I thought, *charming or tedious*. Bellagio was splendid. But relying on three ferries a day had me seeking more independence. By the end of the day we had rented a small boat.

Anne and I quickly settled into a routine which we kept up for the whole week: setting off by water to a corner of the lake, energetic exploring, a long Italian lunch, slow afternoon meandering and then a salad at home for dinner. It felt like a second honeymoon, especially after so many weeks apart.

Luckily, Anne and I share a love of films, and we were keen to visit two famous movie settings. Villa del Balbianello had featured in a *Star Wars* and a Bond film and was open to the public for tours. Villa La Gaeta, however, a lakeside mansion that appeared in *Casino Royale*, was a little more difficult. In the closing scene, the villain, Mr White, is shot in the leg by Bond, and dragged off for an interrogation – a plot line that leads into the follow-up film, *Quantum of Solace*. Once a private home, the villa is now divided into apartments that aren't accessible to the public. But a couple were up for sale or rent. Some were even on Airbnb, so I contacted one and requested to inspect it as a potential renter. An appointment was scheduled for later that day.

On the last day of our most splendid week together, Anne and I arrived in our little runabout and tied up to the jetty. The beach was private, the grounds exquisite, the apartments spectacular and the cost affordable, even for a few nights. We loved it. Without a hint of an Austrian accent, I made a silent vow: *We'll be back.*

16.

The Flying Squad

'Don't tell me I can't do it; don't tell me it can't be done!'
HOWARD HUGHES, *THE AVIATOR* (2004)

For a quiet town, Saint-Nazaire played an important role in French economic and military history. Situated at the mouth of the famous Loire River, it was a major German submarine base during World War II. The U-boats were housed in concrete bunkers, the most monolithic and brutal structures I had seen. Sitting there, unloved for such a long time, they were kind of cool – in a historical and construction sense. I had sailed into the port in 2003 while competing in the Tour de France à la Voile, on the first boat I christened *Southern Sun*, a Mumm 30 yacht, with a young Williamstown crew racing as 'Team Australie'.

Perhaps ironically, the river is now home to a French naval base, and large sections over the water are reserved for military pilots. Europe's biggest aircraft manufacturer, Airbus, builds fuselages at the airport. Once finished, they are inserted, like big Russian dolls, into a giant Beluga plane and flown to the south of France for final assembly.

The *Sun* arrived in Saint-Nazaire at 8.30 p.m. on 10 June, a day later than planned, via Marseille, where the Qantas Imperial flying boats and many others once refuelled. I had hoped to land on the water runway just off the shore of Marseille airport. But it was rough and wasn't worth the risk when a long concrete runway was available too.

147

My small delay was due to the twenty-four hours I found myself at St Lucia airfield, in Lombardy, Italy, where I had planned a quick pit-stop. By good fortune, on enquiring with the *Southern Sun*'s propeller manufacturer in the United States whether they had an agent in Europe who could service the pitch motor, it turned out that Aviare S.R.L. was only an hour south of Como. On arriving, I was helped by aero mechanic Luigi Grasselli, who discovered it was a bigger job than it first seemed: he would need all day to collect the necessary parts and then repair the propeller hub properly. It turned into a huge day and night of work – although not without a classic 'get your priorities right!' long Italian lunch in the middle. But the work was done, and very well, as Luigi sorted out a few other things he noticed along the way. Reaffirming my wonder at the generosity of strangers, not only was he a lovely chap and fantastic engineer, but he refused to let me pay for the long hours he had worked, just the parts and fuel used. Thanks, Luigi.

By contrast, after landing at Marseille airport, I was chastised by an official for not having hired a ground handler to escort me the eighty metres to the terminal building. I apologised, but part of me was resentful at the criticism. I didn't know the rule, and many light air-craft, including a flying school, used the airport. That meant there were a lot of amateur pilots like me walking around the place all the time. It was hardly Dubai or Heathrow. Later that night, making the most of the long summer days and 10 p.m. sunsets, after a long day of flying I arrived late at Saint-Nazaire's airport and found it completely empty. I locked up the *Sun* and caught a taxi into town. The Loire River here was the final stop for the Qantas Imperial flying boats before Southampton, where the passengers disembarked and caught trains to London. Of course, the atmosphere in France in 1938 was tense. World War II began on 1 September the following year, when Germany invaded Poland, but the Spanish Civil War was well underway, and Germany had already absorbed Austria, and in Ocotber 1938 annexed part of Czechoslovakia.

For me, Saint-Nazaire brought a mixture of nervousness and excitement. The following day would be the last of my two-month-long trip, much more leisurely than the Qantas Imperial ten-day passage, although even slower than the six weeks the Cunard line took at the time. I would briefly touch down on the water at Southampton, and then fly to a nearby airport to clear customs. Anne would be waiting for me in London. The *Southern Sun* would be disassembled, placed in a shipping container and sent on a lonely, slow journey home.

My ambition to re-create one of the great and little-travelled routes of international aviation would be complete. I would return home to Williamstown and resume my life running our cinemas. *Is this really it?* I thought. I didn't dare ponder going further than London for fear of jinxing the last leg, which would be a long flight.

○

The French payments system tried hard to stop me getting to London. The fuel bowser at Saint-Nazaire airport only accepted French credit cards – a problem encountered nowhere else along the route so far – and no one at the airport would take my euros and help out. The *Southern Sun* didn't have enough fuel in her tanks to make Southampton, which meant I had to find an airport on the way where I could fill up – a kind of aerial pit-stop. Appreciating my problem and wanting to help, the Saint-Nazaire control tower telephoned little La Baule-Escoublac aerodrome, which was 10 kilometres away, and confirmed that it was technologically advanced enough to accept payment from a foreign credit card.

The five-minute flight to La Baule-Escoublac was the shortest of the entire journey. Established as a military airfield during World War I, it is located in a gorgeous spot by the seaside, and has a classically French cafe and picnic tables. The *Sun* caused a minor sensation at the aerodrome's flying club, where she received that oh-so-French pouty look and a remark I heard regularly: 'No! In that?'

Some respect, please, I thought. *She's looked after me very well.*

Wanting to look my best for England, I polished my boots on the clubhouse's shoe-shine machine, the first I had ever seen at a flying club; I expected to see that sort of thing in England, but hey, *vive La France*! After taking off, I looked across at the Loire River and was reminded that it was once the last stop of the flying boats' epic journey. The breeze was moderate and the water calm, so I turned, descended and eased the *Southern Sun* onto the river near some boat moorings and a lovely beach. After kissing the water, we turned north.

The flight took me over Brittany, one of my favourite places from previous sailing travels, and the famous Mont Saint-Michel monastery, surrounded by tidal flats. I looked over the rocks and islets that surrounded the island of Jersey and thought about how treacherous they must be to sail. About an hour from the British coast, at 2500 feet midway across the English Channel, the *Sun* hit turbulence so severe it would have launched me out of my seat if I hadn't been strapped in. The gentle tailwind was replaced by a strong headwind, which slowed her down. I didn't care, as long as it wasn't too rough to land on Southampton Water. I was euphoric at the thought of finishing the trip – alive and with the *Southern Sun* in one piece – and couldn't stop grinning.

While relaxing on a yacht in Croatia a few weeks earlier, I had called the Southampton airport control tower. The city lies on the river-like Southampton Water, an estuary that drains into the Solent on its way to the English Channel. Southampton's waterways provided a perfect landing spot for the Empire flying boats. The city is a two-hour train ride to London, and the water is shielded from the open sea by the Isle of Wight.

Today, the whole of the airspace above Southampton Water is under the control of the airport. But the water is supervised by a harbour master, employed by Associated British Ports, a company based in the city. The airport controllers described my plan to land briefly on Southampton Water as 'interesting' – a very British adjective, the precise meaning of which in this context was unclear. Flying a few feet above the water was all right, I learned, but I would need AB Ports' permission to get the *Sun* wet.

The port manager, Clive Thomas, put me in touch with the Deputy Harbour Master, Ray Blair. Although he sounded helpful, there was a problem. Southampton is Britain's biggest port for shipping, a busy location for ferries coming to and from the Isle of Wight and France, as well as a popular yacht-racing venue. The famous 'Round the Island Race' starts and finishes from Cowes, on the Isle of Wight, each summer. To reduce congestion, seaplanes were not allowed to land on Southampton Water. That was bad news.

I summarised the *Southern Sun*'s mission to Blair. As a former Royal Navy officer and long-time port manager, he was familiar with the link between Southampton and the historical flying boats. He was also, to my huge relief, sympathetic to the idea of trying to retrace their journey. We amicably negotiated two areas of Southampton Water that would be suitable. He had just two conditions: it would have to be a touch-and-go only, and on a weekday, when there would be fewer recreational sailors to dodge. I would then fly to nearby Southampton International Airport to clear customs and immigration. I was ever so pleased.

So, after six hours of flying, at 1.48 p.m. British Summer Time on Friday, 12 June 2015, the *Southern Sun* descended over the town of Hythe, a patch of coastal land and a sandbar abeam several dozen moored boats, and landed gently on a shallow stretch of Southampton Water for several seconds. She had made it.

Fifteen minutes later, having landed at Southampton airport and been advised by my ground marshal that I had 'a welcoming party inside', I walked into the private aircraft terminal. There were indeed over a dozen people awaiting my arrival. I was still on a high, and I remarked aloud: 'Wow, now that is a welcoming party! That deserves a photo!' I pulled out my phone and took a snap.

When I look at that photo now, I see hints of an uncomfortable encounter I didn't know was about to take place. A few people off to the side are laughing at me, while several men in the front and middle of the room have their backs to me. In the time it took me to take my phone from the pocket of my flying suit, they spun around to hide their faces from the camera. The group was made up of officers from three law-enforcement agencies: Immigration, Customs, and Special Branch, which is a Metropolitan Police unit responsible for national security. The agent from Special Branch was impeccably dressed. *The British really know how to cut a fine suit*, I thought. The other men wore uniforms. They told me they were investigating my 'unannounced arrival' in the United Kingdom.

'Huh?' I said, now surprised. 'I've been in contact with British authorities for weeks. So has my clearance agent, and I filed a flight plan in France this morning stating that Southampton was my destination.'

One officer told me that the French aviation officials hadn't transmitted any plan, which meant the British officials were unaware of my impending arrival. That seemed strange, if not unlikely. I had been handed over from controller to controller on the route from France without any suggestion that I wasn't expected, including by British air-traffic control.

I was so happy about arriving in Britain – for the first time since the year before, when I'd faced a photo of the Queen at the British Consulate in Melbourne, put my hand on my heart and pledged allegiance to Her Majesty, in doing so obtaining British citizenship – that I was amused by a situation that should have worried me deeply. The officers didn't see it that way. The British government takes the security of its borders very seriously. So too does the British public, as evidenced by its vote to leave the European Union the year after my arrival. And of course, since the 9/11 attacks on New York and Washington, aviation security has become much stricter, even if it's an amphibian aircraft retracing a 1930s mail and passenger air service.

I didn't believe I had done anything wrong but the officers were in control – and it seemed they did. Although I was potentially in deep trouble,
I was determined to keep a positive frame of mind and not become angry,
defensive or resentful. They asked detailed questions about the trip, my
reasons for visiting Britain and my professional and personal background.
They emptied my bags, went through all my clothes and electronic devices
and examined all my paperwork. There was no more demeaning moment
on the trip than when a customs officer wearing latex gloves held my
boxer shorts up to a light and ran his fingers over the seams to check for
contraband. *Perhaps he's just appreciating the amazingly lightweight and
breathable merino wool?* I mused, hoping it was a clean pair.

While the search was taking place, a few of the immigration officers
wandered over to a counter used by Signature Flight Handling, which I
had hired to manage my arrival in the United Kingdom. Two of the
company's staff, Chloe and Helen, were perusing my website and reading about the trip, and oohing and aahing at some of the photos. Soon
the customs staff were checking out the screen too, leaving me to answer
Special Branch's polite but firm questions. At the same time, there was
a flow of airport staff and airline crew coming into the lounge, saying
hello, taking photos of the *Southern Sun* and asking disbelievingly:
'Seriously, from Australia ... in that?'

After two hours, the security staff concluded that flying from
Australia at 80 knots would have been a fairly elaborate cover story for
someone trying to sneak into Britain. I was free to go.

To celebrate – my freedom, my arrival and the completion of my
voyage – the Signature Flight Handling staff gave me a coffee and a slice
of a chocolate cake that had been bought for a colleague's birthday. In
an unexpected and gracious act, they also waived their fees, perhaps
because they found my trip amusing and interesting, or maybe just
because they couldn't believe I'd actually made it.

As for my unannounced arrival – it turned out I was in the wrong.
Talking to pilots in London later, I learned that when entering or

leaving the United Kingdom, a 'General Aviation Report' must be sub-mitted to the UK Border Force in addition to a flight plan. The GAR, as it is not so affectionately known, requires very basic information: the name of the pilot and aircraft, where they took off and arrived, and the addresses of where the crew would stay in Britain. It would have taken about three minutes to complete, tops.

I had been grateful for Mike Gray and White Rose's work and quick responses whenever a problem came up, and every other part of the sixty-day journey had gone flawlessly. But I was annoyed he hadn't mentioned this simple form, which was required to enter his own country. Perhaps he had assumed I knew about it; and of course I was now a UK citizen, so I was effectively 'returning home'. But Mike really had done a sterling job overall, and we laughed about this soon after.

○

Even though I had flown across the world, I was nervous about the short flight from Southampton to London, which would be along a narrow corridor between restricted airspace around Gatwick and Heathrow air-ports. I had to get it right.

Alistair, a commercial pilot who had checked out the *Sun* while I was being questioned, helped me work out a flight plan. I texted Anne, who was at the Tate Modern in central London, and confirmed I would soon arrive at Damyns Hall, an aerodrome in outer East London which has an old-fashioned long grass strip and is popular with vintage and modern light aircraft. I took off from Southampton and turned east for the first time since leaving Rose Bay.

The sky was crowded with planes. The intricate green countryside of England was lovely, and I passed over Surrey, where my mother was born in the pretty town of Carshalton. London air-traffic control gave me permission to fly over the Thames River and London City Airport, which is the home of many private jets serving London's big financial sector. It was like Disneyland for aviation enthusiasts.

The *Southern Sun* landed at Damyns Hall at 6.01 p.m. The Air Sport Australia Confederation recognised that the trip had set two world records: for a flight from Melbourne to London, and simultaneously from Rose Bay to Southampton, in an amphibious aircraft.

No one at the aerodrome knew I was coming. I had obtained permission from the chief flying instructor to store the *Sun* there for a few weeks, but he was away on a flying trip when I arrived. The temperature had hit a blistering (for Old Blighty) 27 degrees that day, and a shirtless and slightly pink member of the local flying club (a new form of high visibility?) directed me to a parking spot.

Anne was waiting to greet me. It had only been a few days, but I was ecstatically pleased to see her, and share with her this moment of triumph. She had been so supportive, and now she helped me tie the *Sun* down. We talked about how to get a container onto the field to ship the plane to Melbourne. We were soon ready to farewell the *Southern Sun* and take a holiday.

Anne told a few of the club members what I had done. Either they didn't believe her or it didn't sink in. 'Did you say from Australia? Really, in that?' This was becoming a theme ...

Club member Alan Sutton kindly dropped us off at the nearest train station, and we headed into London. I planned to rest and relax, and to consider a question that had been nagging at me for months: could the *Southern Sun* go all the way?

17.

The Trip

'Life is a journey, not so much to a destination, but a transformation.'
CHRIS VAUGHN, *TO SAVE A LIFE* (2009)

'How on Earth did you make it here to London when you can't even find the room?' Anne asked when I took a wrong turn, for the third time, in the corridors of the Royal Thames Yacht Club.

'There's no compass and the GPS doesn't work inside,' I muttered.

I loved staying at the Royal Thames Yacht Club in Knightsbridge, which offered reciprocal visiting rights to my club in Melbourne. It overlooked Hyde Park, so you'd often see the Household Cavalry Regiment, which protects the Queen, trotting by on training rides. The traditional bar and dining room, the small but comfortable bedrooms – known as 'cabins' – and the atmospheric library and room of model boats celebrate history, boating and adventure tastefully but in a tangible way. It feels very British – tally ho indeed.

I slept ten hours after landing in London. The next day, after arranging to deliver Sophie's rather slow airmail letter to her grandmother, Anne and I began a three-week holiday through England and Scotland. We walked along Hadrian's Wall, the millennia-old defence against wild Scottish tribes built by the Romans, we toured various country estates that appeared in period movies, we visited Winston Churchill's two residences and we also dropped in on a few cinemas. Never had a holiday been so wonderful. I felt constantly elated, and truly at peace with myself for the first time in years. The sky was bluer, the grass greener and the faces cheerier than I had ever seen.

At the time, I wrote in my journal that my flight 'had been a wonderfully rewarding adventure'. That was a true but somewhat glib description. A year later, I still felt incredibly proud. I have thought about the trip every day since it ended; a random encounter or event would remind me of tiny details of my experiences.

The trip had enriched my understanding of the world in a way nothing else could. It revealed incredible physical beauty, human hardship and endurance, and let me know the terrifying but rewarding experience of putting your life on the line for personal ambition. My most powerful discovery was of the generosity of strangers. In nearly every country, at least one person went out of their way to assist me. I became convinced that what I had thought of as regional and outback Australia's 'country kindness' actually flourishes everywhere. The world is awash with good people.

Perhaps that is because human experience is more universal than many of us realise. Regardless of a nation's politics, the average man and woman on the street is just trying to feed and look after their family, educate their children and take comfort and pleasure from being part of a community. We all want to belong.

Government does shape societies, though. I realised there was an inverse relationship between the efficiency of a country and the amount of paperwork required to get stuff done. In a sense, this was profoundly disappointing, although not surprising. The inefficiency and underemployment I saw in parts of Asia, the Subcontinent and the Middle East was dispiriting.

But there is hope. Mobile phones are changing the developing world in the way computers reshaped the developed world. Social media, in particular, is liberating communication. Mobile phone usage in the developing world has leapfrogged mere voice calls. Mobile devices are ushering in an economic revolution, one I hope will help make the citizens of developing nations as rich as those of the developed world.

In 1938, air travel was limited to the super-rich. Now almost everyone in wealthy countries can afford it. The new mobility has created a global tourism boom, so much that famous sites are swamped by people seeking the all-important selfie, which they will then immediately post online. All this drives an ugly trade in tourist kitsch. But discovery through travel is still possible in the twenty-first century. In India I visited Chittagong, Patna and Gwalior, towns I had not heard of until I was planning my trip, and they were immensely enjoyable. In each of those cities I didn't once see another foreigner, which made me feel greedily pleased to have them to myself. The road less travelled is worth taking.

While not cheap, a private aeroplane is one of the most wonderful ways to explore. From the air – but not too high – the gaps between cities, national parks and monuments are filled in. The giant jigsaw that is the physical world starts to fit together. In far north-west Saudi Arabia I was stunned to see mile upon mile of green farmland emerge from the dry-as-dust desert. I captured the memory in photos. Watching the sun rising after flying all night is also implanted in my mind.

Strangely, I felt some sympathy for the passengers of the Empire flying boats. As incredibly privileged as they were to undertake their ten-day journey across the world, it was made at break-neck pace in 1938. They had time for just a taste of some of the greatest luxury hotel outposts of the British Empire, most of which would soon be shut down amid the darkness of World War II.

I like flying and I like boating – but I love travelling and exploring, especially with friends and family. While this was a solo trip, the experience was enriched by sharing it with others via my online journal. I didn't know if anyone would find it interesting, and I was worried about being criticised for trying to undertake a dangerous journey with such little flying experience, so I had kept it very low-key. To my surprise, as word slowly spread, a lot of people who didn't know me started following the *Southern Sun* online to make sure I was okay. They and others sent notes of support along the way. It felt like there was a community out there wishing the little *Sun* safely home on its great adventure. I was flying solo but I didn't feel alone.

For thousands of years humankind has had a need to share stories, whether around a campfire or in a public gathering. Cinema is one of the latest incarnations of that need. If done well, it brings people together. The experience varies from culture to culture, but I consistently saw that comfortable and well-run cinemas were better attended and more popular than bare-bones supermarket-cinemas, no matter how wealthy or poor the host society. This observation might seem obvious, yet poor-quality cinemas are still being built. Those who make the extra effort to provide an attractive, comfortable environment with a community focus seem to be rewarded.

There is one simple improvement available to the cinemas I had visited in the eighteen countries thus far: the choc-top. This is not a universal delicacy: a scoop of gourmet ice-cream in a chocolate-lined wafer cone, dipped in liquid chocolate, adorned with nuts or a lolly, and bagged ready for consumption in a comfortable movie house. They are only sold in Australian cinemas. The rest of the world is poorer for this.

Act ii

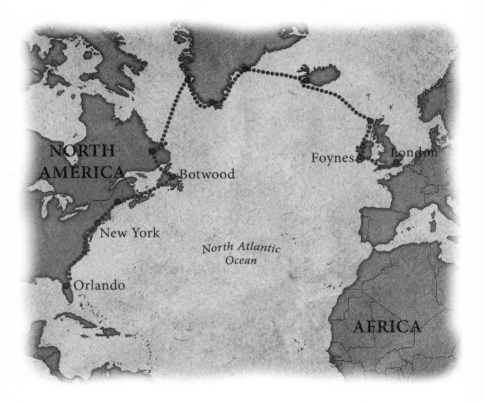

'All we have to decide is what to do with the time that is given to us.'
GANDALF, *LORD OF THE RINGS: FELLOWSHIP OF THE RING* (2001)

18.

The Year My Voice Broke

'I still believe in paradise. But now at least I know it's not some place you can look for because it's not where you go. It's how you feel for a moment in your life when you're a part of something, and if you find that moment, it lasts forever.'
RICHARD, *THE BEACH* (2000)

A s a teenager, I wanted to study overseas, in part to escape my high school. I loved the stone fruit orchard my family lived on in Seville, a working-class small-allotment farming district on the fringes of Melbourne, but I knew there was a bigger world that I needed to explore.

I never really managed to make any good friends at that school, certainly none I recall today, and I still have a scar from when I was stabbed in Year Nine. My attacker didn't welcome my suggestion that her black moccasin slippers were an overly broad interpretation of the school's uniform requirement of black shoes. Looking back, she was probably right: I should have minded my own business. My lack of an inner monologue can sometimes cause problems. It's a small scar anyway.

Before the internet and email, organising an international school exchange was pretty hard. It often meant repeating a year, too, because the different seasons in the Northern Hemisphere put your classes out of sync. Instead, I arranged to spend a year living with my maternal grandparents in the English county of Devon, and I was generously accompanied to London by my paternal grandparents. Over this splendid year I discovered how comfortable I was with my own company. I lived in an attic room at the top of a narrow staircase. I completed Year Ten by airmail correspondence.

I became a creature of routine. My grandparents and I had breakfast at the same time every morning. My schoolwork was done by lunchtime. Once or twice a week we would drive to another town, or Dartmoor National Park, or a quaint pub for a ploughman's lunch, or a tiny church. On other days I would walk around Brixham, our seaside fishing village, for hours. I got to know some of the fishermen and a man who ran a bookshop. I walked every street, laneway and the breakwater, which is over a mile long. I practised throwing a boomerang in a park until I got quite good at it. I spent a lot of time sitting by the shore, looking at the small boats at anchor and the seagulls soaring on the afternoon sea breezes. I dreamed of sailing one of those small boats to Australia, and of flying like the gulls.

Several books I read during that period of solitude helped shape the man I became. I still read them today. Robin Lee Graham's *Dove* captivated me. As a sixteen-year-old boy, Graham set out from California in a tiny sloop, intending to sail around the world. He took years to do it, struggled physically and mentally, but made it eventually. Inspired, I researched which boats I could sail from England to Australia. I bought a sextant and taught myself how to navigate by the sun. I had learned to sail on a dam on our farm, and graduated to the waters of Western Port Bay and the Gippsland Lakes. *Surely I can do this*, I thought. My father vetoed the plan, which was probably just as well.

Born to Win was the story of John Bertrand, the skipper of *Australia II*. The book details the years of build-up and the campaign that led to Bertrand's victory in the 1983 America's Cup, the first time the famous boat race wasn't won by the American team – a triumphant ending of the longest winning streak in sporting history. That was powerful stuff for a fifteen-year-old. The central message was that success doesn't just happen. The boat's winged keel wasn't a magic bullet, and Bertrand led a team of skilled and focused athletes. To achieve something like that, you have to be determined, work at it, be smart about it. Bertrand won the America's Cup the year before I lived in Devon. I watched the races at night on a five-inch black-and-white television, and they had a powerful effect on me as a young sailor. Bertrand became my boyhood hero.

Within Bertrand's book was a reference to another book that had influenced him so much that he carried it around like a personal bible. *Jonathan Livingston Seagull* was a novella published by Richard Bach in 1970. At fifteen, I had never read anything like it before. It is written like a fable, the tale of a seagull learning to push the boundaries of flying. It is really about the search for perfection. Given the hours I spent watching seagulls on the harbour, dreaming of flying, and my growing realisation that I didn't want to wander through life but strive for great things, the book became very important to me. I would read it many times over the years. By coincidence, Bach is a highly accomplished pilot himself, and until recently flew a Searey which he loved and had christened *Puff*.

My English grandparents are no longer alive. But I wanted to introduce Anne to the seaside village where they had shown me great warmth, love and hospitality, and the place that, I realised, was really the starting point of the *Southern Sun*'s journey. We spent a morning in Brixham, where we looked for my grandparents' old house and visited the pier and the harbour. It was strange returning. The town brought back some powerful, distant memories, but seemed small and rundown compared with thirty-two years earlier.

Having arrived in England, I wasn't certain what my next step would be. Going home was the least interesting option. My long-held ambition to circumnavigate the world, which I had suppressed thus far, suddenly seemed plausible.

'You've been talking about doing a circumnavigation most of your life,' Anne said. 'You thought it would be on a yacht but the *Southern*

Sun is still a boat. Just keep going.'

Just keep going.

But I didn't want to get too far ahead of myself. We had plans for a few weeks' exploring the north of England and the Scottish Highlands, so I decided that, after that, we'd return to London, reunite with the *Southern Sun* and fly to New York. After that, I could plan a crossing of the Atlantic. And then we could see what happened next. *Bite-size pieces.*

I rang Mike Gray, my flight agent, and told him what I wanted to do. I would need clearance to fly through Ireland, Iceland, Greenland and Canada. The United States would not require it, as the plane was registered there. If that went well, I might then be heading for Russia, Japan, the Philippines and Indonesia again. For the first half of my trip, he'd had six months to organise the permissions. This time I gave him two weeks.

The *Sun* needed a thorough maintenance check. Gary Masters, an aircraft engine mechanic, performed a once-every-200-hourly service. Fortunately, he reported that the *Sun* was in perfect condition, except for her radio, which had been getting worse and worse. The problem had first surfaced in Darwin, when early-morning moisture from grass had seemed to short-circuit the connections. In India it got really bad. After leaving Ahmedabad I lost contact with the control tower in less than half an hour, which was only about 70 kilometres. Sometimes I could transmit a respectable couple of hundred kilometres ahead of me; at other times 50 kilometres seemed the maximum. This had happened all along the way, and I wondered if the propeller's stainless-steel edges were interfering with transmissions. Or maybe it was the engine's electrics. In Australia I'd never tried to transmit so far, I realised; perhaps the radio had always been that way.

A fully functioning radio was crucial. While over the Atlantic and Pacific oceans, the *Sun* would be hundreds of kilometres from land. I had to be able to communicate with air-traffic controllers, not just in an emergency but also to update them on my position. If I couldn't reach them, I needed at least to ask overhead jets to relay messages. I could only enter controlled airspace with a radio.

An avionics technician tested the radio. Something was definitely wrong. He wasn't sure what, although he was convinced the aerial and other components were okay. I sent the radio for repair to the manufacturer in Australia, XCOM Avionics. The company's owner, Michael Coates, had been following my progress online, and very kindly sent me a new radio without charge when he learned of the problem.

The day before I got started on stage two – the *Sun's* second act – I held court at the Damyns Hall Aerodrome clubhouse. Speaking to a few dozen pilots and aviation enthusiasts, I used a portable projector I'd bought in London to show photos and video of the trip. The audience seemed fascinated, and I felt a bit like Alby Mangels.

I finished with a revelation. 'Tomorrow I'm flying to New York in the *Southern Sun*, and from there I hope to continue all the way to Australia,' I said.

The room was silent. Rather than the whoops of encouragement I had expected, there was just muted shock. I knew what they were all thinking: *Really? In that?*

The airfield's chief flying instructor, Deepak Mahajan, retrieved a book from his office. It was called *Decision Height: England to Canada in a Microlight*, and the author was Jon Hilton. 'You'd better read this,' he told me.

I would soon realise he was wrong.

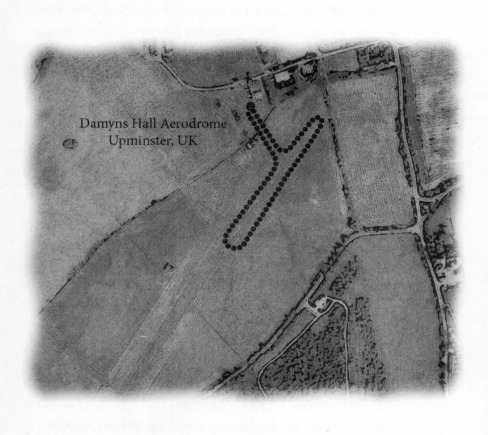

Damyns Hall Aerodrome
Upminster, UK

19.

Dumb and Dumber

'Just when I thought you couldn't possibly be any dumber, you go and do something like this.'
HARRY DUNNE, *DUMB AND DUMBER* (1994)

mperial Airways and Pan Am flew between London and New York in 1938. Pan Am was *the* American international carrier, while Imperial was the dominant carrier of the British Empire. Owned and subsidised by the British government, Imperial later merged with other airlines to eventually become British Airways. Imperial transported 50,000 people between 1930 and 1939. Its long-range services for wealthy passengers and mail were a model for the flying boat service between Sydney and London, which was operated jointly by Qantas and Imperial.

Just like the 'Kangaroo Route', the transatlantic trip began in London with a train to Southampton. From there it was a quick flight on Imperial's Short C-class or Pan Am's Boeing 314 flying boats to Foynes, landing on the Shannon River, near Limerick on Ireland's west coast, for refuelling. Next the passengers flew across the North Atlantic to a small Canadian town – Botwood, on the island of Newfoundland – and then south to New York.

Even with its extra tanks, the *Southern Sun* didn't have the range to fly direct from Ireland to Canada. Striking a balance between history and modern-day exploration, I came up with a modified route: London, Southampton Waters, Limerick, the Faroe Islands, Iceland, Greenland,

Newfoundland and New York City. I could have done the trip in half as many stops, but I wanted to explore on the ground as well as in the air. The shorter legs, of four to six hours each, should make weather delays less frequent, I reasoned, because I wouldn't require good conditions for a full eight or ten hours.

My departure date was set for 7 July, which happened to be Jack's twenty-second birthday. Anne dropped me at the aerodrome and said a quick goodbye. We planned to see each other later that day in Limerick. How hard could it be to cross the Irish Sea? After a few days holidaying on the Irish west coast, we would have a more serious farewell.

Anne headed to the other side of London, to Heathrow, to catch an Aer Lingus flight. Confident I would beat her to Ireland, I decided to give the *Sun* a thorough clean and double-check the engine, which had just been serviced, for anything that looked loose or out of place.

I noticed a tube coming from the air box hanging next to a bottle that catches overflowing oil from the main oil reservoir. A hole in the top of the oil bottle seemed to be the same size as the tube. So I inserted the tube into the bottle – it fitted perfectly. *It must have popped out during the service*, I thought, proud of my minor repair.

After checking there was enough oil and fuel I said goodbye to Deepak and a few club members, and turned on the engine. The *Sun* taxied to the start of the runway. I lined up the runway and applied full power.

The *Sun* felt like she was slipping on wet tiles. The engine misfired and lost all power. I immediately cut the throttle to idle. The engine sounded fine. Maybe it was a glitch? I taxied back to the start of the runway and opened up the throttle again. The same problem occurred. At 4000 revolutions per minute the engine was fine, but at 4500 revs it wouldn't run properly.

It was the beginning of a long and frustrating day of self-doubt and embarrassment. Elated after the success of the flight from Australia, I thought the *Sun* was fundamentally reliable. I prided myself on my ability to fix faults. Within the cinema industry I have often been able to solve technical problems that others couldn't by going back to the basics. So, what could possibly have caused this?

With a mooring rope I tied the *Sun's* tail to a fence and started up the engine to re-create the problem while stationary. It sounded like there wasn't enough fuel getting to the engine. I tried leaving the throttle in position. The revs would plunge, then return, then plunge and then return again.

What had been done in the service that might affect the fuel flow? The primary fuel filter had been changed. Maybe it had been put in backwards? It was an easy mistake to make. Alas, it was in the right way. The next suspect was the gascolator, a device that filters out fine debris from the fuel and creates a swirling motion that separates any water. The bowl was dropped out and cleaned during the service. I completely disassembled it to be sure it hadn't been damaged or reassembled incorrectly, but it was fine.

It was time to use a lifeline: I called the mechanic who had serviced the engine. He seemed stumped. He was in another part of England and couldn't get down to help me. He suggested partially disassembling the carburettor, which injects fuel into the pistons. That didn't fix the problem either. I really wanted to call two Searey maintenance experts I knew, one in Melbourne and another in Florida, but the time difference meant they were probably asleep.

An awful thought dawned on me. Had I mistakenly bought diesel instead of petrol? For the next hour I convinced myself I had. I smelt and felt the fuel, which didn't seem right. Using the wrong fuel can damage an engine; if I had made this basic mistake, the second leg of the trip could be over before it began.

Deepak suggested putting a few drops of the *Sun's* fuel onto a piece of white paper next to a drop from some fuel of his we knew was okay. Once it had evaporated, the residue and colour would indicate if one contained diesel. We conducted the rudimentary test. Thankfully, the drops appeared identical, which meant there was no diesel in the tanks.

After I'd spent half a day trying to fix the *Sun*, it was morning in Florida. I rang Russell Brown, a Searey expert who does all of the factory annual inspections and had travelled to Australia to help prepare the *Sun* in February. He knew the *Southern Sun* and her engine backwards. Everything he suggested I had already tried, or didn't have the skills or equipment to do.

Depressed, I was ready to put the plane into a shipping container and go home. Maybe I had only enough luck to get me to England, and I just wasn't supposed to go heading off across the Atlantic Ocean?

By this time Anne had landed in Ireland, and I called her with the news that I wouldn't be joining her that night. As I had no idea what was wrong, I might not see her tomorrow either, I said. Guilt welled up inside me. She had flown to another country to meet me and was now stranded. Her opinion was that it must be something simple and would be fixed by the morning. I wasn't convinced.

Faced with my distress, the Rotax mechanic who had serviced the *Sun* a few weeks earlier, Gary Masters, put off another job and promised to get to the airfield by 7.30 a.m. I was filled with relief that he had agreed to help me out, but also guilty that he would be making a three-hour drive before dawn. There was nothing else to do but book into a hotel. Alan Sutton again provided the transportation, kindly driving me around until we found a room.

I didn't want to do anything other than have an early dinner and go to bed, but I started reading the book Deepak had given me. Amateur pilot Jon Hilton decided in 2013 he wanted to cross the Atlantic. He got in his two-seater aircraft, a similar size to the *Sun*, although much sleeker and faster, and flew to Canada pretty much along the route I planned. Upon arriving, he promptly turned around and flew back. Along the way he encountered a lot of bad weather, especially low cloud, and found himself flying only a few hundred feet above the water for hours at a time, which is physically exhausting and very dangerous.

It was not what I wanted to hear. Increasingly anxious, I couldn't stop reading. The author seemed to write with such glee about the weather he had to fly through. To me, the flying was risky and not to be bragged about. He was awarded the Britannia Trophy by the Royal Aero Club of Britain for outstanding aviation achievement.

I had a very restless night's sleep.

I got up early and headed to Damyns Hall. *What disappointment will today bring?* Gary was already there when I arrived and we got stuck into the fault-finding. He'd never seen a problem like it. The pain in the pit of my stomach grew more acute.

He checked the carburettors again. They were fine. He took out the spark plugs, which had some unusual oil stains. Oil could be leaking from the turbocharger into the cylinders, he said.

'But that's why there's a drain tube on the air box – so that any oil that finds its way up there can drain out,' I said. 'In fact, I popped the tube back into its bottle yesterday.'

Like a thunderbolt, it hit us. The breather tube was the only equipment that had changed since the service, when everything was fine. Gary explained that the tube was to allow air to bleed from the air box, which provided the oxygen needed to combust the fuel. It wasn't meant to sit in the bottle. We took the tube out and started the engine, with the *Sun* still tied to the fence; we revved her to 5000 revs. The engine sounded fine – it was now running perfectly. *Oops.*

A simple hose, put in the wrong place by an at times misguided and now apprehensive man. Me.

20.

A Good Year

'Venture outside your comfort zone. The rewards are worth it.'
RAPUNZEL, *TANGLED* (2010)

The first stop, if only briefly, on the way to New York was Southampton Waters. The Deputy Harbour Master, by now familiar with a rather enthusiastic Australian obsessed with historical re-creations, granted the *Southern Sun* permission for another touch-and-go. Strong winds buffeted the *Sun* as she climbed back out over the trees along the shoreline and headed west. Just past Bristol, a large rainstorm loomed ominously over her route, which I avoided by flying through the outskirts of airspace under the control of Cardiff airport.

The sky cleared over the Irish Sea but closed in again over Ireland. It was striking how different the Irish farms looked from the British. They were much smaller. Lines of trees, acting as windbreaks, ran along almost every boundary. In England, the eldest son usually inherited the family property. In Ireland, it was traditional to leave property to all male offspring, which resulted in estates being carved up into ever-smaller farms with each generation.

A band of low cloud and rain hung over Shannon, my destination. The *Sun* struggled through 30-knot headwinds. The weather wasn't really good enough for VFR flying, but I dropped below the cloud and followed the Shannon River.

Shannon airport is the busiest on Ireland's west coast, with about

1.7 million travellers passing through it every year. There is a local plane-spotting community too, which I discovered was following my progress online. Malcolm Nason turned up at the airport with his tele-photo lens and took some very dramatic photos of the *Sun* landing on a wet and dreary runway.

I had half-expected to be forced to divert to another airport along the route, so I was relieved to arrive and see Anne. My next priorities were to visit the Foynes Flying Boat Museum, give a presentation to the Limerick Flying Club, and show Anne the stunning west coast of Ireland.

Foynes is a small town on the south bank of the Shannon Estuary. The airport is on the north side of the estuary, which flows into the North Atlantic. The nearest city is Limerick, which sits on the mouth of the Shannon River and has a population of 100,000.

In 1938, when flying boats dominated the transatlantic air route, Foynes was one of the biggest civilian airports in Europe. The estuary had two main advantages: it was sheltered from the ocean, and it was one of the closest points in Europe to North America. Ernest Hemingway, Eleanor Roosevelt and John F. Kennedy flew through Foynes. The Pan Am Yankee Clipper became the first commercial flight to make it from the United States to Europe in one day when it landed at Foynes on 9 July 1939. Going by sea took ten days.

This rich history makes Foynes the perfect location for the world's pre-miere flying boat museum. Its founder, Margaret O'Shaughnessy, has assembled a full-scale replica of the 32-metre-long Boeing 314 Clipper, the flying boat with which Pan Am opened up the world in the late 1930s and early 1940s; incredibly, it's a flying boat similar in size to today's Boeing 737. There's a large collection of memorabilia and displays in the museum, which launched in 1989 and is located in the original shore-side terminal building and control tower, which have been wonderfully restored.

Anne and I had lunch with Mrs O'Shaughnessy, who would be retired if only her mind would stop thinking of great ideas. She was charming, organised and driven, just the qualities needed to pull off a venture like this. The fact she was still running it, and as enthusiastically as ever, was a great personal achievement.

The next day we drove north, to the city of Galway, where I wanted to buy safety equipment for the Atlantic crossing. Denmark's aviation authorities, who control access to Greenland and the Faroe Islands, have equipment requirements for small planes. They include a life raft and an emergency radio beacon known as an EPIRB, which I already had, but also flares, rations and survival gear, such as a stove to melt snow or ice for water in the event of an emergency landing. I was surprised that a drysuit wasn't on the list, given that the cold Atlantic water could kill a person in hours, even in summer, and hence was keen to acquire one.

Galway has a long maritime history, and I expected to find everything I needed at the city's ship chandler, which sells maritime equipment. It had flares but little else, and I regretted not looking when we were in England. At a camping shop I bought a small, expensive stove burner with a gas canister housed in its own cooking pot. While I accepted that it made sense to carry one, I suspected the flame would easily blow out. And I certainly wasn't going to light a naked flame in an inflatable raft.

At an electronics store across town I bought a couple of small torches and a new phone charger. I was amazed to find a stove system that was not only perfect but – ironically, given it was an electronics shop – ran on a concept straight out of high-school chemistry. Shaped like a small thermos, it had a removable inner liner and a teabag-like pouch, which sat between the inner and outer shells. When a small amount of water was added and the inner lining reinserted, the water on the pouch would trigger a chemical reaction that generated enough heat to boil water in five minutes. It was a brilliant, self-contained and reasonably priced stove without a naked flame, which made it eminently safer. I wondered why the camping store wasn't selling them. I bought one and set aside the gas stove.

Now I had everything the *Sun* needed, except a drysuit, which was worrying me. But I had run out of shopping options.

The next day we took an old-style ferry to the Aran Islands, which are brutally stunning islands off the west coast that have been inhabited for thousands of years. We had a private tour with a retired fisherman in his van. As well as detailed information on the history of the islands, he complained bitterly about the damage done to Irish fishing by European quotas. He was very angry about his livelihood being taken away by policy-makers in Brussels.

We considered visiting Dublin but Google stopped us. As I was typing 'things to do in Dublin', I said to Anne, 'If the number one thing to do is "drink Guinness", we're not going.' Sure enough, it was. Neither of us drink beer, let alone Irish stout, plus we only had a few days left together and were enjoying exploring the rugged and isolated west coast.

After a few more great days, it was time for me to push on and for Anne to return to Melbourne. I dropped her at Shannon airport for an early-morning flight home via London. As is often the case, the airport and morning rush left our farewell all too brief. 'Have fun,' she said as we parted, 'but please be careful.'

I returned the rental car and took a taxi to the small Coonagh Airfield. It felt very lonely in the cab. The goodbye with Anne had been too quick – I felt sad at its inadequacy, and daunted by what lay ahead. A few members of the Limerick Flying Club were there to see me off, which helped calm my nerves.

I planned a fly-by and a brief water landing in front of the Foynes museum. It would be a nod to history and a gesture of thanks to Mrs O'Shaughnessy. A one-hour flight would then get the *Sun* to the city of Sligo, where I'd refuel before pushing north to the Faroe Islands, which are about halfway between Scotland and Iceland in the treacherous North Atlantic.

John Brennan, an Irish Searey pilot who had served as my host in the area, was escorting me. I followed his plane for half an hour, around rain and clouds that seemed to be getting lower and darker by the minute. Just when I was considering turning back to Shannon, I heard John announce over the radio that he was diverting to Abbeyshrule, a small village in the middle of Ireland that was named Ireland's tidiest town in 2012.

We landed mid-morning, expecting the weather to clear within a few hours. We officially gave up at 6.30 p.m. To keep us company over the course of the day, John's wife, Caroline, drove from their home an hour and a half away. We had lunch at the local pub, the aptly named Rustic Inn. Fancying a coffee, I was pleased to see a commercial coffee machine behind the bar. When I ordered an espresso for myself and a latte for Caroline, the barmaid admitted she not only didn't know how to use the machine, but was scared of it.

Still in my flying suit and with the pub all-but empty, I went behind the bar and trained the barmaid on the machine, which was similar to the ones at our cinemas in Australia. By the time we left, she was confidently making espresso and was able to heat and froth the milk quite well. Although my contribution was small, I felt I left Abbeyshrule a better place than when I arrived.

So, with a whole day passed, I was only 100 kilometres closer to New York. A local pilot lent us his hangar to house the planes overnight, and we drove to Sligo, where John and Caroline lived, and went to their favourite restaurant for dinner. Despite the seafood-heavy menu, I relished the opportunity to order a whole bottle of red wine, which I reasoned would be much more drinkable than the 'by the glass' fare I'd drunk for most of the journey. From a not-so-extensive wine list I splashed out on what I suspected would be the best option, with a touch of age, and asked for it to be decanted.

'De-what?' the waitress asked.

'A decanter,' I replied. 'It's what you put the wine in before serving it.'

'I'm so sorry, sir, but we don't have one.'

I have never been good with 'no'. I asked for an empty water jug, and into it I poured the wine. The transfer caused much consternation. Some might think I was being pretentious. Really, the blame should fall on John, whose cheeky Irish nature brought it out in me. Anyway, we had a great dinner, and I was amused to be sent, a couple of days later, a photo of a fascinating article in the local newspaper under the head-line 'Globetrotting pilot stops off in Sligo'. It didn't mention the decanter.

~ ~

A dozen Sligo pilots and their friends gathered the next morning for the *Sun*'s departure. They helped me fuel up, polish the screens and top up the brake fluid. A minced beef bun from a nearby fair was provided as in-flight catering. Two local aircraft, John's Searey and a perfectly restored Piper J-3 Cub, were waiting in the air to see me off, and took the only airborne photographs and video I have of the *Sun* in flight.

I was deeply touched by this farewell. The Irish flying community had shown me great support, boosting my confidence. Somehow it made the trip feel like more than just a personal mission. When I met some of the people following my journey, I felt a sense of connection that meant I did not want to let them down. In John, I suspected, I had made a lifelong friend.

My original plan had been to fly to Iceland via the Faroe Islands, a self-governing territory overseen by Denmark. After choosing that route a few weeks earlier, I looked up the island's weather records. More often than not, cloud completely covered the Faroes down to 300 feet; trying to land in conditions like that would be like high-diving into a metre of water.

Plan B was to follow the west coast of Scotland until I ran out of land, and then head straight for Reykjavík, the capital of Iceland. Although that would involve a lot more time over the sea, the route would have two advantages: a healthy tailwind, which would increase my speed and reduce fuel usage, and two alternate landing sites if the weather turned bad, Stornoway, on the Isle of Lewis, the largest island in the Outer Hebrides, or, if I was really desperate, Vágar, the largest island in the Faroes.

The coastal flight was pleasant. But by the time I crossed into Scottish airspace, it was touch and go as to whether I could get to Reykjavík before its airport closed. As I was flying along the remote

Scottish west coast, I had a phone signal coming in and out, which meant I could use the internet to check the weather at Vágar airport. The cloud there was between 300 and 800 feet, and it was raining so hard you couldn't see anything. *No thanks*, I thought. *Scotland it is.*

The diversion was a great excuse to check out the Isle of Lewis. Like so much of Scotland, it is ruggedly beautiful and packed with physical history, including stone circles, old castles and prehistoric stone towers known as *brochs*. Stornoway, the main city, has a stunning castle that at the time I visited was being turned into a museum, and a very busy harbour which was home to a professional fishing fleet and many visiting yachts. There was even a yacht Anne and I had seen transiting the Caledonian Canal at Loch Ness two weeks earlier.

On our trip to Scotland a couple of weeks earlier, I had visited an innovative cinema I'd read about years before. The Screen Machine is a mobile movie house bankrolled by the Scottish government. Much like the travelling library that came to my primary school in rural Victoria, the cinema was built into a truck, and tours remote Scottish towns. Like a Transformer, the trailer expands to three times the width of the truck, and seating platforms and a screen unfold to construct an eighty-seat indoor cinema.

The audiences are hugely appreciative, and the system is relatively cheap to run. There is a single operator, who acts as driver, cinema 'unfolder', ticket seller, projectionist and usher. I had been doodling ideas for travelling cinemas for many years, and the Scottish project drove my conviction to push ahead when I returned to Australia.

Our East Timorese charity, Cinema Loro sa'e, was a good starting point. But the system would need fewer staff to be financially viable on a larger scale. I needed to transfer the concept out of my head and sketchbooks and build a working prototype. We could show movies in regional, rural and northern parts of Australia without cinemas, and eventually share stories in remote areas across the globe. I had spent countless hours thinking about it on this trip, sketching notes and ideas along the way. I planned to call it Screens Without Borders.

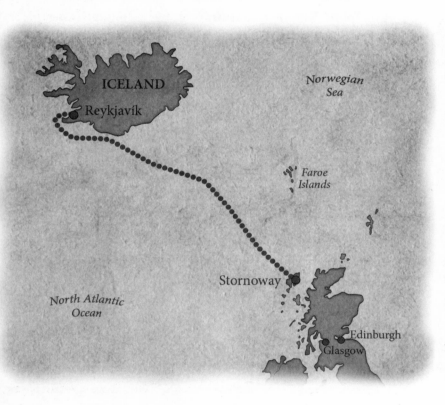

21.

Midnight Sun

'A little nonsense now and then is relished by the wisest men.'
WILLY WONKA, *WILLY WONKA & THE CHOCOLATE FACTORY* (1971)

The weather in Reykjavík looked good. Even though there would be headwinds of between 10 and 20 knots, I expected to make the 575-nautical-mile trip with three to four hours' worth of spare fuel. That would be enough to get to Iceland and back to the Faroe Islands if a wild storm or fog – aviation's silent assassin – made landing impossible.

I woke before dawn and, after my morning coffee ritual, conducted a very thorough check of the *Southern Sun*. I had read the North Atlantic Operations and Airspace Manual, published by the International Civil Aviation Organization, and had been given a crash course on preparations and procedures for an ocean crossing, which included the possibility of ditching at sea. I had all the safety gear I'd brought from Melbourne and the extra items from Ireland. With those specific operating procedures to be followed for the journey ahead, the gravity of the undertaking sunk in. If something went wrong, I would be a long way from help.

Instead of flying straight, the *Sun* would travel in a leftwards arc. The route would include two imaginary markers over the ocean, known as boundary points and used by aircraft to report their position: the intersections of 61 degrees north and 11 degrees west, and 62 degrees north and 13 degrees west. There is safety in numbers: if the *Sun* went down, I wanted to be on a common air route. The slightly northerly path would make for lighter headwinds too.

Flying by visual flight rules over the Atlantic Ocean requires pilots to stay clear of what is known as 'controlled airspace'. That is the part of the sky reserved for aircraft under the supervision of air-traffic controllers. Between Scotland and Iceland, the controlled airspace started at 6000 feet, which meant the *Sun* would have to fly at 4500 feet. Westerly flights are always at 2000-foot increments starting at 2500 feet, as long as there isn't cloud, a system designed to eliminate the chance of VFR planes running into each other.

The staff in the Stornoway control tower were reassuring. I spent nearly an hour with them, studying the weather, discussing procedures, and making sure both that my flight plan was approved and that they knew how to look up the *Sun*'s location on my satellite tracking website if they couldn't raise me on the radio. (I'd created a simple weblink for the tracking, which is still active every time I fly today; check it out at www.southernsun.voyage/where.) Even so, I was feeling more nervous than at any other time on the trip, or indeed in my entire flying career.

The weather conditions were only just acceptable as I left Scotland. Once the *Sun* was clear of land, the sea was pretty calm and the cloud was high enough for me to climb to 4500 feet, an altitude I maintained until I was an hour shy of Iceland. Not for the first time, I wished I had an autopilot. There were no other planes to check for, and nothing to see but water and clouds. With an autopilot to keep the plane flying straight, I could have written in my diary, started a novel or calculated pi to a gazillion places. Instead, I hand-flew all the way.

Autopilots used to be restricted to commercial aircraft. Howard Hughes was one of the first to use one, back in the 1930s, and he did a lot of work in their early development. It wasn't until the 1980s that autopilots became common in light aircraft, in part because they enhanced safety, but also as solid-state technology had made them smaller and more affordable. In a difficult moment, such as when you run into cloud or experience heavy turbulence, it can be safer for a machine to fly. Just like car drivers, pilots can become drowsy after flying many hours and not realise they are in a slow descent. I had heard about people falling asleep while flying on autopilot, and thought it might be safer if I always had a job to focus on.

The further north the *Sun* ventured, the colder it got. To save weight, before leaving Melbourne, the engineers and I decided to remove the heater system. I couldn't see any need for it while flying from Australia to London. Now the situation was rather different. The sun was out, keeping my upper body warm, but despite two pairs of socks I was starting to lose feeling in my toes. I discovered that doing a hundred toe crunches warmed them up. Then I remembered the typical airline announcements about deep vein thrombosis and started trying to stretch, clench and crunch my muscles in my restricted position. It was probably a waste of time, but was something to do.

I found myself focusing on the fact I wasn't wearing a drysuit, which is like a wetsuit for really cold water because it doesn't let any water in at all. I looked out at the inhospitable North Atlantic Ocean, imagining how cold it must be. It dawned on me just how much trouble I would be in if I had to ditch.

The long passages over sea from Australia to Britain had all been over fairly warm water. I could have survived the elements in the life raft with what I was wearing. But if the *Sun* went down in the Atlantic, my overalls, merino T-shirt and cashmere sweater weren't going to withstand the cold. I would die of hypothermia long before I ran out of food or drink. I mentally kicked myself for not trying harder to find a drysuit in Ireland, or even looking when I was in London. I was determined to find one in Iceland.

For the first time since leaving Australia, I had radio contact with air-traffic control continuously over the sea. Even 300 nautical miles from land I was able to reach Shanwick control in Ireland, which handed the *Sun* over to Icelandic control, and they were perfectly clear too. I had expected to have to relay position reports via airliners flying overhead, and so was very pleased with my new radio.

The first visual sign I had reached Iceland was the large rainclouds extending almost to the ground. I approached from the south-east. Reykjavík sits on a north-facing area of the south-west coast. I had a choice: fly above the cloud and a mountain between the coast and the airport, or descend through the cloud and follow the coast all the way around. While it would take nearly an hour longer, I chose the latter option, which would be much safer.

Before I got too close to land, and while there were breaks in the cloud cover, I dropped to 1200 feet, where I could make out white caps on the ocean below. I tracked just offshore. With the cloud ahead seeming to be lower, it was more reassuring to be above the sea, rather than land, which has a habit of creeping up on you.

Checking out the sparse but green landscape was fun until the weather deteriorated. The forecast that morning said there would be a few scattered clouds around the airport at 600 feet. By the time I got close, the overcast cloud completely covered the sky at 600 feet. For the last twenty minutes I flew at 500 feet, through drizzling rain.

Before arriving over Reykjavík, on radio I was handed over to the airport control tower, which cleared the *Sun* to approach below the thick cloud. There were no other planes around. I had a clear view of the runway, which was reassuring. Despite the tiring flying, I felt a great sense of relief and joy at seeing the unique landscape of Iceland. For a fleeting moment I considered reaching out of the window so I could install my camera in a bracket above the cockpit and remotely photograph the spectacular approach. But the *Sun* was barely above the ground now, and flying was more important than tourist snaps.

After nine hours and ten minutes, the Sun touched down on the huge runway at 6.30 p.m. A marshal led her to a parking bay next to – to my absolute glee – a perfectly restored Catalina, the plane my grandfather served on in the Royal Australian Air Force, and the Qantas flying boat used on the Perth–Ceylon nonstop service. I felt like a chick tucking itself under its mother's wing for the night.

I later photographed the *Sun* under the Catalina's giant wing. Whether deliberate or not, the design similarity of the two craft, sixty years apart, was remarkable. The Catalina, which was based in Britain and owned by a tourism company called Plane Sailing, had been chartered by an English private school to transport a leadership group of students on an adventure trip. The Catalina had dropped them off at a lake in Greenland, where they were hiking for a couple of weeks, and would pick them up when they finished. It was an impressive project, although I wouldn't have wanted to pay those school fees.

✦

Reykjavík airport is close to the city, and I was quickly at a hotel and changed out of my flying overalls. The 'old town' has a three-screen arthouse cinema and bar, which was not only very cool for its style and range of films shown, but also charged more for Icelandic films than Hollywood movies, such was the demand. I tried – and failed – to imagine selling that idea back home.

I walked the length of the city and found a highly recommended grill for dinner. They were proud of their beef, but, coming from Australia, with Iceland's proximity to a vast ocean, I was more interested in trying the seafood. The crustacean bisque was probably the most delicious seafood soup I had ever consumed. There was another local speciality on the menu I wasn't expecting; it was exotic, and ethically troubling, but I had to try it. The seared fillet of minke whale, served with mushroom, was delicious. I drew the line at eating a puffin, though.

With the brief sunset occurring around midnight, I still had plenty of time to look around. One of the best ways to see Reykjavík is on one of its new fleet of electric tuk-tuks, three-wheel vehicles that are like overgrown golf carts. My driver was a lovely young guy who was proud of his country. As we crisscrossed town, he gave me a lesson on Icelandic history – from settlement in the ninth century, to Danish rule, farming and fishing. In 1944, while Denmark was occupied by Germany, Iceland simply declared its independence. It was a very adroit move: Denmark had no power and Germany had bigger problems to worry about. So that was that.

Reykjavík has a population of 220,000, and its old town is small enough to be explored entirely on foot. The next morning I left the hotel with a pocketful of leftover euros. While the local currency was the Icelandic króna, I was hoping to use up the coins in a touristy place that catered to the cruise ships that often called by.

A few doors up from the hotel I came across a museum established by a University of Iceland academic. The entrance charge was eight euros. The exhibits were bottled specimens of penises and lampshades made from stretched whale foreskins. I had heard of the museum from the film *The Final Member*, which had screened at the Melbourne International Film Festival years earlier. It followed the academic's search for the last missing penis for his collection – yes, he had one from every mammal, except one of us, a *Homo sapiens*. The whale penises were really very large.

Seven minutes later I had seen enough and began my search for a drysuit. A marine store at the docks had a couple, but the best one wasn't in the right size, and the one that fitted was too heavy to fly in. I caught a taxi across town to a small kayak shop, which had an amazingly thorough range of drysuits at reasonable prices. Buying one in Iceland was going to be as easy as picking up a pair of board shorts in Bondi.

Spoiled for choice, I must have spent an hour trying on different suits before settling on one that was flexible and fitted well. It had one very vital feature: the full-length zip could be undone in flight, allowing use of the all-important red bottle. I felt an almost physical sense of relief at the purchase – which, with hindsight, I now think was a sign of my inner fear about the trip ahead.

○

The next destination was Kulusuk, a tiny island on the east coast of Greenland, and 700 kilometres away. It was the closest airport in Greenland to Reykjavík, and would be the starting point for my tracking of the Greenlandic coast over the following days. The weather looked good too.

Early the next morning I was at the airport. As I was filling out my paperwork, a smartly dressed older gentleman asked if I was flying the old silver seaplane. He had a few questions, and I explained my trip to him. He returned soon after and introduced me to his family. They had stopped in Iceland for a couple of nights, as they did every summer, on their way from the United States to Europe in their private jet. He told his grandchildren, daughter and son-in-law what I was doing. 'This man is an adventurer,' he said.

I was pretty chuffed.

GREENLAND

Kulusuk

Nuuk

ICELAND

Reykjavík

Narsarsuaq

North Atlantic
Ocean

CANADA

22.

The Village at the End of the World

'Ah, the serenity.'
DARRYL KERRIGAN, *THE CASTLE* (1997)

The five-hour flight to Greenland was smooth. One of the advantages of flying in near-freezing temperatures is that there is often less turbulence. There are few or no thermal updrafts caused by geological features or man-made objects on the ground, such as metal roofs, that heat the air above them. A drawback is that very few planes can land on snow, and it's dangerous for seaplanes to land where there might be sea ice, as it can pierce fuselages and sink planes.

About two-thirds of the way, the cloud all but disappeared. As the *Sun* neared Greenland, what I feared at first was low cloud, perhaps even fog – which is impossible to land in, even for instrument pilots – turned out to be broken ice covering the sea to the horizon, a stark if foreboding white visual feast.

Kulusuk airport was hidden from view by a mountain. The US government built the gravel runway in the 1950s so it could access a radar dome on top of the peak. It left in the 1980s. The indigenous Inuit population of 250 now relies on the airport for supplies when ships can't get through the ice, which is most of the year. A few adventure tourists exploring the Arctic region use it too. There is one rather basic hotel, next to the airport.

Flying in over floating ice and beneath the rocky, snow-covered mountains was thrilling. Sitting in the cockpit, I was no longer a short, balding, middle-aged businessman from suburban Melbourne, but a daring and resourceful pilot touching down on a remote landing strip skirting the Arctic Circle.

The temperature was about 9 degrees, which was warmer than expected, and the sky was clear and blue, the colour so vivid it felt almost unreal, like the work of a celestial painter.

My plan was to walk. It didn't take long to execute. I walked from the airport to the hotel. I walked along the only road to the village. I walked around the village. I walked back to hotel. There wasn't a lot to see, but what was there was interesting.

The humble village was set inside a small, semi-circular harbour. The houses were constructed from basic materials and had the same concrete half-ground floors I had seen in Iceland. Their timber top halves used a lot of plywood sheets. With only one supply ship a year, building materials would all have been planned for the one delivery. That led to the houses being built in the same style with the same roofing material. Most of the windows were the same size, either singles or in pairs. All the doors seemed identical. The only real point of difference was the paint jobs, which were all done in primary colours. White was used for window frames and nothing else. I never expected physical isolation to create such architectural homogeneity; I would have assumed the opposite.

There were lots of husky dogs, which power the residents' primary form of transport for much of the year: the sled. Children were running around, playing and enjoying the outdoors. There were even a few trampolines; perhaps one year the transport ship had decided to bring trampolines for the whole town.

There was one store, one hotel, a church and many burial areas. The owners of the one public place to eat – the hotel – had to plan their purchase of supplies with great care. The nearest villages were over 500 kilometres away to both north and south, or on the other side of Greenland.

I spent one night in Kulusuk, the most isolated place I had been. Its rugged beauty was so unexpected that it became, for a time, the most culturally memorable stop of the trip for me, surpassing even the classic charm of Lake Como or the chaotic stimulation of Ahmedabad. Even though I doubt I will ever return, I will always remember the sense of community I experienced there. Very few pilots visit. I was glad I had decided to opt for multiple stops in Greenland.

Another beautiful clear sky greeted me at 6 a.m. I walked from the hotel to the airport, where the *Southern Sun* had spent a solitary night outside on the bitumen in front of the terminal. The helpful airport handlers sold me some of their snowmobile petrol, instead of the much more expensive and less desirable avgas. I started up the *Sun* and tried to manoeuvre her alongside the bowser, but couldn't get close enough. We had to use a couple of jerry cans instead, and one of the tower staff kindly spent half an hour helping me transfer fuel to the plane.

I farewelled Kulusuk by flying off directly over the town. I snapped a few photos and levelled off at 500 feet, so I'd stay out of the way of an inbound commercial flight, although it was also a great way to enjoy the view. After clearing the area, I pushed the *Sun* up to a safer height. The GPS indicated that her ground speed had fallen by ten knots, which meant that the wind at the higher altitude was a five-knot headwind. This minor change in speed would add nearly an hour to my flight to Narsarsuaq, a town near Greenland's southern tip. *Well, there's only one thing to do*, I thought, and dropped back down to 500 feet and the favourable five-knot tailwind.

With the wind to my back, and the land – well, an ice-laden sea – closer to my feet, I enjoyed the ride immensely. The air was smooth and I looked down to see a few seals basking on ice in the sun. To my right was the landmass of Greenland, which rose brutally from the sea.

More ice was visible than rock, and it literally towered above me. An hour out of Kulusuk, the tailwind dissipated. I climbed up to my planned 4500 feet, which wasn't as exciting, and followed the coast most of the way. Reassuringly, the air-traffic controllers were in contact the whole way through VHF radio repeaters. I had expected to lose them a few hours out.

I could have flown across Greenland rather than go around it. But the ice cap that covers most of the country, which is five times the size of California and almost as big as Western Australia, reaches 10,000 feet high. Even with the sea full of ice, I felt more comfortable flying over water. I'd been watching the weather for a while, and the winds seemed to swirl around the top of the ice cap, which is a large heat sink that has a drastic effect on the surrounding atmospheric conditions. The coastline also offered spectacularly dramatic views.

About 120 kilometres from Narsarsuaq, I turned inland. Continuing to follow the coast would have added nearly a thousand kilometres to the trip. At 8500 feet the *Sun* was well above the ice cap. I weaved through several fjords and past green hills that would have looked at home in rural Victoria.

When I switched to the Narsarsuaq airport radio frequency, I couldn't raise the control tower. I suspected the *Sun* was flying so low that the hills were blocking the signal. Most flights arrived from the north or the west, but I was coming in from the south-east. I didn't like entering the airport's 12-mile control zone without making direct radio contact first, but I didn't seem to have a choice. I had at least spoken to the only other plane in the area, an Air Greenland Dash 8, whose pilot told the tower I was coming in.

The landing was simple. No one appeared when I parked – handling agents aren't required in Greenland – so I just wandered into the terminal building.

Narsarsuaq was even smaller than Kulusuk. It seemed to exist only to serve the airport, which was a transfer point for helicopters, ships and boats going elsewhere. A tiny museum provided a brief history of the lush area, which gave Greenland its ironic name. The Viking Erik Thorvaldsson, known as Erik the Red, was banished from Iceland in 982 after provoking a fight that killed two of his neighbour's sons. He moved to the uninhabited Greenland. When others followed, Erik allocated fjords to each family and kept the best for himself. It was like assigning rooms in a ski lodge: whoever arrives first usually gets the biggest room.

The airport, which was long enough for B-52 bombers, was built by the US military during World War II. A major transit base on the way to Europe, it was active for decades. Many of the buildings still there were built during the Cold War. I suspected there were way more dormitory rooms than the base would ever need now; the majority of beds were certainly empty.

I wandered down the only road to a dock where a few fishing boats and lots of runabouts were tied up. It seemed that nearly every resident had a little boat in the water or on a trailer. Teenagers in wetsuits were jumping from the jetty into the sea. University researchers were loading equipment onto a ship. Without much else to do, I helped them carry boxes and crates on board.

The sun was hanging just above the horizon, which meant it was dinnertime. After perusing the menu, I felt it would breach the spirit of the trip if I didn't order the reindeer roll. *Tastes like kangaroo*, I thought, *and I always thought that tasted like deer – oh, of course . . .*

One of the remarkable aspects of the entire trip was my meteorological good fortune. From Australia to England, I lost only one day to bad weather. Since leaving London, I'd lost a day in Ireland. A week earlier it had been so bad in southern Greenland that planes couldn't take off. A French couple flying across the Atlantic were stuck in Narsarsuaq for seventeen days. There isn't a lot to do there. I don't know if the marriage survived.

I was waiting at the airport tower when it opened at 8 a.m. the next morning. A Swiss airline pilot was delivering a high-tech four-seat Cirrus, the private aircraft equivalent of a BMW 7 Series. The Cirrus flies about 100 knots faster than the *Sun*, and he was transporting it from the United States to Europe. He seemed to be laughing at me without actually making any sound. *Hey*, I thought, *while we can both land on water, I can do it more than once.*

My plan was to follow a fjord to the sea. I would then fly north just inside the coastline and check out the fjords, lakes and glaciers all the way to Nuuk, Greenland's capital. There were some magical spots along the way, including a mountaintop that was so flat on the summit you could land a plane on it. I marked the location in case I ever returned.

Two hours into the flight, I realised I'd made a terrible mistake: my beloved cashmere jumper was still in Narsarsuaq. Light yet warm, and with a zip-up neck, it had been given to me by Tim for Christmas in Boston two years earlier. It had great sentimental and practical value. It was also the only jumper I had packed, so I seriously considered turning back. But the winds would have been against the *Sun* the whole way. Instead, I radioed the control tower and informed them of my sartorial emergency. They promised to send out a search party.

Nuuk is inside what may technically be a wide fjord. Or perhaps it's a bay – I'm not sure. But it is protected from the sea, which is why it has the main shipping port for goods arriving in the country, and is Greenland's biggest city. Transport hubs drive economic activity, which in turn attract people.

Air Greenland operates small Dash 8 passenger planes from Nuuk airport all day, and a new pilot was practising landing when I arrived. Made by Canadian manufacturer Bombardier Aerospace, the Dash 8s need the whole runway – which is carved into the side of a mountain, and a relatively short 3117 feet – to take off and land, which meant the pilot had to nail it, each and every time. For an amateur pilot like me, that was pretty impressive. If I had been a commercial pilot, I would have loved to fly Dash 8s for Qantas Link around regional Australia. It looked like real flying, planes with propellers connecting communities.

The *Southern Sun* was the airport's only overnight visitor, and I tied her up next to an avgas storage tank. A tall man bounded over; he seemed happy to see me. Thomas Branner Jespersen used to be an air-traffic controller and now worked for Air Greenland as a ground handler. He was also a private pilot and owned a Lake Buccaneer, one of the most popular small seaplanes in the world. Greenland's flying boat community had exactly one member, so Thomas was excited to see a flying boat in town. After a quick introduction, we agreed to meet for a drink after dinner.

I had wanted to spend two nights in Nuuk, where there was a lot to explore. But it was a Friday, and it turned out that all airports in Greenland are closed on Sundays. It would have to be one night or three. I bought a coffee in the airport terminal and studied the weather. The *Sun*'s entry point into my next destination, Canada, would be determined by forecast cloud and rain. I was tossing up between Iqaluit, due west, a town of 7000 people well inside the Arctic Circle, or Goose Bay, a photogenic air force base much further south, in Newfoundland.

Iqaluit was only 800 kilometres from Nuuk, or five to six hours of flying. Goose Bay would be a 1300-kilometre, nine-hour Atlantic Ocean marathon. The weather on Saturday looked good, but it would not be so benign on Monday. To be safe, I needed to ship out in the morning. The forecast winds favoured the longer route, which would get me a lot closer to New York.

On paper I was choosing the sensible option – but in my heart I knew the longer flight was inherently more risky. It would require more time over the almost-freezing sea. I told myself to trust the *Sun*. She hadn't failed me before, mostly, and I believed she would get me home safely. I filled out my flight plan – destination Goose Bay – and dropped it off at the control tower to avoid any delays in the morning. The staff helped me fax the required form to Canadian customs to advise them of my likely arrival time.

Having decided on my destination, I now had to top up. Getting ready to fill the tanks with avgas, I noticed a stronger than usual smell of petrol, and suspected a leak. A fabric bladder in the *Sun's* passenger footwell had been full of fuel since Scotland. It helped balanced the plane and provided extra fuel, just in case. I lifted it up to check it wasn't leaking from the hose outlet and, sure enough, it was. As I examined the fitting, the thread separated from the bladder in my hand and fuel gushed into the bottom of the plane. As fast as possible I manhandled the thirty-kilogram bag into a position where it wasn't spilling fuel, but a lot had already flowed out, creating a fire hazard, as well as a mess.

I needed to empty the bladder, which was useless in its damaged state. Trying to keep the bladder upright with my right hand, I reached over with my left and switched on the electric fuel transfer pump, which drained the bladder in fifteen minutes while I precariously held it to avoid further spillage. I then removed the bag, shook out some remaining fuel and had a close look.

The nylon fitting where the hose connected to the bag had given way. It was a serious equipment failure, which I was relieved had happened on the ground and not in flight, when I would have been forced to fly the *Sun* with my legs while leaning over to the passenger seat to try to stop thirty litres of fuel draining all through the cockpit.

The separate fuel bladder under the cockpit floor had brass fittings, which weren't going to give way. To save weight on the footwell bladder, I had chosen nylon fittings, which are commonly used in the industry – and, it turns out, a mistake. I made a mental note to revisit that decision once the *Sun* and I got to the United States.

Being a craft that travels on water, the *Sun* has a bung, or screw-in plug, at the back of the hull. When I opened it, fuel gushed out for what seemed like at least a minute; I estimated it was about five litres of highly flammable petrol. I had dodged a bullet.

I checked into a hotel in the centre of Nuuk, quickly changed and started exploring. It was too late for the city museum, but with sunset not till 11.30 p.m. I had plenty of time to look around. I walked briskly for a couple of hours, which helped me decompress both physically and mentally.

Nuuk has one cinema, which doubles as a theatre and community hall, although the staff told me it is mainly used to show films. The movies are a mix of Hollywood and art films, much like our cinemas in Australia. I wandered along the shore and back to the hotel for dinner, where I was told there was a very good steak restaurant on the top floor. Coming from the world's biggest beef-exporting country, I was keen to try the Greenland version. The restaurant had a great wine list and, with Thomas joining me, I was excited about ordering a bottle of good red. It would be a nice break from my usual: 'Do you have wine by the glass?' 'Yes, sir, both a red and a white.'

The steak menu was impressive, perhaps too impressive, so I enquired about the provenance of one cut.

'Australia,' the waiter said.

'How about this one?'

'Australia.'

All the steak was imported. The ox fillet was local, though, and delicious.

Thomas had grown up in Greenland and worked all around the world. He and I had a long, interesting conversation, from travel, to flying, to living in a remote part of the world. After dinner he drove me around on a tour of the town, and dropped me back at my hotel at dusk, which happened to be midnight. You can certainly squeeze a lot into a day with so much daylight!

I stayed up for a while, studying maps and weather forecasts. The route from Melbourne to London had been arranged months in advance, each stop rigidly locked in, so deciding where to go the following day was unsettling. I was convinced Goose Bay was the right call, but it was going to be a long, foreboding flight.

23.

Saved by the Sun

'Set the controls for the heart of the sun.'
ROGER WATERS, *PINK FLOYD: LIVE AT POMPEII* (1972)

Gerry Humphries was a Royal Air Force pilot. On a sortie over the Atlantic Ocean, his Harrier jet suffered a catastrophic instrument failure. Not knowing exactly what was beneath him, he landed on the fog-covered ground where he thought the airport was. He walked away unharmed. When the fog lifted, the wingtip of his Harrier was three inches from another Harrier.

Humphries is now retired and living on a farm with its own landing strip near the Irish city of Limerick. He had been following the *Sun's* progress online, and I had met him, along with other members of the flying club there, when I did a presentation about my trip. He made a point of flying to the airfield the day before I was leaving for a quiet word. As he described what had happened to him when his instruments failed, I was forced to focus on the danger of crossing the Atlantic Ocean in a light aircraft. Humphries later emailed me a manual on Atlantic crossing procedures, which helped with my planning, and suggested I download an iPad app called MeteoEarth, created by the German MeteoGroup, one of the world's leading private weather-forecasting companies; it supplies the data used by many TV stations. The app presents a seven-day forecast map of wind, cloud or rain over any area of the planet, at any altitude, which is invaluable for aviation.

The app is a great example of how technology is making flying safer and easier. MeteoEarth's accurate maps helped me decide to fly to Goose Bay, rather than make the shorter crossing to far northern Canada. While the weather suited flying to Iqaluit that day, I was able to determine that the *Sun* would have had to slog through headwinds for the two following days and would likely be grounded by weather another day.

For a flight of 1300 kilometres over remote sea, the trip from Greenland to the Canadian coast was remarkably straightforward. The tailwinds started in the *Sun*'s favour and kept getting better. After one hour they were 10 knots. After two they were 20 knots, which gave me the equivalent of a 20 per cent discount on flying time and fuel.

Icebergs dotted the sea for the first hour. A couple of hours later, having seen none for a while, I came across one so big that it was emanating waves in concentric circles. The sight was incredible, and one that would have sent a chill up the spine of any long-distance sailor. I marked the berg on my route as 61 degrees north, 54 degrees west. If the location were flipped to the Southern Hemisphere, it would have been at the tip of the Antarctic Peninsula, which juts out from Antarctica towards Argentina. *I would hate to be sailing around here at night,* I thought, but it also made me realise just how far north I'd trekked in the *Southern Sun*.

I flew at 4500 feet all the way to the Canadian coast, a journey of six hours. The air was so calm that I was able to write in my journal, the notepad resting on my knees. I looked up at the instruments and out the windscreen between every sentence, rather than every few words. I enjoyed the solitude, and the opportunity to put my thoughts down on paper. I felt satisfaction at seeing a complicated plan come together.

Maybe I got ahead of myself. Perhaps it could have happened to any amateur pilot. The ease of the flight could have made me overconfident. Either way, the trip would not be quickly forgotten, perhaps marking a turning point in my life. That night in my hotel, safely on the ground at last, I cautiously described on my blog what it had been like to get caught in cloud on the Newfoundland coast. Not wanting to scare Anne, Jack and Tim, I wrote the following under the headline 'Some bonus extra flying time':

> I had already planned a route that brought me down the bay rather than direct, but even crossing the small peninsula below wasn't possible. I started venturing in, got very uncomfortable with the view ahead and turned back, and decided to stay over water or very low land. This is the beauty of carrying extra fuel. I quickly worked out I had four hours' spare fuel, so even flying an extra 60 miles just didn't matter.

The reality was a lot more complex. After six hours' flying, the Canadian coast appeared on the horizon under a blanket of cloud. A second layer of menacing white sat above it. There was a narrow, cloudless gap in between. After such a straightforward flight, I was going to have to finagle the *Sun* through the poor weather to the airport, which was still 150 kilometres away inland. It was going to be hard work.

I could have flown over the upper cloud bank and, unable to see the ground, used my GPS mapping to navigate to Goose Bay. All I would have to do was follow the map and enjoy the clear sky. But if there wasn't an opening when I got overhead of the airport – and the forecast suggested there would be a few gaps – I would have to descend through the cloud. As a VFR pilot, I was only allowed to fly through cloud when there were no other options, and I always tried to avoid that situation. But going over the cloud would be easier, and possibly safer, than flying between the two cloud banks. I had no way of knowing how far the gap extended.

Another option was to fly along the coast to Brig Harbour Island, at the mouth of Hamilton Inlet, which connects to Lake Melville. Goose

Bay sits on the lake's western edge. If at any point the clouds got so low that I had to land – which was possible but unlikely that day – I could have put the *Sun* down on the wide lake. This simple, safe option would have added forty-five minutes' flying.

I called Goose Bay airport on the radio for assistance. They would have the latest weather information and could advise on the safest route in. 'Goose Bay, Searey amphibian, November Four Seven Three X-ray Papa, request.'

No one responded. I was on my own.

Eager to land and celebrate a successful Atlantic crossing, I made a rookie error: I took the shortcut. I flew between the two cloud banks, hoping for a clear path all the way to Goose Bay, which was about an hour away.

I wasn't sure but the cloud below me seemed to be getting higher, and the bank above lower. A few minutes later there was no doubt: the cloud banks were merging. The *Sun* was flying into a tightening vice.

Even small aircraft like the *Sun* can't reverse their direction quickly. It takes a full minute to turn 180 degrees in regular conditions. In an emergency, the *Sun* could switch directions in half that, but even that wouldn't be fast enough on this day. I was flying at 1500 feet, which is low enough on clear day to see people waving up at you. It also takes less than a minute to hit the ground if you lose control.

Being in cloud is like flying on a moonless night – except more dangerous. All you can see is white. If you are not changing direction or speed rapidly, you lose all sense of motion. The plane could be heading straight for the ground and you wouldn't know. All you can rely on are your instruments. And I had been repeatedly warned that visual pilots who inadvertently enter cloud have an average life expectancy of just thirty seconds. A few times on the trip I hadn't been able to avoid flying through clouds. Even with time to prepare and focus on the instruments, I was always relieved to emerge into sunlight.

Now I knew I needed to escape this situation fast. I tipped the *Sun* into a gentle 180-degree turn – but instead of turning to the left, which would have given me a better view of the sky, I instinctively turned to the right, as though I were driving a car in Australia or England. The *Sun* ran straight into a cloud I didn't realise was there.

Caught by surprise, I didn't process properly what had happened. *Why am I in cloud?* I asked myself, which was absurd, because there was no reason I wouldn't be. I was in denial.

If the *Sun* hadn't been in a turn, I would probably have been fine. I could have put her into a gentle climb and popped out above the cloud a few minutes later. Now the instruments indicated the *Sun* was slowly turning and losing altitude. That didn't make sense to my overwhelmed brain. I adjusted the controls but couldn't get her to fly straight and maintain altitude, which would give me a chance to pull myself together.

Fearing I had just thirty seconds to escape the cloud, I panicked. I slammed on the rudder to pull out of what I wrongly thought was a descending spiral. The instrument indicated the *Sun* was banked at 80 degrees – almost on her side – and started diving towards the ground. The warning system was screaming 'terrain, terrain, pull up, pull up' and 'speed, speed' through my headset. I should have been looking *inside* the plane, at the instruments, and using my limited (and dryly named) 'recovery from unusual attitude' training to regain straight and level flight. But instead I kept looking *outside* and only saw white.

She was going so fast that the rigid plastic windscreen started caving in – something I hadn't known was possible. My heart was racing with a sense of dread and mortal fear; it had all happened so quickly. She was about to slam into the ground. I all but gave up, realising I'd lost control, and expected the plane to break apart before I hit the ground. I felt the deepest sense of sadness. It was over. I was about to die.

I thought of my family – I had let them down. But then something appeared, like a dull streetlight on a foggy night, or the first glimpse of light at the end of a long, dark train tunnel. The sun.

Still engulfed in white, the sun looked like a tiny, silhouetted dot. It was late in the afternoon and I was so far north of the equator that the sun was close to the horizon, making it an ideal beacon to steer towards. Even though I couldn't see anything else, it was enough and I regained my sense of orientation. My hands and feet moved instinctively in unison. I levelled out, and eased the throttle a little and flew towards the shining white dot in the cloud. A minute later the *Sun* broke free of the cloud. The ground was only a few hundred feet below. At the speed I was descending, that would have been roughly ten more seconds.

My body was shaking, and my heart was pounding so hard that I thought I was having a heart attack. I knew I had to pull myself together – it was still at least an hour to the airport. *Think of your family*, I told myself. *If you want to see them again, focus. You know what to do. You've been flying for ten years. You've flown half way around the world. Get to the coast and navigate the safest way, back to the water's edge and follow the coast all the way to the airport.*

I flew until I saw the beach and turned right – I would follow the shore to safety. The path ahead was clear. The sense of relief I felt quickly became something else: my shoulders slumped and I blubbered like an inconsolable child.

～

Goose Bay is an air force base that was once home to thousands of troops. When I arrived it had a skeleton staff. That meant a huge concrete runway with few other planes, which was very welcome, given my emotional state. I parked next to two Canadair water bombers, and after shutting down just sat in the cockpit, silent and still, barely knowing what to do next. Was I really here?

The moment was broken by the arrival of the customs and immigration officers. I opened the window, climbed out and got on with the procedures. I tied down the plane, walked into the handling agent's office and arranged to be taken to the closest hotel. Exhausted, I didn't want to rush back to the airport the following morning.

That night, with good internet reception for the first time since Iceland, I downloaded all the detailed aviation maps for Canada and the United States which I'd been unable to get over the last week. I couldn't bring myself to call Anne to explain what had happened. I was barely coping emotionally as it was. I told myself that to share it would have been unfair on my family. They would have been very worried for me, and other people would have contacted them to discuss it. There was no need to start those conversations when I was on the other side of the world. In truth, once the news of what had almost happened was 'out there', I don't think I could have continued.

My angst was of my making. I needed to own it. I confessed the truth to my personal journal in a handwritten script so jittery I could barely read it later. I didn't hold back my anger at myself. I had a very quiet dinner and went for a long, lonely walk. I didn't want to be alone in my room. I broke into tears a few times. It was a horrifying experience, one I still can't help but think about often, but don't like to discuss. I choke up when trying to explain it.

One welcome email had arrived: the Narsarsuaq airport tower in Greenland had found my soft, comforting cashmere jumper on a couch in the tower and promised to post it home to Australia. I breathed a deep sigh. At least something good had happened that day.

24.

Canadian Bacon

'This box is full of stuff that almost killed me.'
SERGEANT FIRST CLASS WILLIAM JAMES, *THE HURT
LOCKER* (2008)

After the trauma of the previous day, I wasn't eager to get back into the *Southern Sun*. Hanging around wasn't going to make me feel any better, though. After a restless night, I slept in. I made espresso and ate a muesli bar in my room, and methodically updated every topographic and aviation map on my iPad. One of the reasons I'd made bad decisions yesterday was lack of information: my charts, made for instrument flying, didn't show the precise height of hills. If I'd had that knowledge, I would have been more confident about flying beneath low clouds.

I was also determined to fix the *Sun*'s propeller pitch controller, which could help me climb out of dangerous situations. My ground agent arranged access to a large hangar. It was a luxury to work inside on a concrete floor, which is much nicer than tarmac, especially when you drop a nut or cog. I wasn't sure why the pitch controller kept failing. There were so many small bronze cogs that pulling apart the device was like playing with the insides of a clock.

While I was working, a couple of firefighter pilots introduced themselves. Based at the airfield, they flew the Canadair CL-415, an amphibian water bomber that could carry thirty people or six tonnes of water. They noticed the Australian flag on the *Sun*'s tail.

'But you haven't come from Australia in that?' one asked.

'Ah, yep,' was pretty much all I could offer. I didn't feel like boasting about my achievements today.

The tough and versatile CL-415 is still manufactured by Bombardier, twenty-three years after its maiden flight. Seeing the beast of a work-horse next to the *Sun*, I fantasised about converting one into a private luxury plane for exploration – an 'air yacht', to borrow a term from the 1930s. The pilots, who were very friendly, offered me a tour, which I was keen to do. I promised to find them after finishing my maintenance.

The work took longer than planned, mainly because I didn't warm up the engine before replacing the oil. In cold climates engine oil becomes very thick and takes a long time to drain. After a few hours the work was complete, and I had a decision to make: to fly or not to fly, that was the question. My intended next stop was only a four-hour flight away, and if I left soon I'd make it before dark. Or I could just stay another day here and head off in the morning. The hotel was pretty depressing, and I thought maybe the best thing for me was to get back into the *Sun* and make the short flight.

I fuelled up, filed my flight plan with the agent and taxied across to the runway, past the CL-415. *Doh!* I thought. *I forgot to get the tour of the fire bombers.* I was really annoyed at myself, but it was 4 p.m. and I needed to keep going. If the flight went to plan I would land in the Newfoundland town of Botwood an hour before sunset.

Cloud hung over the vast, empty wilderness around 1500 feet. I comfortably skimmed along at 1000 feet. There were almost no signs of human habitation, just millions of hectares of forest, rivers and the occasional river boat.

Botwood was the North American refuelling stop for the trans-atlantic flying boats of the 1930s. They flew straight from there to Ireland, a distance of 3200 kilometres. It would have been nice to have that range, I thought, but they never got to explore Iceland or Greenland. I'd take the longer route any day. The town, which has a population of 3100, is proud of its cameo in aviation history. Like Foynes, Botwood has a museum dedicated to flying boats, which I was keen to see. While the water landing area on the well-named Bay of Exploits looked calm, there didn't seem to be any fences or a yard in which I could lock the *Sun* up overnight. So I landed at a small airfield on the edge of town at what I thought was 8.15 p.m. It turned out that Newfoundlanders pride themselves on being half an hour ahead of those Labrador mainlanders, which meant it was actually 8.45 p.m. No wonder the sunset seemed early.

The weather had been kind. I needed an easy flight to rebuild my confidence after the Goose Bay incident. I had come a long way, I told myself, and I did actually know what I was doing. The fact that a four-hour flight felt short, when only a few years ago it would have been a major undertaking, was reassuring.

After tying down the *Sun*, I called Mary, a local cab driver, and asked her to take me to the nearest hotel. There wasn't one, but she suggested a bed and breakfast called the Dockside Inn. Neat and welcoming, it was a very comfortable place to sleep, which was fortunate because Botwood didn't have a raging nightlife. With almost the entire town closed by 9 p.m., the only food I could find was from a takeaway chicken joint.

The next day – the 100th of my trip around the world – I planned to spend a day checking out Botwood and its museum. I took the short cab trip to the airfield, took off in the *Sun* and several minutes later touched down on the bay and taxied to a parking area near the museum, which was built on the grounds of the original 1930s flying boat base. Getting up onto the land was easy as the original concrete ramp and hardstand were still in great condition. I taxied out of the water and – something I'd never done before – down the road to the museum.

The Botwood Flying Boat Museum is small and run by enthusiastic volunteers. Its eclectic collection includes photos, models, artefacts and a cinematic news feature from the 1930s about the flying boats coming to town. The original terminal and speedboat house still stand, and are kept in good shape.

Word got around that a flying boat had arrived, and soon the *Southern Sun* was surrounded by a small crowd, including the mayor, Jerry Dean, and his deputy, Scott Sceviour. Their surprise at seeing an Australian flag on the tail turned to astonishment when they heard where she had come from. The *Sun* was the first flying boat to fly from Foynes to Botwood in thirty-seven years, they said. Hearing that was pretty good. The mayor presented me with a flag of the city and then asked to meet after dinner for a chat over a drink.

After meeting and taking photos with many locals, I flew back to the airfield, where Mary was waiting to pick me up. After I had a quiet dinner alone at the Dockside Inn, she took me to the local branch of the Royal Canadian Legion, where quite a crowd had gathered. They had decided to do me the honour of an old Newfoundland initiation known as the 'Screech In' ceremony. This requires the subject to wear a bright yellow raincoat and talk like a Newfoundlander while standing with one bare foot in a bucket of iced water, and then downing a swig of locally made rum, or Screech. The talking was the hardest bit but I must have come close enough, because I was presented with a certificate that said I had been inducted into the Royal Order of the Screechers. I promised it would go straight to the pool room.

Due to the impromptu nature of the evening, I gave a quick talk. I focused not so much on details of my trip but on the great sense of community I had experienced in towns across the world, including that day in Botwood. The audience was very interested and I moved from table to table casually and answered their questions. It was lovely to be surrounded by such hospitable people. One of the reasons for their enthusiasm was the strong bond that exists between the Irish and the Newfoundlanders.

Sleeping in is only relaxing when you don't have an agenda. My alarm went off at 5.30 a.m. I then woke again at 6.09 a.m., which left me just twenty-one minutes to get ready for my ride. A shower and morning espresso were not optional if I wanted to fully wake up, so I decided to check the weather and file my flight plan at the airfield, hoping there would be some 3G reception. Mary's husband, Gary, arrived in his pick-up truck ready to collect eight containers of fuel on the way. He refused to accept payment for their taxi services – not just for that morning but the previous day too, even though Mary had run me all over town. Such kindness from strangers never failed to move me.

The *Sun's* destination that day was North America. The city of Bangor, Maine, has an airport that is today used by the US Air Force as a stopover for flights to Europe, and it is also the most common gateway for smaller private aircraft crossing the Atlantic.

The United States is the most defended nation on Earth, even more so in the air since the 9/11 attacks. Which is why I was concerned, as I approached the border at 4500 feet, that I had lost contact with Canadian air-traffic control and couldn't raise anyone in the US either. If there was anywhere in the world the *Sun* was going to be intercepted for non-contact at a border crossing, I felt this would be it.

I entered US airspace over the sea and, when the time came, turned right towards the airport, still nervously unannounced. Bangor was forty-five minutes inland. I soon found myself in depressingly familiar territory. The morning weather report said there would be a lot of clouds around, but 'broken', meaning there should have been plenty of holes to fly through. But as I closed in on the coast, there was one long, unbroken cloud as far as I could see, and it reached almost to the ground. I had been flying for over eight hours. The chances of the weather forecast still being accurate after that amount of time were not very good.

Almost due east of Bangor, I had to make the same fateful decision I'd faced three days ago at Goose Bay: go under or over. In an instant, I decided to fly over the cloud at 4500 feet. I didn't have the nerve to do otherwise. If I went under, I could have become caught between a hill and cloud, with no water or runway to land on.

I hoped the cloud would open up before I hit the 30-mile circle around Bangor airport, which I had to seek permission from the tower to enter. If I couldn't see the ground, I wouldn't be allowed to land under visual flight rules. The tower might refuse me clearance to enter its airspace, and it would be up to me to find an alternative.

After fifteen minutes I was close to the 30-mile marker, 50 kilometres to the airport, yet there was no break in the cloud. I had always felt more comfortable descending over water, because I knew there would be no nasty surprises in the shape of mountains or radio towers. The chart said the *Sun* would be safe from obstacles as long as we didn't go below 1300 feet above sea level, which would mean we were a good 500 feet above the nearest obstacle. A sizeable lake ahead was a landing option.

I came up with a plan. I would descend through the cloud to 1500 feet. If the sky wasn't clear, I would drop another 200 feet. If that didn't work, I would climb out, continue towards the airport and think of something else. I reduced power and put the *Sun* into a slow descent. I concentrated on the altimeter, the rate-of-descent gauge which indicated how fast the *Sun* was falling, and on the artificial horizon. I even deployed the flaps, which slowed the *Sun* down and made the handling more docile and the wings less likely to stall.

After a few minutes, at a descent rate of 350 feet a minute, I entered the cloud. Just like near Goose Bay, the cockpit was enveloped in an impenetrable white. This time, though, I was in control. The *Sun* was flying in a straight line, and was level with the horizon. Her speed was only 70 knots, which slowed everything down nicely and gave me more time to react and keep the situation under control.

I reckoned it would be two to three minutes before we emerged from the cloud. After three it was still a whiteout. Approaching

1500 feet, I looked out the side window for signs of land. It might as well have been the middle of the night during a power blackout. In the back of my mind, the memory of Goose Bay haunted me. But I stayed calm and focused. *Okay*, I thought. *I'll give this another thirty seconds. If I can't see through the cloud by then, I'll climb back out.*

I slowed the *Sun's* descent rate to 200 feet a minute. After thirty seconds that put her at 1400 feet, which meant there could have been a hill just 600 feet below. I glanced sideways and downwards. There was nothing but white. I gently opened the throttle, moved the control stick back a few millimetres and jabbed the electric switch with my thumb that trimmed the tail and locked in the climb. Within seconds the *Sun* started gaining altitude, and was soon climbing under full power at 500 feet a minute. I felt a surge of relief as she emerged from the cloud into safe blue sky.

I levelled off at 3500 feet. Having spoken to no one for a couple of hours, I felt quite lonely as I tried, for the umpteenth time, to raise the Bangor air-traffic controllers on the radio.

'Bangor approach, Searey November Four Seven Three X-ray Papa,' I said.

This time a voice came into my headset loud and clear: 'November Four Seven Three X-ray Papa, Bangor, go ahead.'

I requested permission to land, stated my position and advised the transponder code I had been given at Botwood. 'X-ray Papa, 35 miles east, 3500 feet, VFR flight, from Botwood, Canada, request inbound with ETA two-three [twenty-three minutes past the hour].'

I was soon 'identified', which meant he had me on radar and I was allowed to continue towards the airport. I still didn't know how I was going to get through the cloud, though, which made me nervous. There were no holes in the white. Nature didn't seem to have read the morning's forecast.

I advised the controller I was 'VFR on top' and asked him to help me find a way through.

'Are you IFR-equipped?' he asked. He was asking if the *Sun* had navigational instruments for flying through cloud, which it did, although they were basic.

'Affirm,' I replied.

I girded my loins for another scary descent. But with his assistance I found an opening in the cloud a little to the left. *Phew*, I thought. This landing was going to be a lot easier.

While I could have flown through the cloud with the controller's guidance, it was much more comfortable and safer being able to see the ground. As the *Sun* descended to 1500 feet two nautical miles from the runway, I thought to myself: *That's it – I absolutely, positively need an IFR rating and a fully equipped IFR plane. This is not the place to be messing with weather.*

Two minutes later I was rolling along the runway. A customs officer was waiting for me, and took only took ten minutes before handing me over to two US Immigration agents.

Although Bangor is probably the most popular entry and exit point for small planes in the US north-east, these two guys, employing some sort of 'good cop/bad cop' routine, subjected me to over an hour of mindless grilling, badgering me about my reasons for entering the country. They didn't care that the *Southern Sun* was registered in the United States, or that I had flown there dozens of times. They treated me with suspicion and disdain. It was fascinating that the most hostile welcomes I received during my whole trip were in the United Kingdom and the United States.

Seriously, guys, I thought. *Loosen up! Every other country is friendlier than you – even the ones you think are your enemies!*

25.

Sully

"First Officer Skiles, is there anything you'd like to add? Anything . . .
you would have done differently if you . . . had to do it again?"
"Yes. I would've done it in July."'
ELIZABETH DAVIS AND JEFF SKILES, *SULLY* (2016)

'New York radar, November Four Seven Three X-ray Papa, Searey amphibian with one POB [passenger on board], inbound for Westchester via Port Washington,' I radioed air-traffic control.

'Four Seven Three X-ray Papa, you are identified,' the controller replied. 'Turn heading two one zero to overfly, then expect to join downwind for Westchester runway three four.'

'New York radar, request touch-and-go at Port Washington, as per my flight plan. Three X-ray Papa.'

'Three X-ray Papa, what are you requesting?'

'Three X-ray Papa is an amphibian seaplane. Final destination is Westchester, but flight plan includes a touch-and-go on Port Washington waters en route.'

'Three X-ray Papa, proceed to Port Washington, which is OCTA [outside controlled airspace]. Contact me on the way back.'

'Cleared for a touch-and-go, Port Washington. Three X-ray Papa. Thank you very much for your help. G'day.'

The number of planes under the supervision of the New York air-traffic controller I had just spoken to was insane. From huge passenger jets down to the tiny *Southern Sun*, coming and going from five or more airports, he moved us around like chess pieces. The controller seemed relieved to get me off the air. He had a lot more to worry about than a small plane planning to kiss the water at Port Washington, a fancy outer New York suburb on the north shore of Long Island, and America's equivalent of Southampton Waters on the transatlantic flying boat route. Did he realise how far I'd come, or what a wondrous moment this was for me? Of course not.

Port Washington is a picturesque and busy little harbour. It was a Wednesday in July, and the water was full of small yachts and dinghies. I'd been advised in Foynes (and it was confirmed in Botwood) that the last flying boat to cross the Atlantic from Southampton to New York was in the 1950s. Today, visits from flying boats are rare, as I realised when the *Sun* touched down. A small fleet of school-aged children sailed over to say hello, and a guy in a speedboat raced over too. I could tell by the way he was looking at me that the phone in his hand was dialling 911. I gave him a thumbs-up, he hung up and sped off.

The *Sun* had now completed the four water landings of the original London–New York flying boats: Southampton, Foynes, Botwood and Port Washington. I felt enormously pleased. Not because I thought I had achieved a great aviation milestone – I hadn't – but because I had wanted to re-create two important flight routes from history that held a deep personal fascination for me.

Once the schoolkids were out of the way, I eased the *Sun* back into the sky. I then flew to Westchester, a secondary airport for New York City, and landed behind one private jet and in front of another. Because it had been an internal flight, I didn't have to clear customs or immigration. I tied down the *Sun* and casually walked over to the airport building, ignored by all. *Hold on*, I thought. *This is what flying at home is normally like!*

I felt like I had just finished my high-school exams. Sitting on a couch in the pilots' lounge, I didn't know what to do with myself. *What's next?* I wondered. I decided to get coffee first, red wine soon and then a

Hannibal, the birthplace of writer Mark Twain, who inspired my Mississippi adventure.

A river carpark at Hannibal, where I left the *Sun* while I rushed to inspect locations that appeared in *Huckleberry Finn*.

Sleeping on the bank of the Mississippi. I had to spend the night in the cockpit because of the swarms of insects.

The great Mississippi narrows to the width of a creek near its source, Lake Itasca.

The State Theatre in Traverse City, Michigan. Its restoration was spearheaded by documentarian Michael Moore.

The inside passage of the
Alaskan coastline. Even
though Russian permission
hadn't come through,
I decided to keep going.

A beautiful day in southern Alaska. The weather could quickly turn bad, forcing me to hole up in isolated towns.

The Aleutians are a chain of small islands and extinct volcanoes. The amazing views belie the huge swells that would swamp the *Sun* if she landed on water.

Adak, the most westerly civilian population in the United States, and my home for three weeks.

A Cold War–era bunker designed to house eighty-four people.

Quad bikes are the transport of choice on Adak, home to an indigenous population of Inuits. I'm about to meet Ruth, one of the school teachers.

Although isolated, the eighty-person community on Atka has a thriving economy.

The withdrawal of the federal government from the Aleutians has left many buildings on Adak abandoned.

A moment of calm and beauty in the notorious Bering Sea.

I couldn't present to a seaplane conference in Sydney in person, so I used Skype from an Adak classroom.

Every child and teacher from Adak's school farewelling me. I left behind a final letter to my family, just in case.

Cloud, low light and rain: the flight from Alaska to Japan, one of the most dangerous of my life.

I had stashed fuel on Attu, an uninhabited island with a Cold War–era runway I found on Google Earth.

Buying fuel at a petrol station in Japan.

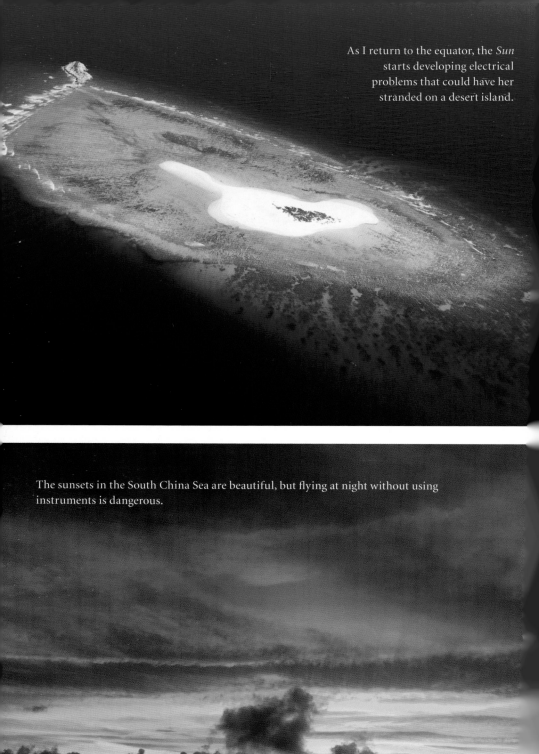

As I return to the equator, the *Sun* starts developing electrical problems that could have her stranded on a desert island.

The sunsets in the South China Sea are beautiful, but flying at night without using instruments is dangerous.

A very intimidating Seahawk helicopter from the Philippine Navy, which I photograph in case something bad is about to happen.

In Rio Hondo in Zamboanga, the public transport is BMX bikes.

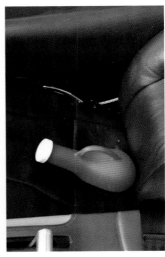

Never drink from the red bottle.

Finally ascending the boat ramp at Williamstown. I'm relieved to be home safely, and so pleased to see my family.

The circumnavigation is completed at the Qantas museum in Longreach, which I rushed to against my better judgement.

My inspirational grandmother, Jean Smith, is part of the welcome-home party.

The rising sun on the roof of the Sun Theatre in Melbourne is a motif for my life.

The setting sun, an inspiration for my adventures, past and future.

good night's sleep. After the coffee, it didn't take me long to settle on my next move, and right now: fly the *Sun* around one of most photogenic and awe-inspiring cities on the planet.

The Hudson River stretches along the western side of the island of Manhattan; famously, it was the site of a water landing by a US Airways plane in 2009. Aviation authorities have established a route above the river for private VFR pilots like me. The maximum altitude allowed is 1300 feet, which is lower than some buildings in the city. Because the airspace around New York is so crowded, there is a very regimented procedure for the route, which intimidates some amateur pilots, including me. Even though I had never flown a plane over or near New York, it was too good not to explore.

I read the Federal Aviation Administration procedures and advice a few times and wrote them out to try to make them stick in my memory. One of the amazing aspects of the route is that air-traffic control clearance isn't needed as long as you follow the rules. You simply turn up and make general broadcast calls, a sign that the tougher restrictions on all kinds of flying introduced after the 9/11 terrorist attacks only went so far.

From Westchester County Airport, north of New York City, I took off and headed west towards the Hudson. My first call on the radio, as I passed over the George Washington Bridge at the northern end of Manhattan, was to let other pilots in the vicinity know I was there. 'Hudson traffic, amphibian, GW Bridge, 1100 feet, southbound,' I said.

There was no reply, response or objection. I could have been in the Australian outback for all the interest I received. Another half a dozen position reports were required, using well-known landmarks. One, for a non-American, was surreal, and I broke into a broad grin as the words came out of my mouth: 'Hudson traffic, amphibian, Statue Liberty, 1000 feet, tracking south and turning east for northbound in one minute.'

The *Southern Sun* was flying so close to the Statue of Liberty I felt I could almost touch it. The sun broke through the clouds, casting a wonderful sheen over the calm waters of Upper Bay. Ferries, boats, barges and yachts created a busy water life that would not have been out of place in a Richard Scarry children's book.

The rules allow aircraft to circle around the statue, which was built to welcome immigrants to America. As a lone pilot and with tourist helicopters in the area, I decided not to push my luck. I was pretty happy as it was. To behold Battery Point, at the southern tip of Manhattan, right up to the Empire State and Chrysler buildings, and so many others I couldn't name, was a high point of my life. It felt like an enormous achievement to have crossed two continents and the Atlantic Ocean. In the thirty minutes of that flight I felt elation, pride and a feeling that I can best describe as approaching bliss. If true contentment is possible, I had found it.

Like most foreigners, I was in awe of the size and density of New York the first time I went there, many years earlier. Seeing it from the air at low altitude brought a new level of appreciation. If you want to find a celebration of American freedom, look no further than the fact that any pilot can fly a small plane the length of Manhattan and, if of a certain ilk, do what I did next.

As the *Sun* passed a few ferries and approached the aircraft carrier *Intrepid*, which has been turned into a museum, I knew what I had to do. I called on the radio: 'Amphibian *Southern Sun*, *Intrepid*, northbound, 800 feet, descending for water operations on the Hudson.'

The *Sun* eased down and landed on the murky waters. I paused for a few seconds to soak up the experience. She wasn't the first plane to land on the Hudson, but unlike some I was able to take off again. I was so happy that I did a second 'splash'n'dash'.

Then I opened the throttle and gently climbed over the George Washington Bridge. A couple of minutes before I reached Westchester, an awful high-pitched squeal came through my headset. I looked across the instruments, scanning for a problem – the lights on the transponder were flashing on and off. I switched off the device and the squealing stopped. As I came closer to landing, I turned it on again but the squealing continued, so I turned it off immediately.

A transponder is mandatory for any craft wishing to land at most airports operated by air-traffic controllers. It sends out a radio signal that identifies the aircraft on radar. It is a vital piece of equipment. I had never heard of one failing like this.

The Westchester control tower advised that it could see the *Sun* and asked me to cycle (switch on and off) the transponder. Rather than say, 'My transponder has malfunctioned,' I said yes – and ignored the instruction. I was apprehensive and keen to land. They could see me. I could see the runway. I had plenty to do before landing. I needed to fly the plane, not start discussing the technical problems I was having. The tower cleared me to land and didn't ask about the transponder again. When I finally pulled up in the parking area, I shut down the engine and sighed with relief. Talk about a roller-coaster of emotions.

Landing on the Hudson was something I'd wanted to do for years, but the transponder problem had given me a big scare. It wasn't life-threatening, but if it had failed during my flight down the coast from Maine, I wouldn't have been allowed to enter New York airspace. I needed a working transponder to access many of the airports I had flown into over the previous few months. I seemed to have become a disciple of a strange 'breakdown just in time' religion.

I tried to turn it back on. The screen stayed blank. I shut down all the *Sun*'s electrics, then took a deep breath and a sip of water. I switched her electrics back on, and turned on the transponder again. This time it fired up immediately, and there was no squealing on the radio headset. This was weird and disconcerting: faults were bound to happen, but I preferred it when there was some logic to them, which made fixing them so much easier.

Even though the transponder was apparently working, I couldn't risk another breakdown. Wherever I headed next, I would have to land at airports without control towers and remain outside controlled airspace. I was already planning to take the *Sun* down to Florida for an annual maintenance check, fix a couple of intermittent faults and get some upgrades. So while it was a concern, it wouldn't stop the trip. But talk about timing.

Putting aside that mishap, it had been a magnificent day. I checked into a hotel near the airport, had an early dinner and retired early. Over breakfast the following morning, I pondered my next move. A lot of people following my flight had encouraged me to fly to the EAA AirVenture airshow in Oshkosh, Wisconsin, which attracted half a million people and 10,000 aircraft. The annual gathering of aviation enthusiasts, which had started the previous day, was only several hours' flying away. I had been promised a hero's welcome on arrival and lots of attention.

I was still reflecting on the trip from London, and I couldn't get the incident near Goose Bay out of my mind. Walking into an airshow in my flying suit with my chest out and being lauded had a certain appeal, but it was the wrong reason to go.

I had always admired the few generals through the ages who, having won their battles, with power there for the taking, returned to their farms and simple lives. I was proud of what I'd done but didn't feel triumphant. I toyed with the idea of turning up at Oshkosh, but decided I wasn't ready to face any big crowds, and that I needed to get to Florida to get on with some maintenance on the *Sun*. The transponder fault seemed like a warning: *You've done well, but don't get cocky*.

☼

The morning television news led with the weather battering the mid East Coast. A tornado was heading for the Carolinas, which meant I wouldn't be able to head south for a couple of days. Besides, I needed to rest, both physically and mentally.

224

New York was by far the most crowded place I'd visited during the whole trip. It was the loneliest, too. As I walked the streets with no real plan, the previous week's events weighed on me. For several moments I had not only thought death was imminent, I had accepted it. The lack of activity and distractions in New York brought this to the surface. I was having a delayed reaction to the trauma of almost killing myself.

I questioned whether I should continue. I didn't want to leave the *Sun* in New York, and she definitely needed some maintenance work. I was starting to think the best thing would be to get her to the factory, get the work done and ship her to Australia. I asked Barbara Pfeiffer, my freight agent of twenty years, how much a container would cost to move the *Sun* from Florida to Melbourne.

I decided to put off making the decision for a few days. I didn't want to be mentally bogged down by it. I had a long trip ahead of me, whatever I decided to do afterwards. New York to Florida I decided I would undertake nonstop. It would be my longest flight ever, around twelve hours, a leg no other Searey, let alone your average Cessna, would dream of making.

○

New York City is remarkable for simultaneously catering to mass and niche interests. As a fan of Winston Churchill, I was thrilled to make a pilgrimage to Chartwell, the only dedicated Churchill bookstore in the world. Located in midtown, it had been in business for over thirty years. Along with books about Churchill, it has many original editions of Churchill's own works. I held an autographed first edition of one of Churchill's many volumes in my hand, in awe of the inky, barely legible inscription penned by Winston himself. The US$12,000 price tag saw it soon safely back inside the locked glass cabinet. Instead I bought a copy of the recently published *Churchill*, by the British politician Boris Johnson – in paperback no less, which struck me as appropriately humble.

Top of my visit list, though, was the World Trade Center memorial and Freedom Tower, the building that replaced the Twin Towers. Two waterfall pools had been built in the foundations of the original north and south buildings, making a very elegant memorial, with a sense of emptiness and loss that was sad yet fitting. The names of all of those lost were etched into a metal surround to the pools.

There's an observatory and restaurant on floor 100 of the Freedom Tower, and the elevator that takes you there has a very nice feature. The three walls have floor-to-ceiling LED screens. As the elevator ascends, they display the physical development of New York over a few hundred years. The view from upstairs was spectacular, although the building owners had created more of an 'experience' than necessary by installing video displays and annoyingly loud commentators, and by trying to make more money by renting out informational computer tablets. Most people just wanted to look out the window in peace.

Although restaurants at the top of buildings don't usually have great reputations, I thought, *What the heck!* The food was pretty good, the wine list fair and the sunset beautiful.

As the sun started making the whole city glow, it had a powerful effect on one guy. He kept nervously walking back and forth, turning and twisting between the tables. After a few minutes of this strange behaviour, he pulled a small box from his pocket and asked his dinner companion if she would marry him. Fortunately, she said yes, and the room applauded most enthusiastically. Bravo.

I was glad to spend a couple of days in New York, and pleased I hadn't left immediately for the Oshkosh airshow. I don't think I would have felt a real sense of arrival in the United States if I'd pushed on. I needed time to reflect, relax, reset.

Although I had decided to fly to Florida in one go, I didn't know what I was going to do beyond that. Perhaps it would then be the right moment to call it quits and return to a more regular life.

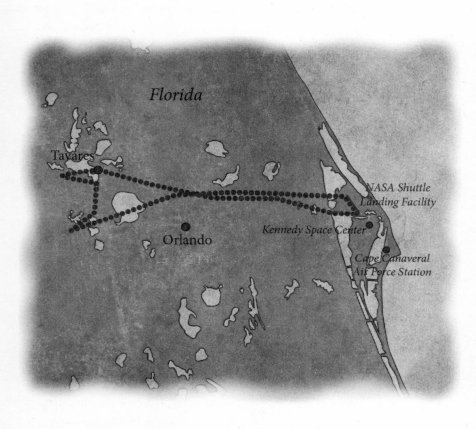

Florida

Tavares

NASA Shuttle
Landing Facility

Kennedy Space Center

Orlando

Cape Canaveral
Air Force Station

26.

Key Largo

'Remember, no matter where you go, there you are.'
BUCKAROO BANZAI, *THE ADVENTURES OF BUCKAROO BANZAI ACROSS THE 8TH DIMENSION* (1984)

Being able to watch a movie with a glass of red wine, walk to the toilet and even sleep was infinitely easier flying in a commercial plane than in the *Southern Sun*. But nowhere near as much fun. After leaving her at the Searey workshop in central Florida for her annual service and helping for a few days, I took a Qantas flight home to Melbourne to see my family. I also attended the Melbourne International Film Festival, caught up on some work and investigated airspace and airport clearances for the *Sun*'s Pacific route home.

I weighed up the options. If I pressed on, I could become the first pilot in history to fly solo around the world in an amphibious plane or flying boat. Given I had travelled so far, it seemed a waste not to go the extra distance. On the other hand, the trip had almost turned into a disaster. And not just the incident near Goose Bay. The numerous equipment glitches could have been far more serious. I had been lucky, and was worried that my luck would run out. Sometimes you should quit while you're ahead.

Without committing to a circumnavigation, I had asked the Searey mechanics in Florida to thoroughly examine the *Sun*. They removed the front deck and re-terminated the wiring, a step I hoped would end the intermittent electrical faults. In Melbourne I commissioned a larger flexible fuel tank bladder that could hold 110 litres, which was enough for five and a half hours of flying. The fuel bladder would be strapped into the passenger seat. Mike from White Rose agreed to seek permission for the *Sun* to fly through the Philippines and Indonesia, but advised that for Russian airspace I would need to deal directly with an agent there. He had never been able to secure permission for solo adventure flights through Russia, and on my analysis I would need this, if I was to cross the northern Pacific Ocean.

After a month in Melbourne, on 8 September 2015 I boarded a Qantas flight bound for London. I arrived the day Elizabeth II became Britain's longest-serving monarch, and pomp and ceremony filled the air. After a quick visit to 1 Savile Row, coffee with a cinema colleague and a visit to the Grand Empire cinema in Leicester Square, I caught a flight from an overcast Gatwick Airport to sunny Miami. It took just forty-one hours from Melbourne to Orlando, via London: the same distance and route the *Southern Sun* had managed in three and a half months. The efficiency of modern air travel was humbling. But I was itching to be reunited with my flying boat, and to start exploring the world from above again.

Progressive Aerodyne had been closely involved in my preparations for the trip to London. Now that I planned to go the whole way around, the company's involvement again became vital. I felt like more than a client. They seemed really proud of the *Sun*'s adventure, which was also creating greater awareness of the plane among pilots around the world. It had certainly given some credibility to the strength and robustness of the design.

I was lent an apartment at the airfield operated by friend and mechanic Russell Brown, who serviced Seareys for the company. I dined with a few local pilots on different nights, and all of them were great company. Jim Walsh suggested many local sights to fly to and visit, and my time with the guru of Searey flying, Dan Nickens, was very special.

Dan is a great adventurer, having flown his Searey across America from Florida to Alaska, with his wife, Anne, following in a motorhome and meeting him each night. He has an enormous amount of experience. I hadn't told him of my troubles at the end of my Atlantic crossing, so he never knew how much his calmness, stories, encouragement and friendship helped me decide to push on. Dan had accompanied Richard Bach on a cross-country Searey journey, which resulted in Bach's later book *Travels with Puff*. He encouraged me to write a book when I was finished, which I had pondered but had not decided upon until talking with him. Dan also gave me great tips on flying up the Mississippi and across to Alaska. Thanks, Dan.

When I was alone, my diet usually consisted of a can of tuna, some nuts and a glass of red wine. I visited just one cinema in Florida, the Aloma Cinema Grille. The 'grille' referred to the fact you could eat a burger at a small table next to you; the seats were comfortable but looked like 1980s vinyl office chairs. The flat floor made it hard for everyone to see the screen. Not the best execution, but on the personal space index in my research it ranked mighty high.

Progressive Aerodyne asked me to give a presentation at the Tavares Seaplane Base, which is close to the Searey factory, an hour north of Orlando. The event, held at a newly built function centre over the edge of a lake, reminded me of my dad pulling out a Kodak slide projector and a carousel of photos from a family trip. This was similar, except I arrived by air and was greeted by a big crowd, including the mayor, Kirby Smith, and the city's business development manager, John Drury. Many Searey enthusiasts had flown or driven long distances to attend, including a couple who had come from Texas. No pressure!

I focused on the flying aspects and the people I'd met, and showed many photos of the sites I'd seen. The audience seemed thoroughly interested, engaged and asked lots of questions. The following day, the local newspaper, the *Daily Commercial*, published an article on its front page under an apt headline: 'Going Solo'. I was so pleased to have been able to share the story like this, especially for Kerry Richter, the designer of the Searey and builder of *Southern Sun*. He had helped me many times over ten years, and so much over the last few especially. He loved all the stories, and saved my photos to his computer so he could share them with his father, Wayne. I think he was pretty proud that the little plane he had designed twenty-five years earlier had gone from 'puddle-jumping' to a circumnavigation.

My planned route home was designed to combine a mix of geographies, sites and cultures. From Florida I would fly to New Orleans, and from there follow the Mississippi north to Minnesota, then west to Oregon, Alaska and the Aleutian Islands. From there it would be across the Pacific Ocean to Russia, then south to Japan and the Philippines, through Indonesia and back to Australia. The whole trip depended, of course, on me getting clearance for every country. One rejection would make the journey impossible and I would have to head home by other means.

One of the upgrades installed in the *Sun* in Florida was a replacement Spidertracks unit, the satellite device that transmitted the craft's position to a website. The new version had in-flight text messaging and access to weather reports from satellites anywhere on Earth. It was a huge safety improvement that would have been very useful when I was out of radio range over the Atlantic.

After ten days in Florida, with me helping complete the service and upgrades, I still didn't have permission to enter Russia. The predominant winds in the North Pacific at that time of year are from the west, which would make the trans-Pacific leg even harder. As an alternative, I also requested permission to land at the most westerly airfield in the Aleutians, a US Air Force base, but that seemed unlikely. If the Russians didn't come through, I figured I'd turn around in Seattle and spend a couple of weeks exploring America before shipping the *Sun* home.

Once the maintenance was finished, I was tempted to pack the plane and fly off straightaway. Prudence dictated a few short flights to check for anything loose, oil or fluid leaks, or electrical problems. Where would I go in South Florida for an extended test flight, I asked myself. Jim Walsh had an excellent suggestion: 'How about Cape Canaveral and the Kennedy Space Center?'

Now that the Space Shuttle program has closed down, NASA allows private pilots to observe the Space Coast from the air, and to 'shoot the shuttle runway' by flying along the entire five-kilometre landing strip at 100 feet, and then past the massive shuttle assembly building. It was a pretty cool thing to do. I was feeling good, and was now ready to venture forth. And who doesn't love rockets?

Act iii

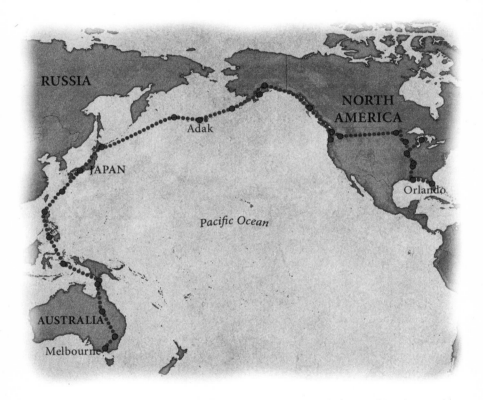

'Man who catch fly with chopstick accomplish anything.'
MR MIYAGI, *THE KARATE KID* (1984)

27.

The Adventures of
Huckleberry Finn

'Don't just fly, soar.'
DUMBO, *DUMBO* (1941)

My route out of Florida took the *Southern Sun* over the Gulf of Mexico and Tyndall Air Force Base, where an air-traffic controller gave me permission to fly through his airspace. After a few minutes he radioed a warning that sent a surge of excitement through my body. 'Three X-ray Papa, traffic at your level,' he said. 'A pair of F-22 Raptors will cross and pass you.'

The two planes, the most modern fighter jets in the world, zoomed in front of the *Sun* from right to left. It felt awesome to see such powerful aircraft in action from the air. Then another two flew past. Just before they disappeared out of sight, I snapped a photo – but it turned out to be two blobs and the inside of the windshield. Either it was the worst photo of the trip, or their stealth technology was that good.

I continued along the coast and landed at Ferguson Airport, a civil airport just north-west of the Naval Air Station Pensacola. This is the national military aviation headquarters, and they have a museum that celebrates nearly 100 years of ocean-based flying – from seaplanes and flying boats to planes that launch from the decks of aircraft carriers. The entry foyer had an imposing floor-to-ceiling picture of an aircraft carrier, and an audacious caption: '90,000 tons of diplomacy, anywhere, anytime'. Only in America! There were some great displays, including the first seaplane to cross the Atlantic, a cutaway Catalina, and various histories of a century of naval aviation.

It was here that an idea came to me: if an *aviator* is someone who flies a plane, then someone engaged in naval aviation would surely be a *naviator*. And if someone who goes around the world is a *circumnavigator*, then circling the globe in a flying boat must be a *circumnaviation*. (Are you still with me?) Finally, if the *Southern Sun* did complete a round-the-world journey, not only would I have made up a new word, I would also be the world's first *solo circumnaviator*!

It was a short flight along the coast to New Orleans, a city I had wanted to visit for many years. The closer I got, the more disparate the coastline became. Mudflats seemed to meander in all directions, and more water came to dominate the scene. At the city's secondary airport, New Orleans Lakefront, the runway was built on reclaimed land that jutted out into Lake Pontchartrain.

After a night spent wandering through the old town, eating gumbo and listening to music wafting from bars along the streets, breakfast the next morning at my French Quarter hotel was different to every other on the journey thus far. There was no flight plan to file. I didn't even know my final destination. The *Southern Sun* would follow the great Mississippi River north, and spend the night wherever she ended up.

From the airport, I followed high-tension power lines across Lake Pontchartrain to the river's mouth. The waterway was busy. Thousands of barges lined the banks, and were rafted together and pushed by river tugs.

The first 200 kilometres to Baton Rouge was wall-to-wall with industry, mainly oil refineries. I had been told that 85 per cent of the United States' fuel passes through there. *If the river levee breaks, America will be redeploying horses and carts for a while*, I thought.

The Ole Miss isn't just the longest river in the US; it carries a great legacy of folklore and emotion. The first sandbar I saw covered in trees immediately made me think of Tom and Huck, the heroes of *The*

Adventures of Huckleberry Finn, meandering down the river on a raft or small boat and pulling up at night to sleep among the trees.

I'd loved Huck Finn as a kid. I read the book and recalled the 1939 black-and-white movie – starring a young Mickey Rooney – being the Saturday matinee on television. I had dreamed for years of building a raft at the source of the Mississippi and floating down to the sea. That was unlikely to happen, so instead I would do it upstream in a raft that flew.

The source of the river is Lake Itasca, which is 1400 feet above sea level. It is amazing to think that a river that is 4000 kilometres long only falls 1400 feet before reaching the sea. If there were a bike path all the way, it would be a very gentle uphill ride from New Orleans to the source.

After a few sweeping bends, I saw a biplane doing what I thought was aerobatics. I was at first envious, but soon realised it was a crop duster, one of many I would see along the way. Five hours and many turns later, I landed at the very large Memphis International Airport, in Tennessee. Within ten minutes I was in an airport courtesy car – a common service for pilots at US airports – and soon I was pulling up at Graceland. Outside the house are the King's two 1960s private jets, the *Lisa-Marie* and the *Hound Dog II*. I am not a huge Elvis Presley fan, but I admire the influence and effect of cultural icons. And shagpile carpet. While it was very dated and at times kitsch, Elvis's house wasn't a palatial mansion, and felt well lived in by a large family. I left impressed.

I got back in the *Sun* and headed upstream, following every bend of the river, wondering where I'd stop for the night. Reelfoot Lake had been recommended as a place to see, if not visit. In the early 1800s, an earthquake in the area caused land next to the Mississippi to subside. According to Native Indian lore, an angry spirit stamped his foot next to the river, causing it to flood. A lake was formed – the only natural lake in Tennessee. The local tribes named it Angry Spirit Foot Lake. From the air, it does indeed look like a foot. But in the 1810s they had no way of getting up high enough to see what it looked like, so how did they know?

I found a small runway inside a national park between the river and the lake, and decided it would make a nice campsite. The *Sun* was the only plane at the airfield, and there was no accommodation anywhere nearby. I broke out an emergency beef stew stowed for the Atlantic crossing and settled in for a peaceful night next to the lake. A swarm of insects descended on my private camp. It was all but impossible to sit still, let alone sleep, and I was forced to spend the night in the cramped pilot's seat with the lights turned off. Rather than sitting in the seat facing forward, I worked out that if I lay on my back with my feet on the rear shelf and my head against the dashboard, I could sleep 'astronaut style'. It was sort of comfortable.

Breakfast was served under the wing. Having raided the emergency provisions kit, I now rediscovered all sorts of goodies, including delicious porridge bars from Scotland. No one makes stodge as magnificently as the Scots!

The *Sun* took off at 10 a.m., having waited a couple of hours due to fog, which gave me time to go for a walk in the national park. Once we were up in the sky, the weather was clear for a while, but the cloud got lower as we ventured upstream until it wasn't safe to fly any further. For most pilots that would have meant turning back or looking for an airport. But I simply flew a loop to check there were no obstructions on the water, and soon landed on the river and headed for a bank behind an erosion barrier, which would shelter us from the current. I nosed the *Sun* up next to a sand bank and tied her to a tree. *Ah, the serenity*, I thought. *Not a bad spot to wait out the low cloud.*

A boat came around a bend. I listened carefully for banjos, but soon the distinctive sound of a two-stoke motor was drowning out the serenity. *Swamp people?*

Three men and a woman, all adorned in camouflage, pulled up next to me in a shallow-bottom motorboat. They were residents of the local town of Perryville on a weekend fishing trip, which they said they hadn't quite got to as yet because they kept meeting interesting folk. I realised I had passed them overhead earlier as they sat midstream next to a two-man Canadian canoe; it turned out they were having a chat with a Boston couple who were navigating the Mississippi from source to sea, and were eighty days in. That was certainly living out a dream.

They offered me one of the beers they were enjoying and the use of their camp while I waited for the weather to improve. It was a nice offer but I didn't want to leave the *Sun*. Plus, the sun was still in the east. Nor do I drink beer. I was thirteen when I saw *Deliverance*, and remain subconsciously terrified of heading off with strangers downriver.

An hour later the cloud lifted. I was soon flying past the Perryville airfield when I heard an unusual call over the radio, which sounded like it was a conversation between someone on the ground and a student pilot. 'Ah, I've just realised I forgot to set the altimeter before you left,' the voice said. 'It looks like you're at 1500 feet, so turn the knob until the small hand is between one and two and the big hand is on five.' I hoped it wasn't some poor guy's first solo flight!

While the Mississippi was a majestic vein of economic activity, it wasn't beautiful. There were many barges on the river. South of Memphis, the banks were marred by a lot of industrial plants that looked like refineries. North of the city, the riverside equipment was mainly digging stuff up – harvesting sand, perhaps.

The further north we flew, though, that started to change. Seeing new topography is always satisfying, and some hills and cliffs appeared. As I neared St Louis, Missouri, I came across the first river lock, and the sign of modern riverfront communities. St Louis was the last city on the navigable stretch of river before locks were built. Geographically the heart of America, it must have been an impressive commercial hub in the era before the locks, which allowed the trading vessels to continue further upstream.

To my great appreciation, St Louis air-traffic control cleared the *Southern Sun* to follow the river through the airport's airspace. The route took me right past the city's famous Gateway Arch. As we passed to the north, I saw the first floating marina complex on the river, and realised there was something I hadn't seen much of thus far: pleasure craft.

All of a sudden there was marina after marina. Some cruisers and even yachts were out sailing. The locks made the river wider and calmer. The environment was prettier, too. Treacherous-looking sandbars were replaced by islands, which boaters could enjoy on weekends – and upon which young trouble-makers apparently spent nights.

My lunchtime destination was Hannibal, the birthplace of author Sam Clemens, whom the world would come to know as Mark Twain. I overflew the town to take a look. A big paddle-steamer was getting ready to embark, so I circled again for a photo and noticed a boat ramp right in front of the town.

I circled a couple more times to estimate the ramp's width, and judged that the *Sun* should just be able to fit. I landed on the river and taxied towards the ramp, but I didn't want to enter the marina until a pick-up truck and trailer had moved on. The ramp was steep and the *Sun* would need speed to get up it. Once she started, it would be hard to stop or turn.

Sadly, the guy on the ramp decided to stand and watch me. He was obviously wondering why a seaplane was going around in circles on the water. After twenty minutes another person – who turned out to be a pilot – went and told him I was probably waiting for him to move, so he finally got out of the way.

It was now after 4 p.m. and I prayed the Twain exhibits weren't shut. The collection was spread across the town. I hadn't studied his books at school – I'd read them at the time, though, and again in later years – and didn't realise that the characters were drawn from his childhood experiences and friends. The houses of people who inspired Huck and Becky were marked, and Twain's own house had a white paling fence. A museum, which was open till 5 p.m., had a treasure-trove of knick-knacks, including Twain's river-boat captain's licence and fifteen Norman Rockwell paintings commissioned in the 1930s for an illustrated edition of his two adventure books. There were reissued hardbacks of this edition for sale in the gift shop, and I wanted to buy one. But books are heavy and I was travelling light. No souvenir shopping was possible in the *Sun* – which unfortunately meant Tim and Jack also missed out on some Elvis sunglasses from Memphis, and I wouldn't get to hear their polite but insincere thanks.

I made it to the town's last Twain exhibit by closing time and then went for a walk down the main street. There were many empty shops, victims of the financial crisis and competition from out-of-town shopping malls. But there were also signs of hope. A fairly new cinema had been built, a theatre had been restored, and new eateries were opening up. In a groovy little cafe I saw my first real coffee machine in two weeks, and thoroughly enjoyed a strong latte. Back at the marina I met some members of the local boat club, and a pilot who helped clear people and vehicles away so the *Sun* could taxi down the cobblestones – a first, apparently – and into the Mississippi.

It was now after 7 p.m., which gave me just under an hour to fulfil the next part of my Huck Finn adventure. I was determined to find an island on the river where I could sleep the night. It didn't take long to locate a suitable spot: an island in the lee of another island, where the current wouldn't drag the *Sun* away while I slept.

Spending a night on the banks of the Mississippi was magical. I had to sleep in the *Sun* again to avoid insects, but I loved cooking and eating dinner on the sand bank. The river trip was an adventure I'd wanted to do for a long time. I drifted off to sleep feeling pretty contented. Florida, just three days past, was already a distant memory.

The river dropped about 15 centimetres overnight, leaving the *Sun* stuck firmly on the sand. There was no point panicking – it wasn't going to change much in the next thirty minutes. Besides, breakfast hadn't been served. After a coffee and an oat bar, I twisted and wrangled the *Sun* into two inches of water. It wasn't deep enough to float the boat but provided a little bit of lubrication against the sandy riverbed. I got into the cockpit, turned on the engine and tried to skid across the sand. Even at full power, she wouldn't budge.

I got out, grabbed the tail and pulled her back and forth to try to release the hull from the sand. It became even more tightly wedged. Was I going to have to get a tug to tow me out?

What I needed was a lighter aircraft with the same amount of power. I had a cunning plan. Standing next to the open cockpit in a few inches of water, with my pants rolled up to my knees, I leaned in and started the engine. Holding on with all my strength, I slowly increased the power and rocked the *Sun* with my hips to loosen her from the sand, keeping a hand on the throttle in case. After a nervous minute, she moved forward just a little. I reduced the power and jumped into my seat. As I upped the power and kicked the rudder from left to right, she jiggled forward inch by inch until she suddenly broke free of the riverbed and was floating. I cut the power and took a huge gulp of air. *Thank goodness!*

The early morning was a lovely time to fly upriver. The air was smooth, with no heat-induced turbulence, and the flying was calm and relaxing. I saw many flocks of birds in formation and quite a few boats that had also spent the night on the river. After refuelling at Tri-Township Airport, I turned east for the second time on the trip since leaving Sydney and set a course for Traverse City, a diversion of around 500 kilometres each way. This is a popular holiday spot on the eastern shore of Lake Michigan, and home to the community-based State and Bijou theatres.

The cinemas are owned and operated by the Traverse City Film Festival, which was founded by Michael Moore. The famous documentary-maker chooses all the films shown at the cinemas (which is also my favourite job at the Sun Theatre, so kept doing it all through the trip). Built in 1916, the State has been meticulously restored and is run with much love. A lean mix of staff and volunteers work year round to keep the cinemas going.

The manager, Kristen, showed me around and chatted. Jim, the projectionist, is an accomplished organist, and performs before screenings. I wasn't aware of the unique 'Bijou by the Bay' before I arrived. It was originally built as a museum and gallery in a park on the edge of Lake Michigan, and was leased from the city by the film festival and converted into a smaller cinema because the demand for moving-image storytelling was so strong.

I'd never seen a cinema so wonderfully plonked inside another building in such a fashion. The result was a very cute venue with a rare vibrancy both inside and on the facing street, where there were interesting and good-quality restaurants, cafes and bars – and not a franchise outlet in sight.

I could see parallels between our Sun Theatre in Melbourne and the State in Traverse City. Both had been abandoned and were surrounded by run-down shopping strips. The resurrection of each cinema was part of the revitalisation of the area at a time when many people were questioning the relevance of cinema in the face of online entertainment and DVDs. These parallel successes in Victoria and Michigan illustrated that a cinema can be the cornerstone of a lively and economically sustainable ecosystem.

The next morning I considered flying direct to Minneapolis, which would have saved me a day by avoiding a big stretch of the river. As tempted as I was, I couldn't bring myself to take the shortcut. I had committed to myself to fly the Mississippi and that's what I was going to do.

I backtracked to the point where I had turned east, refuelling at Tri-Township Airport. I then continued north, following every turn of the river, which was becoming more and more picturesque, to Minneapolis, the sixteenth-largest city in the United States. After landing at its medium-sized airport, I quickly packed up and got to a nondescript hotel by dusk. A huge AMC cinema glared across the street, so I walked towards the foyer to see what was showing. After the previous day's wonderful experiences, though, I couldn't bring myself to cross the threshold of the commercial, soulless monolith, so I had dinner alone and got an early night.

The further upstream the *Sun* progressed, the younger the Ole Miss got. The lake-like views of the previous day were replaced by rapids and a couple of small waterfalls. She was now looking like a small river, like Melbourne's Yarra or Boston's Charles, and was wandering all over the place, seemingly posing a question: north, east, west or south?

As I flew upstream of Grand Rapids, Minnesota, the Mississippi passed through several shallow lakes and kept getting smaller, carving more intricate curves into the earth, and creating marshes and bogs. Ultimately she terminated at Lake Itasca, which happens to be the same shape as Lake Como, although much smaller. Their geographic similarity has no real relevance, although for me landing on both for the first time was sheer joy.

In the last hour of flying the river became so small it was hard to follow. But once the lake appeared on the horizon, I knew where to go. There was almost no wind. I landed on the lake at noon, shut down the engine and drifted while I soaked up the peace and ate some lunch. It was the fifth day of my adventure since leaving Florida, yet felt much longer, like a momentous achievement. The *Southern Sun* had conquered the Mississippi.

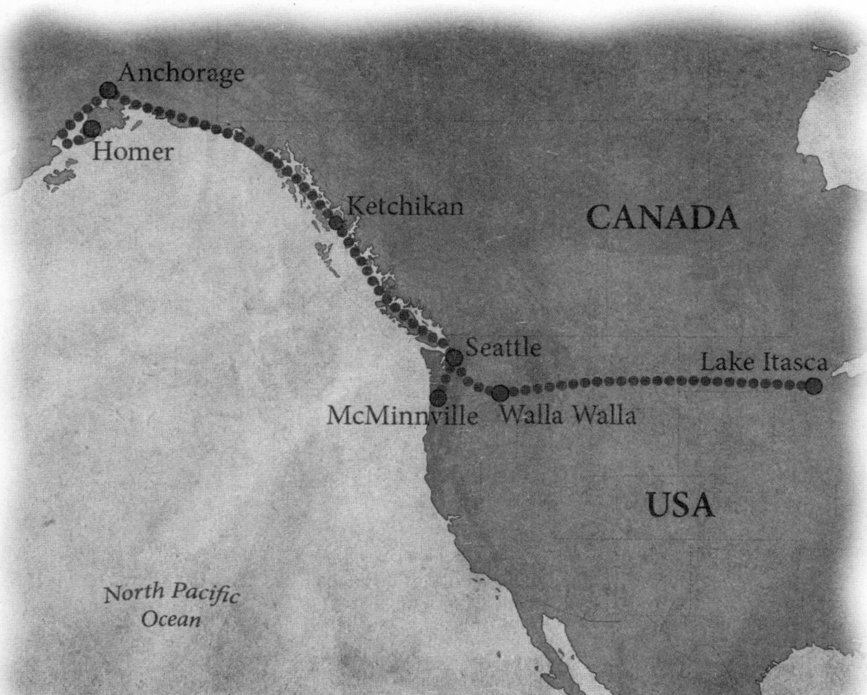
Anchorage
Homer
Ketchikan
CANADA
Seattle
Lake Itasca
McMinnville
Walla Walla
USA
North Pacific
Ocean

28.

Call of the Wild

'At some point, everything's gonna go south on you ... and you're going to say, this is it. This is how I end. Now, you can either accept that, or you can get to work. That's all it is. You just begin. You do the math. You solve one problem ... and you solve the next one ... and then the next. And if you solve enough problems, you get to come home.'
MARK WATNEY, *THE MARTIAN* (2015)

Sitting in a Seattle coffee shop on the first day of October with a bunch of seaplane pilots who knew their way around Alaska, I started to fear that I had flown as far as I would get. The Russians hadn't come through with permission for me to fly through their airspace, let alone land at one of their airports. Alaska was billed as a no-go for newcomer pilots after September. I was scared of the wild weather and long distances between the Aleutian Islands.

Common sense said the trip was over. Winter was not far away. The Bering Sea was getting colder, and the Arctic ice sheet was advancing south. Ferocious headwinds would soon tear across the sky from Siberia, slowing a small plane like the *Sun* to the speed of a car in peak-hour traffic. After losing control near Goose Bay, I was even more nervous about being caught in a storm or cloud traversing the notorious Aleutians. And without a refuelling stop in Russia, I didn't know how the *Sun* could get from Alaska to Japan.

I could have called it quits right there in Seattle, packed the *Sun* in a shipping container bound for Melbourne, and headed home after the greatest adventure of my life. I had set four records, travelled further in a tiny seaplane than anyone had ever before tried, made new friends and met generous strangers, and experienced the enormous personal satisfaction of pursuing a dream that had its gestation in a lonely teen-age year far from home.

On the other hand, I had come this far, so why stop now? In a century of flight, no one had ever conducted a solo circumnavigation in an amphibian plane or flying boat. Becoming the first to do so would be rather splendid. Aviation world records aren't set easily. The body that certifies them, the Fédération Aéronautique Internationalé, has strict requirements, including that a round-the-world trip must be completed in no more than 365 days. That ruled out storing the *Sun* and returning the following spring. Realistically, continuing now was my only chance to make a mark on aviation history, even if it was just a footnote.

More importantly, I wanted to keep going. For reasons I found it hard to articulate to anyone, including friends and family, I needed to arrive at Williamstown in the *Sun*, slowly motor up the yacht club ramp and walk the short distance home to our house. Flying home in a commercial plane would be a failure. Finishing was everything. Besides, what else was there to lose, apart from my life? And what is a life worth without discovery?

Decision time had arrived. I could continue to Alaska and try to cross the Pacific Ocean, or accept that the circumnavigation was beyond a small plane like a Searey. I was leaning towards shipping her home. Perhaps I could try again in a few years if I could find a bigger flying boat.

Then, over coffee with some local flyers, Captain Karen Stemco, a commercial seaplane pilot, piped up. 'You really need to talk to Burke,' she said. 'Burke Mees. You know Burke?'

Burke is a veteran commercial seaplane pilot who flies the Aleutian Islands, which extend from the Alaskan mainland across the North Pacific. He is a legend, with incredible experience, which he shares through articles in aviation magazines. Karen knew him well. I'd read his articles but never met him. We called him on the spot.

For years Burke had flown a 1950s Grumman Goose, one of the most rugged, reliable and utilitarian amphibious flying boats, through the Aleutians, all year round. It was possible to do, he said, but there was an important ingredient for survival: patience. 'Yes, there is bad weather, and plenty of average weather,' he told us down a crackly phone line. 'In between, there are glorious days. Take your time, accept getting stuck here and there for a few days, and you can make it.' He had an ominous warning too: 'There isn't a crashed plane in the Aleutians that doesn't have sun shining on it soon after.'

Wow, I thought. *That is sobering. But ... maybe I can do it.*

I decided to weigh up the decision over the next couple of days while I enjoyed Seattle. I had wanted to visit for years. Not only is it the major American city that is probably most similar culturally to Melbourne, but I also admired its record of world-leading businesses, including Amazon, Boeing and Starbucks. Any place that can make a decent cup of coffee is okay in my book.

As much as I treasured my portable espresso machine, I was looking forward to real coffee shops. Ones that used porcelain. I wasn't disappointed. My first Seattle coffee, with my host Walter, at Zoka on North 55th, was fabulous. It was made on a Slayer, a machine that is the Rolls-Royce – no, more the Bentley – of coffee machines, and built in Seattle. My hipster barista was oh so cool, with his carefully manicured facial hair. The double-shot skinny latte was magnificent. So good I had to have another. I spent the afternoon buzzing.

Boeing's first aeroplane was a seaplane, the cleverly named Boeing Model 1. A replica was on display at the company's Museum of Flight, next to its enormous assembly buildings at Boeing Field airport, where green primed-but-unpainted 737s waited on the tarmac to be dispatched to airlines around the world. The museum had prize exhibits for aviation enthusiasts, including a Lockheed SR-71 Blackbird, which could fly at three times the speed of sound, a former Air Force One and a Concorde. At the smaller end of the scale, the museum had a drone used for surveillance of the Somali pirates who hijacked an American cargo ship in an incident portrayed in the movie *Captain Phillips*, starring Tom Hanks. It even had used shells from the sniper rifle used against the pirates by US soldiers. The Boeing museum was very impressive, but there was another that was beckoning me to visit, one housing the granddaddy of all flying boats.

The Evergreen Aviation and Space Museum is in McMinnville, Oregon, a couple of hours south of Seattle by air. Its star exhibit is the Hughes H-4 Hercules, the largest flying boat ever. Built by Howard Hughes and flown but once, briefly, it was nicknamed, much to his chagrin, the *Spruce Goose*, because it was constructed mainly of birch ply due to lightweight-metal restrictions during World War II. Hughes hoped that the plane would revolutionise transatlantic travel, help the Allies win the war and neuter the threat of Germany's U-boats. But the prototype, which was designated HK-1 and had eight engines, wasn't completed until 1947.

It is unclear if the plane could have flown more than a short distance. Sitting in the cockpit, I was in awe of its size, and couldn't imagine trying to get her to take off. I felt a strong connection with Hughes as I sat in his seat. He had been one of the great inspirations of my life. I've read every book I could lay my hands on and seen all the films that feature this unique character. Great achievements take determination and risk, and Hughes never gave up on his flying boat. Finally, and famously, she flew.

Sitting there, it became clear to me there was only one way home. A day later, the *Southern Sun* left Seattle, northbound for Alaska.

There were glorious blue skies for the flight, which I took as a good omen for the difficult journey ahead. I flew around the famous Seattle Space Needle on my way. There was a long flight ahead but I had travelled too far not to have a little fun, so I orbited the UFO-like restaurant atop the Needle. Not far north of Seattle, amid farming land, I saw the oddest thing: an eighteen-wheeler semi-trailer rig speeding around an oval racing track. *I suppose they have to test them somewhere*, I thought. *Or perhaps it's another niche American pastime?*

The *Sun* headed north-west, over San Juan Island. I had planned a brief rendezvous en route. Soon I reached Orcas Island, where pilot and author Richard Bach lives in a large home on top of a hill. While lining up to land *Puff* at San Juan Island in 2012, Bach clipped some power lines and flipped upside down. At the age of seventy-six he was forced to spend four months recovering in hospital. The near-death experience inspired him to write a fourth part to *Jonathan Livingston Seagull*.

Having read the book many times after discovering it as a teenager, I wanted to pay homage to its author. Dan Nickens had explained how to recognise his house, which was quite easy as it was alone, perched upon a hill. In salute I flew an orbit around the home, as I tried to fly higher, faster, further. *Thanks, Richard, for a lifetime of inspiration.*

To avoid having to clear customs and immigration twice in two days, I planned not to land in Canada. I did, however, fly for most of the day at 2500 feet through Canadian airspace, over the rugged coastline, dense forests and windy broad bays. The last couple of hours of the seven-hour flight forced me to weave between taller and taller mountains. Normally such flying would be stressful, but with such clear weather it was joyous. If it stayed like this, getting through the Aleutians would be a cakewalk.

The *Sun* arrived in Ketchikan, the oldest town in Alaska. Small and pretty, it faced the Inside Passage, a protected route north that provided safety for smaller aircraft and was popular with cruise ships. During peak cruising season, up to 10,000 tourists could descend on the town in a day, a number that astonished me – and that I was pleased to be avoiding. I had hoped to see *The Martian* at the town cinema, but by the time I arrived the film was half an hour in. At least I could get straight to bed. I knew that, when I awoke before dawn, I would wish I'd had more sleep.

○

The flight from Ketchikan to the Alaskan capital of Anchorage, my next destination, reminded me of Greenland. While the scenery was different, both towns were so different from what I was used to that I found them deeply beautiful in an almost surreal way. For much of the leg, out my left window I saw sea that was so clear it could have been the Caribbean. To my right, the scenery switched from fjords with glaciers eeking their way down to the sea, to snow-covered rocky mountains, to river deltas of sand flats and tributaries.

Anchorage's large harbour and lakes are popular with seaplanes. But I chose to land at the international airport so I could grab a courtesy car and get to work chasing up my airway clearances, which were becoming a more pressing problem by the day. I needed either the Russians or the US Airforce to come through. I couldn't see another way to get across the Pacific.

I managed to make contact on the phone with someone who worked in the control tower at the remote air base. Shemya Island has to be one of the loneliest military postings in the world. It was abandoned after World War II and then reopened during the Cold War as a long-range weather station and refuelling stop for the B-52 bombers that patrolled the border with the Soviet Union in case a nuclear war broke out. Today it has no civilian residents, and a small Air Force airport that can be used in emergencies by passenger aircraft.

A man in the tower said he couldn't give me permission to land there, and that I would have to talk to his superiors at the Air Force base in Anchorage. I called the base, but they wouldn't help.

'Can I come down and speak to you?' I asked.

'No point,' he said. 'No civilian aircraft are allowed on the island, and even if we gave you permission, we don't have any gasoline or avgas out there.'

Now I really needed the Russians to cooperate.

Anchorage has a Regal Cinema, which is probably the best national multiplex chain in the United States. The cinemas have big screens and slightly reclining, if sometimes creaky, seats, which are pretty comfortable. *The Martian* was the main feature they were showing, and the screen was so large it almost felt like you were watching it from the front row at an Imax cinema. The central message of the fabulous film was that there is always a way through. You just need to go back to the start, look at what you have to hand, reframe the data and keep rethinking the problem. The timing of this message was good for me.

The next day I planned to head to Dutch Harbor, with a refuelling stop after six hours' flying at Cold Bay, the last airport with avgas on the Alaskan Peninsula, which juts out into the North Pacific. Because I needed to do some maintenance on the *Sun*, as well as buy some freeze-dried food and gloves and socks, I wouldn't be able to leave Anchorage early in the day. Still, I estimated I'd get to Cold Bay a few hours before sunset.

Within an hour of leaving, the *Sun* hit low cloud over the Gulf of Alaska. There was a solid wall of white at 500 feet. Then 200 feet. Trying to fly under it, I was now so close to the water that I could make out every ripple in the churning sea. I started to get worried. Then the *Sun* ran into a layer of mist. Visibility fell to only a kilometre, and only patches of the sea peeked out below me.

Unprepared for this bad weather, I was on the verge of panic. Memories of plunging through the sky on the other side of Canada returned. This time, the *Sun* was so low she wouldn't even have thirty seconds before crashing. *Stay calm*, I told myself. *Stay calm. You need to find a way to safety.*

My original plan had been to cross the land mass and approach Cold Bay from the north, which would have meant flying over some mountainous terrain, but that would have been suicide in this low cloud. So I cleared the cloud and took what I hoped would be a safe route along the southern side of the peninsula. Thirty minutes later, the weather wasn't much better. I flew back and forth, trying to find a way through. I considered diverting to a large island about halfway between Anchorage and Cold Bay, Kodiak Island.

I didn't want to stop. Every extra day reduced the *Sun's* chances of making it across the Pacific, and I was focused on getting to the Aleutians as quickly as possible. *There must be a way*, I kept thinking. Niggling at me was my promise to Anne to be safe, and also Burke Mees' warning: 'There isn't a plane crash in the Aleutians that doesn't have sun shining on it soon after.'

I turned to my satellite-connected iPad and checked out the weather at the airports within a couple of hundred kilometres. There was low cloud everywhere. Wherever I went, I'd be flying into life-threatening weather. I turned around and headed back the way I'd come.

I had been defeated, but I was making the prudent choice.

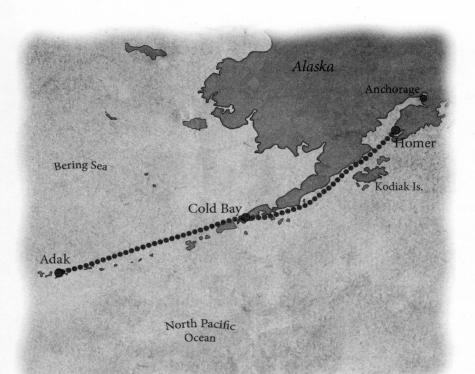

Alaska

Anchorage

Homer

Bering Sea

Kodiak Is.

Cold Bay

Adak

North Pacific
Ocean

29.

The Odyssey

'Adversity is the state in which man most easily gets acquainted with himself.'
LIEUTENANT HOPPER, *BATTLESHIP* (2012)

Homer, Alaska, was the first town on the way back with a proper runway, a control tower, fuel and accommodation. Its name alone beckoned to the *Southern Sun*, on her odyssey.

Relief washed over me when the *Sun* touched down. I went straight up to the control tower and viewed the latest weather information. The controller called me a cab. While I waited downstairs, it dawned on me that I had been a fool. I had been so busy running around picking up supplies in Anchorage that I had forgotten to download the latest weather charts and radar images.

Satellites reveal clouds, while radar shows where it is raining. There was a huge band of cloud right where I had turned back. Had the *Sun* pushed on, she would have run into heavy rain. I had been mentally wrestling with a decision that, in hindsight, was simple: turning back was the only sensible option. Information was readily available that would have helped me understand this, but I hadn't used it. American services for amateur pilots are the best in the world. I had become so used to not having it while flying that I hadn't downloaded the information. It was a stupid mistake I kicked myself for making.

One nice surprise was the Homer Cinema, a classic 'Mom and Pop' country cinema. From the outside it looked like an old timber barn, but inside it had a lot of character, including couches at the rear of the cinema, which had found favour among the town's teenagers in particular. It showed a mix of new releases and alternative and art films, much like we did at our country cinema in Bairnsdale. There was even a Halloween screening of *The Rocky Horror Picture Show* imminent – which is where you find yourself asking, 'So you just happened to have a set of fishnets at home, did you, John?' (There's always at least one!) The *pièce de résistance* was the old projector, which after being replaced by a digital system had been reimagined by a local artist into a robot *objet d'art*.

The next morning I studied the weather radar over and over. While there was rain about, the clouds were stable and not too low for flying. There was bad weather coming, though, and the following day it looked like cloud would close in over a huge area around the Alaskan western peninsula. Wherever I got to today, I would likely have to stop for a few days, so I tried to find somewhere interesting. The historic town of Dutch Harbor was achievable. It was one of the few American towns bombed by Japan during World War II – and a place *Playboy* once described as having the toughest bar in America.

Departing Homer took me straight out over water. The previous day's weather system had barely moved, but now I was mentally prepared for a difficult flight. After thirty minutes at 500 feet, I descended to 250 feet for an hour – such ultra-low-level flying is allowed only when it's absolutely necessary. Once the *Sun* was clear of the low-pressure system, the day become gloriously clear. *What a bizarre part of the world for weather*, I thought as I looked across at the land out to my right and the sea below.

The *Sun* got to Cold Bay in plenty of time to refuel and make Dutch Harbor by dusk. I called ahead to check on accommodation, which I almost never did, and found that the one and only hotel in town was booked out. It must have been my sixth sense kicking in.

Cold Bay was a good place to store a plane, but not so good for humans. Recognised as the most overcast town in the United States, on average it lies beneath a blanket of cloud for 304 days of the year. Not something to put on the tourist brochure. During World War II, large dugouts along the side of the runway were created to protect American bombers from Japanese air raids. They are now used as weather shelters for private aircraft.

The *Sun* was safe from the wild wind gusting in from the Bering Sea. Sadly, though, there was little for her owner to do. There was no mobile phone reception in the town, and the internet was painfully slow. There was one store, one bar, one rather basic library and a post office. The school had closed due to lack of children. After an eighteen-minute walk I had seen all there was to see. The town store had a choice of magazines: *Duck Hunting* and *The Rifleman*, the journal of the National Rifle Association. The Cold Bay Lodge, where I was staying, was like a boarding house.

On my first day in Cold Bay the weather was so horrible that I spent it entirely in my sparsely furnished room, apart from a short visit to the store. I sent emails, booking some films for our cinemas back home, but with the internet so bad I couldn't watch trailers; I just had to trust the details I could glean from IMDB. I also chased up my requests to fly through Russia. Amid the isolation, my mind started wandering, and I couldn't help but ponder if they knew about my Soviet passport ...

I watch a lot of movies. Sometimes, on reflection, when I wonder what I was thinking, I question whether too much cinema has dulled my sense of reality. In the mid-1990s, before widespread use of the internet, I was known to peruse the esoteric mail-order ads in the backs of magazines such as *Popular Science*. That's how I came to purchase a USSR passport.

It was what's known as a novelty passport, and was issued after the USSR had ceased to exist. The ad said it was a great safety net if you were ever kidnapped. Like I said, my sense of reality may have been somewhat dulled.

A few years later I secured the 2000 world 2.4mR class sailing championships for Melbourne. People from over a dozen countries were coming to compete, and I was determined to make it a successful event for our club and city. I had one of the small yachts and wanted to race. I don't quite recall why – I think just to have as many countries as possible – but rather than enter as myself, I decided to enter as Mikhail Smetinsky, the name in my 'other' passport. I set up a hotmail account under that name and emailed the manager of a boatbuilding company, asking to charter one of their boats. I happened to own the boat company, and the manager who received the email, Marie-Cecile, sat three desks away from me.

I could hear her excitement each time she received one of Mikhail's emails. She was especially enthralled when a brown paper bag with cash for the charter fee arrived mysteriously at the reception of our building. As the event got closer, the reality of my silly idea dawned on me. Each team was expected to participate in a street procession behind their national flag. How could I turn up without being recognised?

Nervously, I arrived hidden behind a hat and glasses. The first day's racing was very windy, so I obscured my face under a jacket hood. No one called out the mysterious 'Soviet' visitor. The waves were quite large, and a lot of water came over the side of my boat – an awful lot. Then it sank. A rescue boat came over to see if the Russian competitor was okay. A volunteer from the yacht club looked down while handing me the hose for a pump and said, 'Um, is that you, Mike?' For the second time that day I had a sinking feeling.

The story soon spread like wildfire through the club and was deemed pretty funny. Now, I couldn't help wondering how far the story had travelled ... Could it be part of the reason that, after months, I was getting absolutely nowhere with the Russian authorities?

The next day, I walked around Cold Bay, took a few photos and checked out the wharf, which other residents of the lodge were repairing. Half in jest, I asked the lodge's lovely owner, Mary, if there was a cinema in town. She told me an amazing story. Cold Bay was once a US Air Force base, and home to some 750 families. They had various community facilities, including a cinema. When the Air Force wound down the base in the late 1980s, it buried all of their buildings, including the cinema, so they wouldn't decay in the open and become dangerous eyesores. Somewhere, under a mound of dirt, was an intact cinema with all its equipment in place. If only I'd brought a shovel.

If my mission had been to find a real-world Basil Fawlty, I would have succeeded at the Cold Bay Lodge. Mary's husband, Bill, a former Navy man, seemed to regard lodgers as disruptions to the tranquillity of his isolated life. He spent his days in a reclining chair, watching *Fox News* and grunting at the parlous state of the world.

The first morning I was there, I came down for breakfast at 8.30 a.m. I had set no alarm, knowing I was going to be housebound all day due to the bad weather.

'Good morning, sunshine,' came the surly greeting. 'Good of you to wake up.'

I was a little taken aback, and gingerly took my seat at the breakfast table, where I was pleasantly greeted by Mary and asked what I'd like to eat. She cheerily poured me some coffee and went about cooking. Then Bill got up from his throne to talk to me at the table.

'Listen,' he snarled, 'I don't know how things are done where you're from, but breakfast here is between 7 and 8 a.m. My wife works hard enough without you making things harder on her, so tomorrow be here on time.'

I felt like there must be a candid camera somewhere. Who talks to anyone like that? I was so shocked that I apologised, saying I hadn't been made aware there was a set breakfast time.

'Well, you've been told now, so don't do it again,' he shot back as he sauntered away to continue watching the repetitive news feed.

My delicious breakfast soon arrived, and Mary asked me about Australia and my trip and couldn't have been more delightful. I felt for her – she seemed isolated by more than just geography.

Everyone else I met in Cold Bay was friendly. There were about fifty permanent residents, plus visitors working on infrastructure projects or hunting during the 'good' weather. Planes were used like pick-up trucks, and it seemed every second person had a pilot's licence. Their Piper Super Cubs were particularly impressive. With their big tyres these can land just about anywhere; the ones I saw had rifles mounted to the wing struts, just in case there were any bears around when they landed.

○

Refreshed with optimism from watching *The Martian*, I spent the day in my room on the dial-up internet trying to work out how to get home. I ripped up my plan and started from scratch. I considered a multitude of options. Maybe south from Adak via Wake Island, and then across the warmer Pacific islands? No, Wake was closed to outside visitors, and I was advised that they didn't have fuel anyway. Everything else seemed out of range – but maybe there were other parts of Russia I had not yet considered? There was still hope. A new plan would take the *Sun* to a different part of Russia. It wouldn't be the closest but the airport seemed more cooperative, and it had the fuel I needed. *Thanks, Matt Damon*, I thought. *I'm busting out of here.*

After three days the weather looked like it would be clear the next morning. I planned to leave at dawn. After an early breakfast, Bill's 'hospitality' peaked as I was preparing to leave.

'Do you pay a bond to be allowed to fly here?' he asked.

'No,' I replied, preparing myself for what I knew was coming next.

'We've had a few of you Lewis and Clark types through here. The last one never made it to Russia. Never heard of again. They wasted millions looking for him. Just doesn't seem right.'

I knew it was just a throwaway comment from a grumpy old man, but Bill's gibe about the lost pilot hurt. Mental framing is important, and focusing on what could go wrong is not helpful when you're in the air. Once I was on my way, I was soon flying over a vast and very rough ocean. As the *Sun* battled through high winds and above huge waves, melancholy descended on the cockpit. I couldn't stop thinking about what Bill had said, and what would happen if I had to ditch at sea. I wondered if I would be able to get the life raft out before the *Sun* sank, if the emergency beacon would work, and how long it might take to be rescued. They were depressing thoughts, and I was annoyed at myself for dwelling on them, especially as I'd avoided them for the rest of the journey.

In Seattle I'd bought a new headset that had bluetooth, which meant I could connect it to my iPhone. For the first time on the entire trip I was able to listen to some music. But I only had a few albums on my phone to choose from. I started with some early Pink Floyd, which can be soothing but now seemed so morose I had to rummage for something else. Oh dear ... The only other album I had was The Complete Speeches of Winston Churchill. The great orator filled the void and lifted my spirits. Tally ho, indeed.

There were strong headwinds en route, so I flew the whole seven-hour leg at between 300 and 500 feet. At one point I made out a ship on the horizon, and as I approached I saw it was a huge fishing trawler. Seeing it smash through each enormous wave highlighted for me how big the breaking seas were – I didn't envy the crew.

I had been roughly tracking a string of uninhabited islands and rocky outcrops. That's what pilots flying visual flight rules do, especially those in single-engine planes: follow any semblance of land to reassure ourselves in case of an engine failure. In truth, most of these remote islands would offer little help if the worst happened. Just short of Adak, my destination, I made out an outcrop with a difference. It was almost conically round, and as I got closer I could see it was a perfectly shaped Mount Fuji–style dormant volcano. I climbed to 1000 feet to get a better look. It was spectacular, magnificent and kind of scary. The centre was filled with calm, iridescent bluey-green water that was starkly different to the sea crashing around it.

Next, Adak Island came into view. The runway was so wide that I was able to land diagonally across it, into the strong wind, which was safer than what is known as a crosswind landing. I taxied to the only building and was surprised to receive a call on the radio offering directions – the tower was unmanned. I looked around and saw a large yellow pick-up truck. After I shut down the *Sun*, the truck drove over and the airport manager climbed out.

'Oh, a Searey,' he said. 'I've always wanted one of those.'

In the 180 days I had been travelling, Vince was the first person at any airport who knew what type of aircraft the *Southern Sun* was.

My heart soared – this had to be a good omen. Maybe I would make it all the way round the world after all.

Attu

Adak

Aleutian Islands

North Atlantic
Ocean

30.

Castaway

'Two little mice fell in a bucket of cream. The first mouse quickly gave up and drowned. The second mouse wouldn't quit. He struggled so hard that eventually he churned that cream into butter and crawled out.'
FRANK ABAGNALE SR, *CATCH ME IF YOU CAN* (2002)

The Aleutians are a string of volcanic islands that stretch from mainland Alaska to eastern Russia. This sparsely inhabited environment (most of it Alaskan territory) is a different world. Among aviators and seafarers, the islands are known for their high winds, heavy rain and persistent fog.

A mostly barren rock in the centre of the chain, Adak was once a naval base home to a few thousand people. By the time the *Sun* arrived, only a hundred remained, most of them indigenous Aleuts. Adak is the last inhabited island and the most westerly outpost of US soil with a population and a post office. The one school has twenty-one children, and there are two shops, one diner and a cafe. There are lots of buildings, but most are uninhabited. It felt like a ghost town.

Michael and Imelda run the Blue Bird Cafe out of an old US Navy home. They keep an upstairs room available for the rare visiting pilots, which was simple, comfortable and furnished in the 1980s, when the Navy left town. Seeing that I was having difficulty walking after my long, cold flight, Michael lent me a pair of old insulated boots, which were deliciously warm.

An Orion navigator, Michael was posted to the island by the Navy decades earlier. After retiring from the military, he returned to Adak to work in the fishing fleet, and ended up opening the cafe. Luckily for him, his wife, Imelda, is a skilled and organised cook. The logistics of maintaining a cafe in such an isolated place are tricky. They rely on two double garages full of dry foods, multiple deep freezers, fridges and irregular supply ships. And a dog called Lucky, who scares the rats away from all the food. And lots of planning. Nothing is easy out there.

Adak would be my home for at least a week. I arrived on a Saturday, and was advised that the earliest I might be granted permission to enter Russian airspace was the following Sunday. The Japanese aviation regulators, who in different ways were almost as difficult as the Russians, had cleared me to arrive on the Monday. The timing would be tight, but I was confident it would work out.

An airport in the far eastern city of Yuzhno-Sakhalinsk had agreed to let me land as long as the *Sun* got a green light from the Russian federal aviation agency for the airspace clearance. The one glitch was that the airport was beyond the *Sun*'s range, and no other Russian airports had responded to my request for landing permission. I needed to organise a pitstop. The perfect place would have been the military airport on Shemya Island, Eareckson Air Station, the second-last piece of US territory at the western end of the Aleutians. But as I had discovered in Anchorage, the Air Force was unlikely to let me in.

There is one last island in the Aleutians, 50 kilometres west of Shemya, called Attu. It's part of the state of Alaska, but Attu's only inhabitants are the large rats which have the run of the empty buildings. Sitting in my bedroom above the Blue Bird Cafe, I scoped out Attu on Google Earth. A runway was still there, and half of it looked in reasonable condition. The surface wasn't broken up or cracked, or covered by debris. The satellite photo wasn't current, so I could not be totally sure, but Attu seemed like my best chance – perhaps my only chance – of getting across the Pacific. If I could leave some fuel there and then return to top up in Adak, the *Sun* would theoretically have the range to make it to Yuzhno-Sakhalinsk in Russia.

Attu was 377 nautical miles away, which would take about five hours in good conditions. If the runway was land-able, I would look for a place to store the petrol and return to Adak. I would go back to Attu once permission had been granted to fly through to Russia and the weather was clear enough for me to safely cross the North Pacific.

I considered spending a night on Attu and leaving before sunrise so the *Sun* could arrive in Russia in daylight. After the difficulty I'd had getting permission to enter Russia – they just seemed paranoid about foreign private aircraft – I didn't want any confusion about who I was or where I was going to land.

For five days, morning and night, I obsessively checked the weather. Twice when I thought it might be clear enough to leave the following day I got up at 6 a.m., adrenaline surging, and looked out the window at a thick fog. Deflated, I went back to bed each time. When I wasn't checking the weather on the dial-up internet, I was staying in touch with home by email. Most work matters were now being handled by others, but it was pretty surreal to think I was on an almost deserted North Pacific island booking movies to play in Australia, via email with people who assumed I was sitting in my office at the Sun Theatre in Yarraville!

On the sixth day the regular morning fog and rain cleared by 9 a.m., revealing a cobalt-blue sky. My hopes soared. I had already filled up five flexible jerry cans with 110 litres of petrol, which I stowed on the passenger seat. I took off and headed west. The 760-nautical-mile round trip would take ten hours, I calculated, which was safely within the twelve-hour fuel range of the *Sun*'s main tanks. My course took me over the few islands west of Adak. If the fuel-laden *Sun* went down, I wanted to be close to land.

The sky was so clear that I began to question the Aleutians' reputation for bad weather. A few hours in, a light-grey dot appeared on the horizon. It grew bigger as I got closer. *Wow*, I thought. *The US Navy has a ship out here protecting the islands. That's incredible for such a remote place*. The ship seemed to be steaming directly towards me. Perhaps it was wondering why an aircraft would be flying at 500 feet at 80 knots, which is very low and very slow, tracking straight for a US Air Force base. I began feeling a little apprehensive.

But the warship was a creation of my imagination. In fact it was a fishing trawler, which looked grey because it was being followed by thousands of seagulls. And it wasn't heading for me; I was heading for it. Fixated on the boat, I had steered the *Sun* 10 degrees left of my course. I laughed at my own paranoia and foolishness.

The islands along the route were all uninhabited, except for the second-last, Shemya (which is sometimes also called Shemiya). Ten miles out, I called the Eareckson control tower on the radio. Acting as though I flew along the border between the Pacific Ocean and Bering Sea every day, I casually advised that the *Sun*, which I knew was not welcome on their runway, would be flying by.

'Shemiya, Searey November Four Seven Three X-ray Papa,' I said.

'Ah, aircraft calling Shemiya?' came the reply. As I suspected, I had taken them by surprise.

'November Four Seven Three X-ray Papa, Searey amphibian, 10 miles east at 1000 feet, transiting overhead Shemiya for Attu,' I said.

'Three X-ray Papa, copy that. Where did you originate?' they asked.

'Origin Adak, visiting Attu for three zero minutes, then returning to Adak this afternoon.'

'Advise when overhead, Shemiya.'

'Advise overhead, Shemiya. Three X-ray Papa.'

Shemiya was the flattest island I had seen in the Aleutians, which made it a perfect place for an air base. The 10,000-foot-long runway, which could accommodate an Airbus 380 in a trans-Pacific emergency, extended almost the whole length of the island. I couldn't see any parked aircraft but there was a strange tall building facing Russia, with an array of white radars on one side. Perhaps that was why they didn't want civilians visiting.

'Searey Three X-ray Papa, overhead Shemiya,' I radioed.

'Three X-ray Papa, copy overhead. We won't be on station on your way back, so have a good flight.'

'Thanks for your help, good night. Three X-ray Papa.'

So simple. *What a shame I can't land there and meet the crew*, I thought.

Attu was 50 kilometres away. Travelling at 80 knots, the *Sun* would get there in just under half an hour. More than 1700 kilometres from the Alaskan mainland, Attu is one of the most remote places on the planet, let alone in the United States. I circled the runways to check their condition, but they looked much as I'd seen on the satellite photo taken a few years earlier. Half of one runway was unusable. The larger main runway had tufts of grass growing here and there but seemed in reasonable condition. There was a light misty rain, and turbulence caused by the wind and surrounding mountains.

My aviation chart suggested there would be dozens of buildings. With no population, I figured the island must be a ghost town. I was nervous and excited. As it came into view I realised that only a handful of structures remained, although there were dozens of empty footings, silent monuments to the buildings that had once housed a busy army base, the scene of a battle some seventy-five years earlier.

Attu and the nearby Kiska Island were the only US land invaded and occupied during World War II. The Japanese believed they could block any American attack on Japan from the Aleutians. Their initial success was kept secret from the American public, in order to preserve morale. When the Americans sent soldiers to reclaim the island in May 1943, the men boarded the ship not knowing where they were going. To avoid the secret getting out, the soldiers, who had been trained for desert warfare, were not given arctic clothing. Many suffered severely in the freezing conditions.

The island was expected to fall in three days. On the second-last day of the nineteen days of fighting, the last of the Japanese forces launched a suicidal *banzai* charge, one of the largest of the entire Pacific campaign. Led by the senior Japanese officer on the island, they broke through American lines and engaged in hand-to-hand combat with rear-echelon troops, losing all but twenty-nine of the roughly 3000 men in the island garrison.

After the war, Attu was converted into a twenty-man Coast Guard navigation station. In 2010 it was essentially abandoned by the US government. The Coast Guard station, which is a robust concrete building on a protected stretch of coast, still stands. There was no vandalism and the building was well secured; I couldn't find a way to get in or even see inside. An anti-aircraft gun had been turned into a war memorial. But I didn't find any other military artefacts or signs of World War II.

Someone had the foresight to turn a small temporary building next to the runway into an emergency refuge. There were a few fold-out camp beds, some emergency rations, a crusty old couch and some fat rats, which scurried every which way when I forced the jammed door open. There didn't seem to be a shelter anywhere else near the runway, so I turned the room into a fuel depot. I put four bags of petrol in an empty closet and latched the doors. I left another on a coat hook. I hoped the rodents wouldn't like the smell of fuel and try to nibble through the bags.

I wanted to spend more time exploring but I needed to return to Adak before sunset, so left after just forty-five minutes. That would see me arriving at the other end thirty minutes before sunset, or forty-five minutes before it was dark. On the flight back to Adak I had a tailwind and the clearest skies I'd seen all week.

If permission from the Russians came through, I'd have to fly at 16,000 feet, higher than the *Sun* had ever been. With the tailwind giving me extra time, and strengthening at higher altitudes, I now took her as high as possible as an experiment. The temperature outside was minus 20 degrees, and the air so thin I had to use an oxygen can. There were beautiful puffy cloud formations for miles either side of me.

At 13,800 feet the *Sun* started fogging up. I wiped off what I thought at first was condensation. A fine powder had coated the inside of the windscreen, and I became concerned it was deadly carbon dioxide building up inside the cockpit. Later I was told it was a kind of snow. It was so cold and dry at that altitude that my breath was turning into crystals. I descended straightaway and arrived at Adak at 7.30 p.m. under a golden late-afternoon sun.

It had been one of the most intriguing days of the entire voyage. Flying through a remote area to an island no one had landed at for years, nor was likely to, was both daunting and exciting. After initially retracing a flying boat route, I was now making an expedition into remote lands surrounded by treacherous seas.

The biggest step in my long journey was close, and everything depended on the Russians. I had been working on them for months now, but didn't seem to be making definitive progress. The weather was closing in and time was running out. It was time to ask a favour.

31.

The Way Back

'So shines a good deed in a weary world.'
WILLY WONKA, *WILLY WONKA & THE CHOCOLATE FACTORY* (1971)

The logistics agent working on my Russian clearance told me to expect an answer from the Russian government any day. That meant I would be leaving Adak within a week. The question was: in which direction? I'd been advised that my request would have to be vetted by the Russian security services. As the difficulties became clearer, I could sense the enthusiasm of Yuzhno-Sakhalinsk airport waning in our email exchanges.

I assumed the main problem was that the *Southern Sun* was an American-registered aircraft, and that I was travelling on British and Australian passports. No one had told me the real problem, which frustratingly I only discovered in the fine print at the bottom of an email trail after a week on Adak. It stated: 'Experimental planes can only be granted permission to fly in Russian airspace with diplomatic approval.' This vital rule seemed to have been overlooked by everyone involved.

As kit aircraft, Seareys were legally classified as an experimental plane – even though mine had in fact been built by the manufacturer itself. This made the *Sun* subject to further regulations. The Russian aviation authorities weren't going to admit it without clearance from their foreign ministry, which meant I needed Australia's Department of Foreign Affairs and Trade to lobby their Russian counterparts on my behalf. This was depressing news. It sounded like a difficult process, and I figured they would have better things to do.

Waiting on an island at the northern edge of the Pacific Ocean, I didn't know where to start. I went for a walk to think the problem through. It was clear that whatever I did, there wouldn't be a resolution quickly. I considered storing the *Sun* on Adak while I returned to Australia to work on the Russians. It wasn't a path I wanted to take. I believed I only had a week – a fortnight at best – before Adak would close for winter, and the *Sun* would have no chance of flying home west. The altitude at which the temperature hit zero – the freezing level – was getting lower every day. Flying above that height would be dangerous, because ice could form on the wings. The westerly winds were getting stronger, too. Soon they would set in for winter, and would reach 100 knots on some days. Flying straight into wind faster than the *Sun's* 85-knot cruising speed meant she would literally go backwards.

If I couldn't get off Adak within a week, I had two options: store the plane and return the following year, or fly back to Anchorage and either leave the *Sun* in storage or pack her into a container and ship her home. My temporary landlord, Mike, said I could store the *Sun* in an old hangar at the airport – if I could open the doors, which weighed tonnes and hadn't been moved for ages. But he advised against that option. When people on Adak don't drive their cars for a while, rats often eat the wiring, and it's almost impossible to repair. Rats could destroy the *Sun* if she was left alone. I wondered if I could hang her from the roof inside the hangar so the rats couldn't get to her. Another option Mike suggested was to take the wings off and store her in his second garage, and Lucky would try to ensure rats didn't get in.

Mike had made a generous offer, which I deeply appreciated. But there was another problem: my ego. I had travelled a long way. Now that it was a possibility, I was enamoured with the idea of becoming the first person to fly around the world solo in an amphibious plane or flying boat. The solo circumnaviator.

In order to complete my round-the-world flight and claim a world record, my deadline to reach Longreach in northern Australia was 13 April, which would mean leaving Adak by mid-March at the absolute latest. I returned to the weather records. February and March looked nasty. April wasn't much better. It probably wouldn't really be safe to fly until May. If I waited, I would have the satisfaction of having flown around the world, but the trip would not be formally recognised as a record.

There was another option, but it was one I had resisted thinking about. The Australian minister for the environment, Greg Hunt, was a university friend. Greg had chaired the student council at Ormond College, where we lived as undergraduates. I was always a bit in awe of his maturity and intelligence, and still am today. Raised by a father who was a career politician, Greg was genuinely committed to public service: he had turned down opportunities to make much more money in the private sector. I thought he was the perfect person to be minister for the environment in a Coalition government. At university he had been a passionate conservationist, committed to making a difference in the world. He was a natural leader, consultative and communicative, who genuinely had empathy for both sides of politics. For the past twenty-five years I had thought he would one day make a good prime minister.

I was reticent to ask for Greg's help, even though I was lonely and desperate. Many years earlier, Greg had been an adviser to Australia's foreign minister, Alexander Downer. I knew he still had a strong interest in international affairs, and a network of diplomatic contacts. But I hadn't seen Greg in nine months; like most of my friends, he had no idea I was even on the journey. I felt terrible intruding on his time and using a personal relationship to seek a favour.

Gingerly and apologetically, I sent an email asking if he knew anyone at the Australian Embassy in Moscow who might approach the Russian foreign ministry on my behalf. Even if he could give me a name and contact details, I wrote, that would save me a lot of time trying to work it out from Adak, where I didn't have a phone and the internet was so slow.

After spending the day trying to solve what had become the toughest challenge of the whole trip, I went to bed deflated. For the first time I was starting to accept that my ambition of completing the first solo circumnavigation was probably not achievable. Mechanical problems I could overcome. Russia and the weather were out of my control.

The next morning was a normal day: cold and overcast. Still despondent, I checked my email. There was a note from the Australian Ambassador in Moscow, Paul Myler. 'How can we help?' he asked. There was an email from Greg as well.

Relief flooded through my body. *Thanks a million, Greg*, I thought as I read his brief email. Greg congratulated me on the trip so far, and told me he'd sent a note to the embassy and asked them to get in touch.

I explained my predicament to the ambassador, who connected me with an aide, Jake Barhonein, who promised to help however he could. I was proud to be a citizen of a country that sees adventure as a great pursuit rather than a frivolous waste of government time. In some small way, I felt a little more connected to the broader world. I wasn't so alone. There were people out there looking out for me. Helping me.

Jake came back a couple of days later with double bad news. It would take at least a month for me to gain diplomatic clearance to fly through Russian airspace. And the chances of approval were only 50 per cent in any case. By then, the icy winds coming across the Bering Sea from Siberia would make a trip almost suicidal. The Russian option was finally shut.

○

I came to the grim realisation that, if I wasn't to give up, I had only one option left. From Adak, I would have to bypass Russia and fly all the way to Japan, a distance of 1800 nautical miles, or 3300 kilometres. The *Sun* didn't have the range to make it in one go. Success depended on almost perfect weather conditions and the fuel bags stored on Attu. Even if they weren't damaged by rats, I would then have to fly hundreds of kilometres out into the Pacific Ocean – over some of the most treacherous and remote seas in the Northern Hemisphere – to avoid Russian airspace. I really didn't want to be intercepted by the Russian Air Force.

The first leg, from Adak to Attu, would take five to six hours. It wouldn't be safe to stay on the uninhabited island overnight because of the changeable weather, let alone the purportedly hungry rats, which could start eating the *Sun* or even me while I was sleeping. The lack of a layover on Attu meant I would have to fly through the night to Japan. There would be no place to land along the way, no autopilot and no toilet. Of the estimated twenty-five hours of flying, with an hour on the ground to refuel, some fourteen to fifteen would be in the dark. Over such a long flight, the weather could easily turn nasty. Sleep deprivation would impair my judgement and ability to fly. I would arrive in Japan's crowded airspace physically and emotionally exhausted. It was the aviation equivalent of an ironman race – after running a marathon overnight and before a triathlon the next day. Okay, perhaps I've overstated it slightly, but you get the idea.

There were several Russian islands along the route about 100 to 200 kilometres to the north and west. International aviation protocol allows any aircraft to land at any airport in an emergency. If the weather deteriorated or the *Sun* developed a mechanical fault, she would legally be permitted to divert to Russia. Even so, would I be comfortable flying into Russian airspace at night, probably out of radio range, and in an aircraft that used the same engine as a Predator drone? *No way.* Having tried to convince the Russians to let the *Southern Sun* in, Jake at the Australian Embassy in Moscow now did the next best thing: he communicated my flight plan and the emergency airports I might need to use to the Russian authorities through official diplomatic channels. If the *Sun* had to divert, at least they would know in advance what this unidentified aircraft was. The information could mean the difference between being received cordially, spending days in jail, or even being shot down. More than anything, though, Jake's actions helped my mental preparation.

Bizarrely, the Japanese authorities required ten days' notice to alter the route. Any change reset the clock. In a country very fond of bureaucracy, it had been almost impossible for experimental aircraft to fly through Japan until a couple of years earlier. A German flight instructor who lives in Japan, Peter Steeger, had all but singlehandedly convinced the government to adopt more flexible rules. He now arranges flight clearances and planning services for aircraft transiting through Japan, an incredibly drawn-out process. The Japanese wanted detailed information about Searey aircraft. Not just the *Sun*'s fuel capacity, weight and speed, but also her original configuration – before she was modified in the Florida hangar.

Thanks to Peter's perseverance, permission came through from the Japanese aviation authority on Friday, 23 October 2015. The *Sun* was given the official okay. Now she just needed a little clear sky.

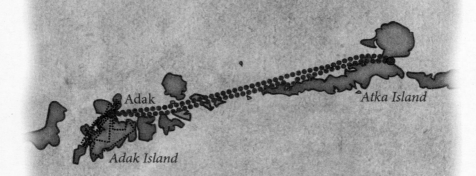

Adak

Atka Island

Adak Island

.... *Local joy flights*

32

The Secret Life of Walter Mitty

'Only if you find peace within yourself will you find true connection with others.'
PALM READER, *BEFORE SUNRISE* (1995)

Twenty-four hours, once a week. Perhaps every ten days. The conditions that would make a flight to Japan possible were rarer than Sundays. The prevailing westerly winds would cripple the slow-flying *Sun*'s ground speed on most days. She needed a nor'easter, and soon.

Two weeks later and it would be November, and the moisture in the air would turn into ice when it hit the *Sun*'s airframe. Instead of raining, it would snow, weighing her down and covering her windshield like white paint. (Or, as has oft been murmured of late, 'Winter is coming.') I obsessively watched weather systems roll across the Bering Sea on my iPad.

By choice, I was stranded on a Pacific island. Used to a life of constant activity, I had been forced to slow down. I did so many sit-ups, squats and push-ups that I was the lightest and fittest I'd been in twenty-five years. I mingled with the residents of Adak Island, feasted at a Community Crab Feast, went on hikes, took residents on joy flights, explored bunkers that once stored nuclear weapons and reread *Jonathan Livingston Seagull*. I befriended the local school's teachers, Julie, Ruth, Molly and Christopher, and talked to their pupils and others about my quest.

I met Ruth first, while walking down the street near my digs on the second day. She was returning home from school. Seeing a new face, she wanted to know the who, where and why of my presence on Adak. I was equally surprised to find a woman in her twenties out here, her Dutch accent suggesting a story of her own. She was in the final year of her studies in Holland to be a teacher, and had taken a four-month placement at the Adak school as part of her practical training. Ruth offered to introduce me to the other teachers and show me a bit of what she'd found on the island. Because she was there temporarily, she was eager to explore as much as possible after school and on the weekends. She had found the permanent residents less enthusiastic: for them the bizarre had become normal. I was pleased to have someone to show me around.

Meeting Julie was a privilege. She had been travelling to Adak to teach for twenty years. It's a tough life living alone there, but she knows that her investment in those children makes a huge difference to their lives. We had a few dinners together at her ex-military house, and even watched some DVDs, including Pixar's magnificent *Inside Out* – a fascinating film to watch with teachers, who spend all day managing the emotions of children.

Adak has the westernmost post office in the United States. In the 2016 presidential election, Julie got to the post office to vote near closing time. She was thus recognised in the press as the last person out of 139 million to vote in the election. I didn't ask whom she voted for, but I suspected it wasn't Donald Trump.

Christopher was relatively new to the island. He was emerging from a painful divorce, and Adak's remoteness seemed to soothe his soul. I had come to appreciate the strange power of isolation while sitting in the *Southern Sun* for hundreds of hours, and exploring remote places like Adak. We shared life stories over a few dinners.

It rained at some point on most days, but there was also plenty of clear weather for exploring. In the grounds of the airport I came across an interesting buried doorway. It was pitch-black inside, but my iPhone torch illuminated some shower cubicles, each with a door at the front to enter and a door at the back to exit to the next room. The tunnel went deeper and deeper, eventually leading to a dormitory. It was an emergency bunker with eighty-four beds, for use in case of nuclear attack. I found many of these around the airport and town – there were enough, I was told, to accommodate the few thousand troops stationed there. *Cripes, imagine being in here with eighty-three other people …*

Elaine was an Aleut woman who ran the only supplies store, and was a regular at the cafe. She recommended some sites that I should visit, and Ruth showed me others. The most harrowing was the locally nicknamed 'seven doors of doom': seven underground bunkers, built side by side, each with a heavy steel door, surrounded by a double row security fence and once by armed sentry posts that suggested something of grave danger and importance. It was the place they had stored the nuclear bombs – at the height of the Cold War, this was the closest naval aviation base from which to lob bombs at the Russian east coast. I slowly opened one of the doors, which creaked and groaned just like in a horror movie. It was very, very creepy.

I walked a few kilometres past the harbour and up a hill to an old military barracks. Most of the buildings' doors were bolted closed, but I found a dorm that I could get into. Further up the hill was an old timber church, which felt like something from a Grant Wood painting. At some point, someone had decided that the only timber building on the island wasn't holding up, and they wanted a church that would stand the test of time. In the big, bold late 1970s, or perhaps the early 1980s, a second church was constructed, a monolithic structure that looked to be the last building erected before the base was shut down. It didn't quite create the warmth and communal feeling that I associated with a church.

It was raining heavily as I walked home, but I was curious when I came across a seismologic research building, with equipment still there, complete with red evacuation lights, rotary dial phones and warning sirens – an ominous sign of what life had been like on the island.

As each day went by, I went in another direction. I walked up hills, along bays, grey sand beaches and many disused buildings. I wasn't sure how long I would spend on Adak, but the long days of walking brought back strong memories of my teenage years living in Devon. Alone, wandering.

I was told there was a cinema, near a former officers' quarters. I went searching. Expecting a small standalone building, upon walking through the area I noticed one end of a large two-storey block had something odd about it – no windows. Of course, the one thing cinemas around the world have in common is no natural light. The building was boarded up and a sign declared: 'NO ENTRY'. However, I pretended that the sign wasn't in English, but rather a strange dialect instead which translated as: 'EXPLORE AS YOU MUST'.

I jimmied the door open and climbed over some rubble to find a still-intact cinema of a few hundred seats. Using my iPhone light, I found the screen had been ripped down and ruined – so that was clearly my first hurdle if I was to reopen the cinema before I left. A typically narrow and oddly placed door led to a projection room. I carefully climbed the steep stairs and discovered a sad scene. A projector lay on its side, rusted and battered. A machine that once brought so much happiness – between a few training films, I imagined – had been ungraciously destroyed.

It struck me as amazing, though, the sense of romance and affection some of us feel for what is ultimately just a machine – yet a machine that for over a century has delivered laughter, tears and joy to people across the globe. Much like a boat, a plane or a car, a projector brings the promise of adventures that transcend its designed function, to flicker on and off twenty-four times a second, casting an image upon a wall.

'I'd love to be on Adak for a week with spare time and a plane,' Burke Mees wrote to me in an email. 'There is so much to see!'

One of Mees' suggestions was Atka Island, which was about an hour's flight away, back east. I arrived just before midday. Walking to the village, I was overtaken by a convoy of quad bikes, with one or two children on each, going home for lunch from the schoolhouse. A small and industrious community of eighty Aleuts live on the island, the indigenous inhabitants of the Aleutian Islands, who were almost wiped out by Russian fur traders and fishermen in the 1800s.

They are a friendly and proud people. The community owns the town's busy fish-processing factory and a power generator, which means they avoid the outrageous US$1.60 per kilowatt hour charged on Adak, ten times the price in Australia and nearly twenty times what most Americans pay.

When I asked a woman in the town's well-stocked store if she had any postcards, she said they were sold in the city office, which was 'over the hill'.

'Thanks, but there's some bad weather coming so I don't really have time,' I replied. 'I need to walk back to the airport.'

'That's okay,' she said, 'I'll drive you up there.'

Lucinda not only drove me to the city office, she also gave me a tour of the township: a simple timber church, the old harbour, houses her father built, the town water tank and a tower of instruments used to measure wind speeds at different heights because the community was considering buying a wind generator to supplement their diesel unit. I met her husband, Chris, who it turned out was the mayor. Their kindness was exceptional, and greatly appreciated.

On the way back, I followed another of Burke's suggestions. I took the *Sun* over Bechevin Bay, on the western side of Atka, where a B-24 Liberator bomber crash-landed during World War II. The wreckage was still there, sitting ominously in the tundra between two hills. When I flew in low for a closer look, the *Sun* was hit by a powerful downdraft created by the strong north-westerly tumbling over the adjacent hill. For two seconds I had the nauseating experience of weightlessness. I would never get comfortable with that.

○

Before leaving Australia, I had agreed to speak at the Seaplane Pilots Association's conference in Sydney in late October 2015, assuming I'd be home by then. Now, as I waited on Adak, it was obviously impossible for me to give the speech in person. But the school kindly let me use their computer lab, which had enough reliable bandwidth to run Skype. I take public speaking seriously and spent a day preparing for the presentation, much of it in the Adak cafe, where the always-on TV was showing CNN hype up a hurricane that was about to hit Mexico. 'The worst hurricane in Mexico's recorded history is nigh,' cried the news. When it turned out to be little more than heavy wind, CNN swapped its on-screen wind statistics from miles per hour to kilometres per hour, so its predictions of '250 mph gusts' wouldn't seem quite so obviously overblown. Was there ever such a perfect example of what is wrong with the 24-hour news cycle?

With a world map as a backdrop, my 45-minute presentation and slide show went smoothly, although I didn't mention my growing angst about the flight to Japan. Those feelings were tightly bottled up inside. I was determined to appear confident, almost breezy, about the dangers ahead. It felt bizarre to be standing in a classroom in a remote part of the world talking to a group of pilots and aviation professionals back in Australia, whom I couldn't see.

At the end of my talk, a spokesman for the Seaplane Pilots Association announced that I had been awarded the newly created Ross Vining Exceptional Achievement Award. Ross was a beloved Australian Searey pilot who, tragically, had died a few years earlier while on a round-Australia expedition. I was moved by being recognised in this way, and even more so by being associated with Ross.

That afternoon, I posted home everything that would not be essential for my flight to Japan. (A year later, it still hasn't arrived ... thanks, US Postal Service!) I needed the *Southern Sun* light so she could carry as much fuel as possible. If the weather didn't open up by the end of October, a mere week away, I would either fly her back to the American mainland or leave her on Adak and take another shot the following year.

Crunch time had arrived.

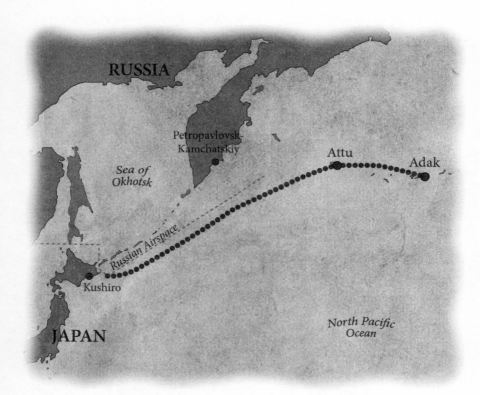

33.

The Right Stuff

'We've always defined ourselves by the ability to overcome the impossible. And we count these moments. These moments when we dare to aim higher, to break barriers, to reach for the stars, to make the unknown known. We count these moments as our proudest achievements ... that our greatest accomplishments cannot be behind us, because our destiny lies above us.'
COOPER, *INTERSTELLAR* (2014)

Two huge low-pressure systems sat over the Bering Strait and the North Pacific, inching towards Alaska. I had watched them for days, studying how the interaction of the isobars affected the winds across thousands of kilometres of ocean. The rotation of the Earth means that, in the absence of other influences, including landmass, winds predominately come from the west. But the boundary between two weather systems could overwhelm the globe's spin and send air back towards Siberia, a north-easterly that the *Southern Sun* could surf all the way to Japan.

The winds between Alaska and Japan were forecast to reverse on Wednesday, 28 October. I awoke that day with a sense of anticipation laced with fear. As the morning hours passed, the predominating winds changed direction to the east. The flight of my life was on.

I methodically fuelled the *Sun*. A plane designed to carry 100 litres of petrol was now carrying 410 litres. With my small backpack stowed, and my life raft and emergency bag carefully placed within reach inside the cramped cabin, I was ready to go. At 2 p.m., just as I was about to set off, every pupil and teacher from the Adak school gathered on the tarmac, holding farewell signs they had made in class. I chatted with the teachers for a few minutes and thanked them for our few weeks together. Each pupil said goodbye, shook my hand and conveyed their best wishes, bringing joy to my heart. Michael, my new friend and host at the Blue Bird Cafe, directed me to take off using hand signals he had learned while flying from US aircraft carriers.

The *Southern Sun* had twenty-one hours' worth of fuel on board. She took off and flew west with a tailwind, thanks to the first easterly to have come over the island in two weeks. She had never been heavier, and I was careful not to make any sudden movements to the controls. I didn't want to put any more stress on her light airframe than necessary.

I had done everything possible to prepare, but still the risks were significant. An engine failure over the Pacific at night would be hard to survive, even in a flying boat. If the *Sun* did manage to land in the rolling seas, the chances of me being rescued in the vast ocean were slim.

I had written a letter to Anne, Tim and Jack. I told them I loved them, I reflected on the many good experiences we had enjoyed together, and I apologised for making their lives difficult from time to time. I offered some positive and uplifting advice to the boys about their futures, although I knew it would be insufficient if they ever read it. I spent two days thinking about the words, and couldn't hold back my tears as I committed them to paper. Ruth agreed to post the letter if I didn't make it home. I stuck a pretty Alaskan stamp on the envelope, and hoped it would never receive the postmark that would deliver it to my family.

I was scared. I worried that I was pushing my luck too far. I knew my determination to lap the Earth could have warped my assessment of the risk. Everything had to go almost perfectly for me to make it, and over such a long flight that was not likely.

Thinking back now, I see that I must have known it was more dangerous than I was comfortable with. As when I left Melbourne for

London, I didn't tell anyone how I planned to get to Japan. I had not sought permission to land on Attu, the uninhabited island where I had stored fuel. It would be safer for someone in authority to decline that permission rather than say yes. And anyway, I didn't know who to ask. I posted a vague message online about my intentions 'to soon do something', but I wasn't specific – I didn't want to be told I was crazy. Anyone following my satellite tracking could quickly work it out.

As far as I could tell, no one had attempted to fly from Attu to Japan before. Certainly I hadn't read or heard of it, and my research was thorough. Without any previous examples to learn from, I planned the flight as logically as possible. It seemed straightforward and reasonable on my flight plan, on my Excel spreadsheet and on Google Earth. But I was about to fly twenty-five hours in a day, crossing the international date line in the process. When commercial flights cross the Pacific in fifteen-hour legs, they have complete changes of crew and beds for the off-duty pilots.

That morning, I had called the US customs and immigration service to advise I was leaving the country by private plane from Adak. I may not have entirely explained my stopover in Attu, which is of course American territory, but I didn't want any last-minute hiccups, such as being told I couldn't land there, let alone depart the United States from Attu.

The low cloud around Adak was soon left behind as the *Sun* ventured out over the ocean. The six-hour flight to Attu was uneventful. The highlight was seeing some gorgeous clouds that looked just like animals, including a blue whale gently floating just above the sea.

The wind gradually shifted from an easterly to a north-north-easterly, which was exactly what was forecast and what the *Sun* needed to get to Japan. Over Attu, turbulence bounced the heavily laden craft up and down. I landed well short of the abandoned runway's full length, taxied up to my makeshift fuel depot, and as I opened it up clearly heard the sound of scurrying rats. But all five fuel bags were intact. If they hadn't been, I would have had to fly back to Adak, and that would have been the end of the trip.

I gingerly emptied the fuel into the *Sun*, while she rocked in the strong wind and light rain. Sunset was forty-five minutes away. I walked up and down the runway to look for potholes or debris, and then rang Peter Steeger in Japan on my satellite phone, requesting clearance from the Japanese authorities to take off.

The answer was no – not just yet. Fog was predicted at Kushiro, my arrival airport in northern Japan, but it would clear by mid-morning.

'You'll need to wait at least three hours before taking off, and prefer-ably six,' Peter said.

Crap, I thought. *That will mean taking off in the dark, on a disused runway, with no lights.*

Waiting would be better for my arrival in Japan, but the conditions on Attu were deteriorating. I decided it would be best to leave in four hours, at midnight, which would get the *Sun* to Japan by late morning. It would mean fourteen hours' flying in the dark out of an expected eighteen-hour flight, which increased the danger. But I wanted tail-winds for as long as possible, and they would dissipate as the night wore on. When I did hit a weather front near Japan, I wanted it to be in day-light. Flying at night, in the rain, over the ocean and with no autopilot would be marginal at best.

I went back into the hut and tried to rest. It didn't work. The wind bat-tering the small shed was one thing; the rain on the roof was another. The smell of rat droppings wasn't very relaxing either. I set an alarm on my iPhone for two hours' time, and then tried to sleep by closing my eyes and lying on my side on the dirty old couch. Hah – as if. With the lights out and my senses alert, the wind seemed stronger and the rain heavier, and I was just waiting for the rats I could hear to climb over me. I lay there for ninety minutes before realising that the rain really was getting heavier.

Outside, I discovered the conditions were getting a lot worse. The sky was overcast and a strong wind was buffeting the *Sun*. The rain was not too heavy but I feared it soon would be. The clouds to the north, where the wind was coming from, seemed more ominous than those to the south. By now it was nearly 11 p.m. Midnight was too far off – it was time to go.

I made an espresso and ate a cold crab cake given me by my Adak hosts, Mike and Imelda. The irony of enjoying a hot coffee on a barren island without electricity or running water wasn't lost on me. It felt very strange leaving the United States from an uninhabited island – a huge contrast to my arrival at the bustling Bangor airport a couple of months earlier.

I decided to take off from the shorter of Attu's two runways, which crossed the longer one. It would take the *Southern Sun* straight out over the ocean, which was safer than flying past hills and a disused communication tower. About two-thirds of the runway was in fair condition. The rest was so rough, with grass growing through the tarmac, that it could damage the *Sun*'s undercarriage. I decided to place some LED torches along the runway as references in the dark.

Still, I was apprehensive. It was hard enough to see where the *Sun* was going while taxiing down the main runway; I couldn't image what barrelling along at take-off speed would be like. I taxied the length of the runway to get my bearings, and then turned on the LED lights. I taxied back along the runway, which was uphill. When I got to the point where vegetation was growing through the tarmac, I turned the *Sun* around and faced the ocean.

Gulp! The LEDs were invisible. It was raining and I couldn't see through the windscreen. When the *Sun* moved forward, I simply wouldn't be able to tell where the runway was.

Okay, this is really uncomfortable now, I thought. *Slow down and have a good think.*

I knew from watching the weather for the previous few weeks that it often rained on the islands for hours at night. A few kilometres out to sea, though, it would usually be clear. There is almost always some rain in the Aleutians. On the days the weather report says no rain, it seems to rain a few times. If it says it will rain a little bit, it rains a lot. And just don't go outside if they ever predict bad weather. I had waited for the best weather window, taken Burke's advice on patience, and thought that this would be the best shot I had.

Prudence called for a test run. The *Sun* has a very good landing light, which should have helped. Without going to full power, I rolled forward to see how visible the runway was. There was too much rain on the windshield and I couldn't see a thing.

I stopped and thought. I could see through the side window, just not the front. Experience told me that rain washed off the windshield at speed, which meant it would only be a problem when I started to move forward. So I opened the side window and, looking out, began taxiing forward. Even though my head was getting wet, the runway was well lit by the landing light. I could see the closest LED blinking halfway along. I took off my headset so it wouldn't get saturated; it wasn't like I had anyone to speak to on the radio out here.

I taxied back to the start point and applied full power. The wet wind pricked at my face, but I forced my eyes open and concentrated on steering straight. The *Sun* lifted off the ground halfway along. I pulled my head inside the cockpit, focused on the instruments and climbed gently to keep up our speed. As soon as her wheels left the ground, the *Sun* jerked 30 degrees towards the wind, which meant the landing light was no longer illuminating the runway. Within seconds she was over the sea anyway, and all I could see was black. I felt a deep sense of dread. I had been so focused on taking off and getting clear of land that I hadn't thought about the next step. The sky was overcast, which meant there was no moonlight. I couldn't see where the sky met the sea.

The view out the window was uselessly black, just as opaque as the white of the clouds that had enveloped the *Sun* off the coast of Canada. I had replayed that earlier mishap in my mind hundreds of times, and I wasn't going to make the same mistake. Carefully and calmly I looked at my instruments and deployed my training. I kept the artificial horizon level, the speed with plenty of safety margin and gently climbed at a slow 100 feet per minute south, towards Japan. After fifteen minutes the *Sun* was at 1500 feet, the highest I was prepared to fly; the icing level was forecast to be 2500 feet. Fifteen hundred feet wasn't even double Melbourne's tallest building. I needed to stay low enough to remain ice-free, and high enough to be clear of the ocean. The prospect of ice forming at night is particularly scary because it is that much harder to detect. I figured the aluminium struts between the hull and the wings would be the first to develop ice, and I shone my torch on them from time to time to check.

The bumpy air gradually became smooth and the rain cleared. Within half an hour the *Sun* was travelling at a groundspeed of 110 knots. This was faster than I expected, so I throttled back to conserve fuel and not arrive too early. After an hour there was just enough moonlight that I could see clouds ahead. The ocean glistened in patches here and there. After several hours all the clouds disappeared, revealing an almost full moon. For six hours I enjoyed the delightful sight of a perfectly clear vista and an ocean sparkling in the moonlight.

In the hours before dawn, though, I became incredibly tired. I could feel myself falling asleep, which I recognised from my young days of driving in the country – back when I thought I was invincible. One night in England I dozed off and sideswiped a roundabout at 2 a.m. Now, memories of that accident helped motivate me to concentrate on staying awake. Without an autopilot I could not risk sleep, even momentarily, because it could take as little as ninety seconds for the *Sun* to hit the water. I nibbled on food, drank and used the red bottle. I splashed water on my face. I slapped myself. I opened the window to let in the freezing air.

Then, far out to the east, I saw the first glimmer of refracted, rather than reflected, sunlight. I was filled with a great sense of relief. Even a small amount of daylight would make it easier to stay awake. But my good fortune was about to end. The weather on the horizon was looking, to quote an old chum, 'cloudy, rainy, no sunny'.

The tailwinds dissipated and turned to headwinds. I began to begrudge Russia. In order to stay out of Russian airspace, I was flying around an imaginary point in the ocean, meaning I had to go many extra kilometres. The *Sun*'s ground speed at one point slowed to 32 knots, or 60 kilometres an hour. In an act of defiance, I cut the corner and entered Russia for about a minute. I can't remember if I actually blew a raspberry in their general direction, but I definitely wanted to.

As it turned out, the tailwinds I'd waited for had been too effective, and the *Sun* arrived a couple of hours earlier than planned. I used the satellite device to get an abbreviated weather update: it was currently impossible to land at Kushiro, which was covered in fog.

The *Sun* was so close to safety, yet ahead of me all I could see was a line of cloud almost down to the ocean. The rain once again started falling on the windscreen.

Nakashibetsu

Kushiro

JAPAN

Kobe

Tokyo

Okinawa

34.

The Terminal

'I think I can, I think I can, I think I can.'
CASEY JR, *DUMBO* (1941)

was by myself in the cockpit, but I wasn't alone. At his home on the other side of Hokkaido island, Peter Steeger was following the *Sun*'s progress on his computer and comparing her position with a radar map of the rain front over northern Japan. He called my satellite phone and suggested I head a little more north, a course that would avoid the worst of the weather.

I was still a long way from land. Although the visibility was not great, I was comfortable that I could see sufficiently well and felt under control. The *Sun*'s groundspeed was now down to 60 knots. With about an hour and a half of flying to go, she had four hours of fuel, which was reassuring. At 160 kilometres from the coast I was not within radio range of the airport. Peter called back with an update. Kushiro was still fogged in, leaving me with two options: circle for a couple of hours, or divert to another airport.

Peter was proving to be a most efficient and concerned handler. He had already made a call and arranged permission for the *Sun* to land at Nakashibetsu airport, further to the north, where the weather was good enough to land without using instruments. This was a relief, because turning north towards that airport triggered a jump in the *Sun*'s groundspeed and meant I only had an hour left to fly. I was exhausted, and just wanted to get on the ground.

It was a bumpy hour. While there was no rain and the cloud had lifted, the turbulence was the worst I had ever experienced. I slowed right down and took my time. At one point I heard another aircraft on the radio. Relieved, I waited for them to finish speaking and then called the air-traffic controller.

'Fukuoka Radar, November Four Seven Three X-ray Papa, Searey amphibian, six zero miles south-east Nakashibetsu, squawking one two zero zero, inbound for Nakashibetsu,' I said.

'November Four Seven Three X-ray Papa, advise your elevation and origin airport,' came back the answer.

'Four hundred feet, Attu, Alaska,' I replied, thinking, *I bet you don't hear that every day*.

'November Four Seven Three X-ray Papa, you are identified, continue direct Nakashibetsu,' he said, rather deadpan.

The further I flew, the more the cloud lifted. I was able to slowly climb to 1500 feet. Twenty-six hours after leaving Adak, with a classroom of kids waving with their placards, I was directed by the air-traffic controller to change frequencies and contact the airport tower.

'Nakashibetsu, November Four Seven Three X-ray Papa.'

'November Four Seven Three X-ray Papa, track direct Nakashibetsu, expect runway twenty-six,' they replied.

Fifteen minutes later I landed on a huge concrete runway and taxied to a lonely parking spot. I could have gone to sleep right there in the cockpit, but I waited in my seat for the airport officials to arrive.

I had just flown across the Pacific Ocean, setting a record for the longest ever flight in a Searey – and, I suspect, the longest solo flight in any amphibian aircraft. After flying through the night, I was physically and emotionally spent. All I wanted to do was go to a hotel and sleep. But Nakashibetsu was a domestic airport and didn't have any immigration officials who could legally admit me to Japan. I would have to get back in the *Sun* and fly the 85 kilometres to Kushiro when the weather improved.

The airport staff welcomed me with a few words of English, which was a lot more than the Japanese I knew. I was escorted to the terminal but was not permitted to leave their offices. They seemed to understand what I had just put myself through, and kindly led me to a small room with mats on the floor. I slipped into a deep sleep almost instantly. A few hours later, at 1.30 p.m., someone knocked at the door. I didn't hear them. They came in and shook my shoulder. Three-quarters asleep, I panicked, fearful that I had slept through the whole day and night. 'What day is it?' I asked. They gestured that someone wanted to speak to me on the telephone.

It was Peter. The fog had lifted at Kushiro and it was time for me to complete this mission. The officials were anxious that I clear customs and immigration as soon as possible. I went to the bathroom and splashed some water on my face and neck. The short sleep had done the trick. I was ready to venture forth.

In yet another example of the incredible generosity encountered during my trip, the airport staff had bought me some welcome presents while I was asleep: products from their region, including Hokkaido gouda cheese, dried beef and baby sausage. Their gifts were humbling and I thanked them profusely.

The rain and cloud had vanished, revealing a clear sky. The short flight to Kushiro was straightforward, assisted by the air-traffic controllers' excellent English. I was greeted on the tarmac by my agents from Japan Airlines, who were very helpful and detailed. It felt like being back in India, with dozens of pieces of paper all needing stamping and signing, except that everything was spotlessly clean and immaculately presented. The care taken with the placement of each rubber stamp highlighted why origami is a popular artform in Japan.

Clearing customs and immigration took a couple of hours. I had to pay tax on the three hours' worth of fuel left in the *Sun* because it was regarded as 'imported'. After a lot of paperwork, reference books, calculators, more rubber stamps and a supervisor checking, the tax was 100 yen, or about a dollar.

It was thirty hours since I had left Adak. I'd flown for twenty-four hours over three legs, the longest being seventeen hours. I was rather glad to be on land.

Later, some people wondered if I had properly considered the risks of such a long flight. I had. Over and over. I didn't want to die, and wasn't taking the risk to look brave. I'd physically and mentally prepared myself for the challenge and its dangers, including the dreaded prospect of landing on the ocean at night. If that happened, I knew my chances of surviving would be less than 50 per cent. Would I take that risk again? No. If there's ever another time, I will ensure that I don't have to undertake such a perilous flight.

On reflection, though, I realise that I had painted myself into a corner. While stranded on Adak, I had developed such a laser-like focus on getting home that I put the risks to one side. I was certainly determined, and I remained calm through that whole day, despite some testing moments.

I had come a long way since nervously leaving Darwin six months earlier. With 900 hours flight time, I was still a low-time pilot, but the experiences I had been through, while flying low and slow in a little plane that never let me down, went way beyond flying. It had been as much a test of my mental fortitude as of my physical endurance and flying ability. Out there alone, I could apply all my resources and climb the highest mountain.

The snow and rain that now came to northern Japan had an upside: an enforced break. After nine hours' sleep, I woke still exhausted. My morale was high, though, helped by congratulatory emails that poured in from people who had been following the *Southern Sun* online, and were happy that I had continued on and made it across the Pacific.

I needed a haircut. I looked like a cross between Krusty the Clown and a mad professor. I found a barber who, it turned out, was fascinated by Australia. He insisted on having a conversation while holding sharp scissors or a cut-throat razor in one hand, and Google Translate on his phone in the other. The haircut was successful; the conversation not so much. But we had fun.

At the Kushiro City Museum I learned that the city had been a trading port for centuries. The residents had once worn clothes and shoes made from fish scales. I couldn't imagine how that would smell on a summer day. There was one cinema in town, an Aeon eight-screen Multiplex. I hadn't had much experience of Japanese cinemas, and was interested to find that the huge building in fact housed a department store, which operated the cinema. It would be like Myer, Marks & Spencer or Macy's deciding to build a cinema inside their stores, and sell popcorn and pretzels covered with caramel.

It was only 2 degrees one afternoon when I arranged to change the oil in the plane, which proved to be slow and tricky while wearing gloves. But the real fun came with refuelling. Kushiro did not have any avgas, nor did they officially allow petrol to be brought into the airport from outside. Generally I've found the plane will fly much further with full tanks of fuel, so I developed a cunning plan. I took my fuel containers in a taxi to a petrol station, but earlier that day I'd gone to a department store and picked up those cheap bags people buy when they have bought too much on their trip for their luggage. I worked out I could fit two fuel bags in each. I felt bad walking my luggage out to the plane past the ever-polite Japanese handlers, but it wasn't hurting anyone and the smuggling solved the problem, even if a little cheekily.

A few days later I flew over several snow-capped mountains and descended into Kobe's island airport just as the sun dipped below the horizon. From that point I planned to spend two nights at every stop. As keen as I was to get home to Australia, I knew they were places I might never see again, and I wanted to continue experiencing new cultures, towns, food and cinemas. Also, every flight from then on was 1200 kilometres or more, and a day off was a nice break.

My agent in Kobe was a retired corporate pilot for the Sony Corporation, Taco San, who showed me where to park and refuel. He had booked me into a hotel at the city's port; 'Please enjoy the hotel; please experience Japanese culture,' he urged me. The hotel was more of a bathhouse and restaurant, with a few floors of rooms for those wanting to stay the night. No shoes or Western clothes were allowed. Once checked in, guests were given traditional dress to wear throughout their stay.

In my room I felt a bit odd looking at myself in the mirror – except that, of course, deep down I love dressing up. All the other diners in the restaurant were Japanese, and dressed accordingly, so I would have been out of place in Western clothes anyway.

After dinner I went to the eighteenth-floor rooftop for a foot bath, which turned out to be a long, hot pool for your feet, with views over the city. I was the only single person. Just when I thought that might make the other people feel uncomfortable, one couple asked me to take their photo. Then another did, and another, which made me realise that no one minded my presence. It seemed surreal, especially after where I'd been just a week before.

From Kobe, I flew seven and a half hours to Okinawa, a Japanese island close to Taiwan. The further south I flew, the more the Pacific looked liked the ocean I had always imagined it to be. There were stunning sand islands and sparkling blue seas. Something else happened too, something I hadn't experienced since Florida: it was warm. In fact, it was hot enough for me to take my woollen jumper off, which was a blissful feeling. *Maybe I can even stop wearing two pairs of socks*, I mused.

Arriving at Naha, the capital of Okinawa, was stressful. A Boeing jet was landing in front of me, several planes were waiting to take off, and a controller told me to hurry up – and then, just before I landed, instructed me how to exit the runway. It didn't help that there were heavy and gusty crosswinds.

If you're told to exit to the left when you're five feet above the tarmac and about to touch down, you can't help but look left, which is what I did. The act of turning my head led me to pull the stick slightly to the left just as the wheels touched the ground. The tyres squeaked and squealed and I was forced to urgently correct the steering to stop the *Sun* from fishtailing down the runway.

Anne was wondering when I was going to get home, and I was finalising what route to take. The most efficient way seemed to be through the Philippines to the island of Ambon, in Indonesia. I could then fly across the Timor Sea to Horn Island, on the northern tip of Queensland. That would mean a comfortable flight to Longreach, where I wanted to explore the Qantas Founders Museum, which I had skipped on the way out. Longreach seemed appropriate for another reason: it would be the first place on the trip I returned to, and so would make the circumnavigation official. I was pleased about that, given this enormous undertaking had started with the simple idea of retracing the Qantas Imperial Sydney–Southampton flying boat route.

Even though I was relatively close to home, I still had several days of flying, each longer than any flight I had done a year before. Such long overwater crossings were not to be taken lightly. It was too early to celebrate. I needed to stay focused. I couldn't know that, after serving me so well for such a long time, the *Sun* was about to suffer two potentially fatal breakdowns.

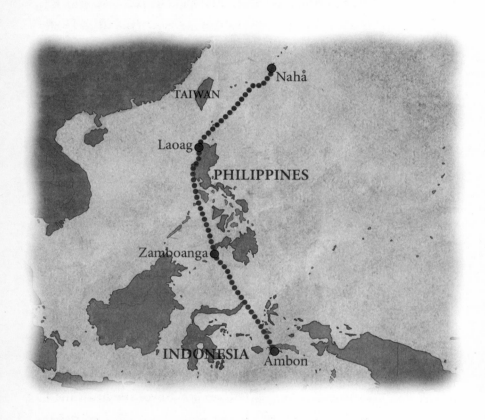

35.

The Final Countdown

'The suspense is terrible ... I hope it'll last.'
WILLY WONKA, *WILLY WONKA & THE CHOCOLATE FACTORY* (1971)

I had been quietly flying over the Philippines, enjoying the view of farmland, seaside villages, reefs and islands for several hours, when a large helicopter flew past in the opposite direction, but at the same height. *Blimey*, I thought, *that was close. And what are they doing out here anyway?*

Several minutes later I noticed a helicopter to my left, about a kilometre away, flying in the same direction and at the same speed, but about 1000 feet higher. Painted grey, it seemed to be a navy helicopter. I wondered if they were looking at me. I assumed it was the same helicopter as before.

There was a large storm front ahead that I needed to dodge. David Geers, a fellow Searey pilot in Australia, had offered to look up weather patterns online if I was ever unsure where to go. For the first time I called him on my satellite phone. He was pleased to hear from me. It turned out he had been following the *Sun*'s progress on the website, which he said he always kept open on an iPad, even taking it to bed, which was starting to wear a little thin with his wife, Cheryl. David said he would check out the weather and call me back.

From where I was located, going right would have taken the *Sun* further out to sea. Going left would have taken her closer to land, where

311

I could find an airport if the weather was impassable. I needed to make a decision quickly, and my instinct said go left.

I turned 10 degrees left, which was towards the helicopter. I looked out at the cloud and then focused on my map. After less than a minute I looked up and was shocked to see the helicopter barely the width of a road from the *Sun*, rocking its rotors left and right – the international signal for 'you have been intercepted'.

What the hell? I thought. I rocked my wings back, acknowledging that I understood.

The side door of the helicopter was open, and manned by a soldier who was aiming a large machine gun straight at me. Standing behind him was another soldier, who was pointing a video camera. A camera mounted on the front of the helicopter was clearly looking in my direction too. I carefully took a photo, all the while thinking, *What if I'm never seen again?*

I tried calling the helicopter on the radio frequency assigned to the area.

'Helicopter intercepting seaplane, November Four Seven Three X-ray Papa, do you copy?' I said.

There was only silence. I repeated the message but still there was no response.

I rang David back and told him what was happening. I wanted to know if he thought there was anything else I should do, which he didn't. Airliners above me were talking on their radios, which was distracting, so I turned down the radio while I spoke to David. We discussed the cloud front ahead, and he said going to the right would get me around the system quickest. The conversation was comforting, and I asked him to note my position just in case something happened. I couldn't chat for too long because I needed to concentrate, and I didn't want to run out of phone credit.

The helicopter was a menacing sight. I tried calling it again, but got no answer. I checked I was on the right frequency, and tried a different one just in case. Silence.

As the *Sun* flew on, I grew more concerned. The international rules of flight dictated that, if intercepted by a military aircraft, I was required to follow it. But why? What was going on? I had heard stories of people being intercepted, diverted to an alternate airport and locked in jail while their paperwork was checked. In most cases they were released within a few days, but still I didn't fancy it.

I looked down and everything became clear. There was an aircraft carrier accompanied by warships between the *Southern Sun* and the Philippines coast. The ships' wakes were parallel to and almost under the *Sun*'s flight path, until they'd made an abrupt left-hand turn to the east. Now they were heading away from me at a right angle. My flight path would have taken me straight over the fleet.

The USS *Theodore Roosevelt*, an enormous aircraft carrier, was patrolling this part of the South China Sea to remind the Chinese who owns it, I read that night. On reflection, I could see how a small plane, especially one using the same engine as a Predator drone, heading straight towards the carrier in the middle of the ocean must have seemed suspicious.

I was still worried, but I now understood why I had been intercepted. I continued to fly, keeping one eye on the helicopter and another on my charting software. After forty-five minutes I was about to hit cloud, and had to change direction. I could follow the helicopter, or turn right through the cloudless air and head for my planned destination.

I didn't want to just follow the helicopter and see what happened. I turned 30 degrees right, towards a clearing between the clouds. The helicopter aggressively followed, but got no closer. I descended to 1000 feet to get under the cloud. The helicopter followed. As I passed under the cloud, the helicopter suddenly turned back towards the aircraft carrier. *Phew.*

Breathing a sigh of relief, it occurred to me that I hadn't heard any noise on the radio for a while, which seemed strange. I felt for the knob and discovered that I'd left the volume all the way down after the phone call. I was mad at myself. As I turned it up, I heard the tail end of some-one's voice: '. . . Seahawk changing frequency.'

A Seahawk is a US military helicopter. I felt sick. *You idiot*, I thought. But then they hadn't answered my first radio calls, which had prompted me to phone David. I could still hear passenger jets flying above me so I listened for a minute. No one was talking about the *Sun* or the helicop-ter. Should I say something? I decided to continue along in silence. I was worried I was in big trouble.

My heart sank ninety minutes later as the *Sun* flew around a head-land and towards Zamboanga airport. A helicopter was hovering right between me and the runway. Were they waiting for me? Had I caused an incident? The questions sat heavily in the cockpit for a few minutes.

As I turned the *Sun* to land, the helicopter slowly flew away. It looked like a civilian chopper. When I landed, it was clear the airport was fairly quiet. But two official cars and half a dozen officials in uni-form with gold braid and stern hats were waiting for me.

I shut down the *Sun* and stayed in my seat. The uniforms approached. As they came closer, my dread dissipated: they weren't soldiers or police officers, but customs and immigration officials. They smiled and wel-comed me to Zamboanga.

My handling agent emerged from the terminal. Still seated inside the *Sun*, I asked him in a hushed tone, 'Is everything okay?'

'Yes, of course,' he said. 'Come in, get a drink of water and sign your paperwork. Welcome to Zamboanga!'

~

My stay in Zamboanga turned out to be one of the highlights of the trip. I knew little about the place, so felt a heightened sense of discovery; it was only later that I learned it was considered a dangerous place for vis-itors. As much as I was in a hurry to get home, I still wanted a day off flying to explore.

Some quick internet research presented a photo of Rio Hondo, a fishing village of houses on stilts over the water. After a morning walking around the old fort, harbour and even a place of pilgrimage, I tried to get a motorcycle sidecar taxi to Rio Hondo. The first two drivers shook their heads and kept going. The third agreed. After fifteen minutes we reached a security checkpoint, where the driver shooed me out of the sidecar. As I wondered what would happen next, the guards motioned to some teenagers who had BMX bikes and rudimentary sidecars. We were soon pedalling down the road in one of them, with every other bike following, and accompanied with squeals of delight.

We came to a walkway. The charred remains of stumps protruded from the water. The fishing village had been burnt to the waterline in a small civil war, leaving the residents destitute. The United Nations had been building new homes for the fishing families. Despite the hardships they had been through, they welcomed me with open arms. Kids flying kites talked to me in broken English and showed me their homes. I was offered a freshly caught fish to eat. It was a simple yet delightful afternoon. As I so often found, those with the least were the most prepared to share.

From the Philippines I planned to fly to Ambon, in eastern Indonesia, my final stop before Australia. About halfway there, I noticed the fuel gauge wasn't moving in the direction I expected. Looking at a glass filter through which the fuel passed, I could see no movement. I put my hand on the electric fuel pump behind my seat – it didn't seem to be functioning.

Oh dear. I had two hours of fuel in the main tank and was four and a half hours from Ambon. After travelling almost all around the world, it was the first time an in-flight technical fault had threatened to force me to divert. There were numerous island airports ahead but I dreaded the paperwork and official encounters of an unscheduled arrival.

I had designed a redundancy into the fuel system in case the pump failed. Anyone who has ever been in a small boat with an outboard motor will have seen the black rubber priming bulbs used to inject a small amount of fuel into the engine to get it started. I had installed one in the *Sun*. The bulb was within comfortable reach behind the passenger seat.

I started pumping with my right hand and the fuel was flowing within seconds. After about ten minutes the fuel level on the main tank had increased a little. After twenty minutes my forearm was getting sore. After thirty minutes the fuel gauge was staying level. The engine burnt 20 litres of fuel per hour. In Melbourne I'd been able to pump at a rate of 30 litres an hour for two minutes. Now, above the Molucca Sea, I was struggling to keep up with the engine's consumption.

After an hour I noticed the fuel gauge drop a little more. I wasn't pumping fast enough. It wasn't clear the *Sun* could make it to Ambon. With the control stick wedged between my knees, and still pumping with my right hand, I searched with my left hand on the iPad for the few airports either side of my route. They were all very small and some had gravel strips. The chance of finding spare parts was remote, and hostile officialdom high, which motivated me to keep pumping.

After four hours the *Sun* crossed the equator. My arm was burning now, but I circled back and crossed again. I wanted to draw a circle on my tracking map as a message to Anne: 'I'm nearly home!' Because the tracker didn't update continuously, though, the *Sun*'s circle displayed as a triangle. Still, you have to celebrate the little things!

A summer haze had turned the horizon into a blur, which made the first sight of Ambon very welcome. The island was twenty minutes away, and there was one hour of fuel in the main tank. I pumped for a few more minutes but was confident now I would reach the airport. I raised my arm and clenched my fist a few times. *Yep, that's gonna hurt tomorrow ...*

A year later, my forearm still feels odd when I make a fist.

AUSTRALIA

PAPUA NEW GUINEA

Ambon

Horn Island

Weipa

Longreach

Rylstone

36.

Australia

'Every human being has a basic instinct: to help each other out. If a
hiker gets lost in the mountains, people will coordinate a search. If a
train crashes, people will line up to give blood. If an earthquake levels
a city, people all over the world will send emergency supplies. This is so
fundamentally human that it's found in every culture without exception.'
MARK WATNEY, *THE MARTIAN* (2015)

Before reaching Australia, I had to get out of Ambon, Indonesia, which lacked the hospitality of the Philippines and Japan. I used my day off to install a new fuel pump from a car parts shop. After the *Sun*'s electrical fault the day before, I was paranoid about the next day's twelve-hour leg. It was a serious undertaking, and I still had a lot of water to pass over to get home. Frustratingly, the Ambon airport authorities would not approve the *Sun*'s clearance paperwork in advance. They told me to return in the morning. That wasn't convenient, as I wanted to leave at first light so I could arrive in Australia before sunset.

After spending half a day sourcing a new fuel pump and installing it in the *Sun*, I visited a small 'twin cinema', which had eight lounge chairs in each room. When I asked what films were showing, the lady motioned her arm across the shelves of hundreds of DVDs and said, 'Anything you'd like.' A quick glance noted that $2 per person seemed worryingly cheap, and when I realised the film titles 'on DVD' were actually still showing in cinemas around the world, I decided I couldn't include this venue in my MBA research on ethical grounds.

I enjoyed a slow dinner by the beach as the sun dipped beneath a golden-red horizon. It was very quiet. I looked across the water and couldn't believe that this was it. I'd come all this way, and had just one leg to go before arriving back in Australia.

I got to the airport before dawn. No one was there to let me in. After waiting and calling, I eventually reached the *Sun* by walking through the public terminal, through an unmanned metal detector and out a fire exit. As always, being in the flying suit seemed to grant me special passage. After my pre-flight checks I searched for my handling agent, who wasn't there. His office manager wouldn't help me. They hadn't prepared my invoice and he claimed no one knew how much I owed for landing there. It was ludicrous. I was tired, wanted to get home and really preferred to arrive in Australia during daylight.

There was a solution. If I paid several hundred dollars extra on my credit card, the manager said, he promised to refund the difference when they worked out the true cost – which of course they never did. It was the only time on the trip I felt ripped off, which was remarkable in itself, and it also cost me two hours of daylight. It was hard not to lose my cool, but I didn't want to take off angry, which would neither help nor get me in the sky more quickly. By the time I was cleared to leave, I knew I'd be landing at least an hour after dark.

The flight itself was glorious. Despite my nerves – including constant thoughts of, *This is too good to be true; something is bound to go wrong* – the *Sun* charged along without a glitch. The weather improved the closer I got to Australia, as though welcoming me home.

Horn Island, north of Cape York, was a low-key way to re-enter my native land. The sun dipped below the horizon an hour from the island, but a brightly lit runway guided me down safely. I parked, shut down and soon had visitors. Customs, quarantine and immigration staff – now known as Border Force – greeted me with cans of spray to fumigate the *Sun*. They had been intrigued by a weblink at the bottom of the emails I'd sent them over the previous week, and had been following the *Sun* on the internet.

'It's very small, isn't it?'

'Yes, but she's got me all the way around the world,' I said, patting her nose.

It was great to be on home soil. I'd made it back to Australia, and with only one more flight my circumnavigation would be officially complete.

Horn Island has a classic country hotel with basic rooms and big steaks. Just like at Cold Bay, the other guests were working in the area. There were a few charter pilots, a plumber and some builders servicing the surrounding islands. There were no tourists except me; the place was too remote to appeal to the grey nomads. I went to sleep early. At sunrise I planned to connect two dots and complete a continuous line on my map.

As word spread about the journey, more and more people had been following the *Sun*'s progress online, including several who were making their way to Longreach to witness the completion of the circumnavigation. I planned a day off there so I could finally have a good look at the museum, and to catch my breath before the last two legs home, which would be on consecutive days. I would stop overnight in Rylstone, New South Wales, where a friend, Rob Loneragan, the Australian Searey agent and airport owner, had organised a welcoming party at my penultimate stop. The next day I would fly home to Williamstown, arriving at 3 p.m. on Hobsons Bay, in front of the Royal Yacht Club of Victoria, where Anne had invited close family and a few friends to greet me. It would be a small gathering with no media.

○

From Horn Island I headed almost due south for Longreach, which was only eight hours away. The fact I was now thinking of such a distance as 'only' said a lot about the trip and my new sense of what was normal. Two years earlier, I had been frustrated if headwinds added fifteen minutes to a ninety-minute trip from Williamstown to Bairnsdale.

As I looked down at the sea, I realised I was passing through too quickly. The bright green and blue sea was spotted by lots of sandy islands. I wanted to get home, but the ocean that had been hidden in the dark the evening before was stunning in the morning. I decided it would be wonderful to come back and explore the islands and crystal-clear waters another time.

Two hours into what was looking like a humdrum flight, a red warning light illuminated on the dash. The word beneath the light read simply 'charge', which meant the battery was no longer charging. My heart sank. I felt it hit the bottom of my stomach, maybe twisting a little as it fell. *Not today!*

It was the second problem I'd had in three flights. While I'd made it through some incredible situations, perhaps this was the final reminder. Maybe I wasn't meant to make it. Had I dreamed too much and pushed my luck too far?

If the warning light was correct, the generator might have died, or perhaps an electrical component. Maybe a wire had come loose. Whatever the cause, I couldn't keep flying. The *Sun* would only stay airborne for another hour or two, and Longreach was still six hours away. If the battery was no longer charging, the electric fuel pumps would stop when it ran out. The engine would then stop.

The fault was serious, but soon my disappointment was tempered with relief. Almost anything can be fixed on land, and an emergency landing in the desert would be preferable to putting down in the middle of the ocean, even in a seaplane.

The mining town of Weipa, forty-five minutes away, wasn't the closest airport. But from the back of my memory somewhere I recalled hearing boarding calls for Weipa in a Qantas lounge. I might need replacement parts, and that wouldn't be easy to organise. The nearest Searey shop was in Florida, and spare parts for the Rotax engine would have to come from Melbourne. Weipa had regular commercial flights that could transport parts or a mechanic, if needed.

Turning 90 degrees right towards the town, I noted my new heading and distance, calculated my arrival time and wrote down the airport's radio frequency and runway headings. I then shut down every electronic device except the radio – including the GPS, which I had now been using to navigate for over 55,000 kilometres. I began steering by compass and timing the flight by my watch, just like I'd done during my first cross-country training flight a decade or so before.

The red sand and scrub landscape was flat and featureless. I was incredibly relieved when Weipa airport came into sight and I could make my inbound radio call. After landing, I quickly parked and began searching for the fault. I couldn't see anything loose, so I called an expert: Wal from Bert Flood Imports, the Rotax engine distributor, was a guru for these engines. He had never heard of a generator failing. There are sometimes problems with the rectifiers, an electronic box between the engine and the battery, he told me.

Oh, are there? I thought. *I wish I'd known that eight months ago.*

After a couple of hours of plugging and unplugging, and studying wiring diagrams emailed by fellow Searey pilots David and Doug on the ground in Longreach, it became clear that the rectifier was the most likely culprit. The plug connection had blackened lugs, suggesting it had overheated. There was only one thing to do: get another one ASAP, most likely from Melbourne.

Rob Loneragan, who had also helped work out the fault, arranged for a rectifier to be flown from Melbourne overnight. I spoke to the freight agents at Weipa airport to advise there was a package coming, and asked what time I should collect it.

'Oh, overnight really means two days out here,' they said. 'If you're lucky it might be here by 3 p.m., but more likely the following day.'

My heart sank. That would force my greeting parties in Longreach and Rylstone to wait a couple of days. Worse still, Anne had put a lot of work into planning my homecoming, and rescheduling that would mean a lot of mucking around. But I couldn't see what else to do. I rang

Rob again and apologised that it looked like I'd be at least a day late.

'Stand by,' he said. 'I've got another idea.'

Rob tracked down Paul Hewitt, who owned a Searey in Innisfail, an hour south of Cairns, which was about 700 kilometres from Weipa. Despite having never met me, he left work immediately and removed the rectifier from his own plane. I rang Rebecca at Skytrans, the airline with the first flight the next morning from Cairns to Weipa, to book in the package. Pretty soon she called back and advised that, rather that send the part as freight in the hold with the baggage, one of the airline's staff, Christopher Palmer, would carry it to Weipa and hand it to me in person.

Paul dropped the package off at 5.30 a.m. at Cairns airport, which was an hour's drive from his home. Christopher handed me the part at 8 a.m. I simply plugged it in, and by 8.45 a.m. the *Sun* was back together and the engine started at first try. The red warning light was off. Skytrans refused to accept any payment. Paul wouldn't be able to fly his plane until I replaced the part. Such generosity was incredible. By 10 a.m. the *Southern Sun* was heading towards Longreach over a dust-red desert.

Headwinds made it a seven-hour flight. I was due to give a talk that night in Longreach, at the theatre of the Qantas Founders Museum. Rather than the day off I was looking forward to, I would now be arriving an hour before I was due to speak. At least I would make it, though, and not disappoint anyone.

In the distance I could see dark clouds, thunderstorms and flashes of lightning. It was an ominous outlook. Flirting with one of the greatest killers in small plane aviation, 'get-there-itis', I threaded my way through gaps in the clouds a couple of miles from the lightning. While my flying remained technically under visual flight rules, I was pushing to land at Longreach because I didn't want to let down the people waiting. This was why, for the whole trip up to that point, I had not made my plans public: I was worried that one of the side-effects would be flying through bad weather to meet a waiting audience.

And so a small, rather old-fashioned, silver flying boat, the *Southern Sun*, landed at dusk on 12 November 2015, becoming the first solo round-the-world amphibious aircraft, and I the first solo circumnaviator. We were directed by fellow Searey pilot David Geers to park in front of the historic Qantas hangar at the museum. A few dozen people were there, including Nicole Kuttner from the museum, who had promoted my arrival on the local radio station. I shut the *Sun* down, climbed out and was handed a bottle of champagne, which was the perfect greeting. As we drank and chatted, I was presented with the inaugural Ross Vining Exceptional Achievement Trophy, which had been 'virtually' awarded by video when I was holed up on Adak.

Inside the museum, I hooked up my iPad to a projector. I should have been exhausted but was on such a high that I spoke for ninety minutes without pause. I loved every minute of it. Telling the tale was like living the journey over again.

There were lots of good questions, the most common being: 'What's next?'

'I need to get home first,' I said.

The next morning there was a 10-knot tailwind and not a cloud in the sky. Soon after the *Sun* took off, my phone rang. It was Jon Faine, an ABC Melbourne radio host who had heard about the trip. Near the end of our live-to-air interview, he asked, 'So where are you now?'

'Four and a half thousand feet, 20 miles south of Longreach,' I replied.

It was only then that he realised I was flying.

After seven hours of flying over increasingly high cloud, I made an inbound radio call from 13,500 feet and the *Sun* descended over the farmland surrounding Rylstone, where Rob had redeveloped a private grass airfield, Rylstone Aerodrome; pilots can buy a block of land there and build themselves a hangar and a home. I circled over the field, landed and taxied across to the original clubhouse and tower, which had been restored by Rob. I was surprised at the size of the welcoming crowd, which was about fifty people, including my friend Ian Westlake, who had watched me depart from Sydney in April.

The local State Emergency Service staged a sausage sizzle. The steak sandwich they made me really hit the spot. Now I felt I was all but home. I spent the afternoon explaining the *Sun*'s systems and regaling people with tales from the trip. In the evening we went into town, where Rob had booked several tables at the local pub, and enjoyed a very social dinner. Just three nights earlier, I couldn't help remembering, I'd eaten alone on the beach in Ambon.

I slept at the airfield in the old control tower, which had been turned into a bedroom. When I woke the next morning, I had a stunning 360-degree view of the field from the bed, which occupied most of the room. It was a glorious way to begin the day of the last flight of my journey in the *Southern Sun*.

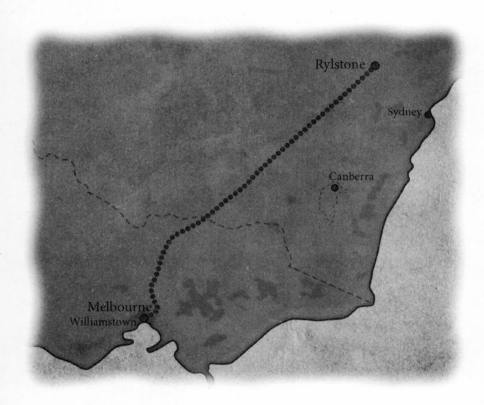

37.

The Wizard of Oz

'There's no place like home.'
DOROTHY, *THE WIZARD OF OZ* (1939)

The final sunrise. Saturday, 14 November 2015. Day 213.

As I looked out at the Rylstone airfield, the first signs were good: some cloud, some sun and blue sky. Everything looked right for the last flight of this journey. After a quiet breakfast with Rob, and a slow, trepidatious pre-flight, it was time for the *Southern Sun* and me to make our way south.

An hour south of Rylstone we were flying in almost clear blue skies, with just a few puffy pillows of clouds for company. With a stronger tailwind than expected, the planned six-hour flight looked like it would only take five hours. Anne would be at Williamstown with family and friends at 3 p.m., so the *Southern Sun* had to slow down or else they'd miss us landing and me alighting. I pulled back the throttle and took my time.

I felt a strange mix of pride and nervousness at being so close to finishing this incredible journey. The weather looked fine and everything was running okay, but only forty-eight hours earlier we'd been grounded in Weipa, so I couldn't help thinking again that this was all too good to be true. I fervently hoped no last-minute gremlins were lying in wait. I thought back on the seven months – so many different peoples, places, cultures. As I write this now, a year later, the scale of the trip has certainly sunk in, but on that final leg the cockpit was filled with a mixture of elation and bewilderment.

I thought of the people I'd met around the world. So many had helped out with acts of kindness – my travel would have been so much harder, and much less fulfilling, without their generosity. I was conscious that it is so easy to feel this way but never connect again with such folks, so I had kept a list and would at least send them all a 'season's greetings' card that year.

Kilmore and the mountain range marking the northern boundary of Melbourne appeared on the horizon, as the tailwind turned to a headwind, and the GPS calculated our ETA was now exactly 3 p.m. Only half an hour to go. As we passed over the eastern suburbs, I was so excited to see Melbourne's skyline that I decided to fly along the Yarra River, and over the Bolte and Westgate bridges.

As we passed the Newport power station and approached Williamstown, it was only 2.47 p.m. The *Sun* flew an orbit over the Royal Yacht Club of Victoria, and I saw Terry O'Hare's huge Australian flag flying proudly from the mast of the *Kookaburra* to welcome the *Southern Sun* home.

To kill some more time I flew south, over the bay, where I could see a fleet of yachts racing in our club's two-day Lipton Trophy Regatta. Was this to be my Bernard Moitessier moment, having completed a circumnavigation, continuing on to avoid the crowds? Not quite. Passing over the yachts and circling once, the *Sun* wagged her wings on the way back, as the clock crept towards 3 p.m. It was time to land on the waters of Hobsons Bay.

It was rather windy, but luckily it was coming from the south, so the water was reasonably protected. Being a Saturday, there were a lot of boats around, which was causing a general sloppiness in the waves that I would have preferred to avoid. Flying back over the club and the landing area, I could see a long line of yachts sailing towards the finish line, at the end of the club marina. It was such a solid line of boats that there wasn't a gap between them to land!

I circled Hobsons Bay several times, waiting for a suitable stretch of water. The view from 1000 feet made it quite easy to judge a good landing area. Finally, as we turned left over Webb Dock, a path became clear. I performed my pre-landing checks – three times over, in fact, to ensure no last-minute mistake led to embarrassment. *Here we go.*

As I felt the hull skim the water, I pulled the power and in a matter of seconds was landed. I slowly taxied towards the boat ramp, and could see a couple of dozen family and friends lining the jetty. I opened the window and waved, and was delighted to hear cheers and clapping from the small gathering, even with my headset on and the sound of the engine.

Now there was just one last hurdle. The boat ramp concrete drops away just below the waterline; I had become stuck here previously, and my greatest paranoia was that I'd come to grief again today, as I left the water. We had timed my arrival to be at high tide, so as to minimise the chances, but it was still the biggest concern I had about the whole day. I had learned to approach the ramp slowly, and then with 10 metres to go to apply the power so I'd almost jump over the end of the ramp.

I overcompensated a tad, and the tail of the *Sun* lifted up as she leapt onto the ramp. But everything was okay, and I continued up the ramp to level ground. Even before I'd shut down the engine, Tim leaned in to hug me. That sense of being so missed by your son is one of life's greatest joys.

I shut down the plane, and found I didn't feel ready to jump out just yet. When I did, the journey would truly be over. As I sat there, Anne and Tim handed me a magnum of champagne, which I jubilantly popped. As I went to take a triumphant swig, I bumped the bottle into my microphone – oops, my headset was still on! I quickly moved it, took a sip, handed the bottle back and climbed out so I could hug Anne, Jack and Tim, be welcomed by my family and friends, and shake many hands.

I was so happy to see everyone – special people from my life, spanning decades. Even my grandmother was there, beaming but also shaking her head in disbelief. I showed people the plane, and there were plenty of questions about food, water and so on. Was that small backpack really all I'd taken? Most hadn't seen the *Southern Sun* before and were horrified at how small she was. 'Really? In that?'

I didn't have the words to describe succinctly what I had just been through. I knew it had been enormous, and I suspected life-changing, but how do you respond to a question like, 'So, how was it?' Just saying, 'Yeah, great,' doesn't cut it. I suspected it was going to take some time for me to make sense of this profound personal experience.

While standing on the lawn at the yacht club, one of my *Kookaburra* crew members asked, in front of Anne, 'Any chance you can sail tomorrow? We need a skipper for the regatta.'

I looked at Anne, thinking, *No, I need a day home with my family*, but before I could even open my mouth she said, 'Oh, go on, the fresh air will do you good.'

She was right: the persistent smell of petrol and avgas had dulled my senses somewhat, and there is nothing quite as relaxing and yet focused at the same time as steering a classic yacht with twelve crew around a racecourse. It proved to be just the day I needed to unwind, and clear my lungs and my head. But there was something I needed to tell my family.

The next day was Monday, and I went back to work. I had many calls and notes of congratulations, but I also continued answering work emails with the multitude of people still unaware I'd been away. Business as usual.

That night, over an emotional dinner with Anne, Jack and Tim, for the first time I shared what had happened at the end of the Atlantic crossing over the Canadian coast. How close I had been to not coming home.

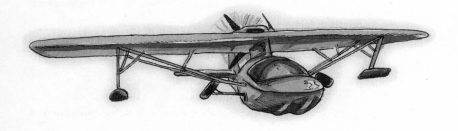

38.

The Way

'Life moves pretty fast. If you don't stop and look around once in a while, you could miss it.'
FERRIS, *FERRIS BUELLER'S DAY OFF* (1986)

G iven half a chance, life can certainly be interesting.

The three most common questions I've been asked since returning home are:

What was the most amazing place?

What did you learn?

What's the next adventure?

I have spent a lot of time thinking about each of these questions – especially the second.

Although I love quoting lines from movies to make a point, I don't think 'life is like a box of chocolates'; for me, it's a journey. We embark on a voyage and hope to fill our lives with adventures of all sizes along the way.

In my journey so far there have been many wonderful adventures: raising a family with Anne, travelling with them to faraway places such as Egypt, Antarctica and Bonnie Doon, helping set up thousands of cinemas across thirty countries, sailing on the historic *Kookaburra* for twenty years, being Commodore of a yacht club. Competing in the America's Cup Jubilee and the Tour de France à la Voile also come to mind.

My bankruptcy meant 2004 was a really bad year for me, my worst yet, while the court case saw me off my game and depressed for three years. I found the courage to fight back, and came out on top emotionally and personally. The flight around the world in the *Southern Sun* was one extraordinary voyage – so grand that I wrote this book and made a documentary to help me make sense of it all. However, I suspect none of it would have happened if not for the hardships in those years before.

But the greatest journey yet – by far – has been saving the Sun Theatre, restoring and reimagining it for the modern era. Although we struggled financially for the first few years, I think it's fair to say it's now a beloved focal point of the village. The voyage of the Sun in Yarraville continues, as she goes from strength to strength. We keep improving the Sun Cinema in Bairnsdale, and we have some other cinemas planned as well: it's at the core of who I am, and we'll keep working to make them even better.

Cinema Loro sa'e, our free outdoor cinema in East Timor, is now in its seventh year; it too has been a heart-warming success, having travelled to hundreds of villages and screened films for tens of thousands of people. In April 2017 we founded Screens Without Borders, our new social enterprise, to expand our Timor model, initially into the Northern Territory and Papua New Guinea, and further afield in the longer term.

One of the great lessons of sailing is that, sometimes, to get where you want to be you may need to go back and forth a little; if the conditions change, you tack. It can be easy to stick rigidly to the path you're on because you don't want to change your mind, but looking to the horizon can sometimes reveal an alternate path – so take it.

We must not forget the lessons of the past: they are our greatest trials. Equally, though, I now realise we mustn't be pulled under by them either. The hours I have spent awake in the pre-dawn, fretting how I could have done certain things differently, were wasted time and mental energy. The future is the only thing I can change, so with strength of mind and lessons learned I will move forward confidently, knowing that when I apply myself I can achieve great things.

Yet I'm just forty-eight, with at least twenty years of work left in me, and hopefully many more years of fun beyond that. I know I'm very lucky to be alive – the irony of saving the Sun and then being saved by the sun is not lost on me – but I am determined to make the most of the second chance I have been granted and ensure that on the continuing voyage of my life I give to those around me. I certainly have ideas for other adventures, but, like the voyage of the *Southern Sun*, an idea without a plan remains a dream; I'll work away at them and keep them to myself till their time comes. One day, when my working years are over, I might even realise my first big dream: to sail around the world. But for now my attentions are elsewhere.

The *Southern Sun*, my silver friend, did so well to take me safely around the world but I feel the time will soon come for her to have a rest. My next long flights and adventures will be for Screens Without Borders, so a larger bird is in order – one with more seats, so that Anne, the boys, friends or colleagues can join me. We'll need room for portable cinema equipment, and definitely two engines for safety. That's a whole new journey I can't wait to start working on.

Did I find the golden meaning of the whole trip? My great takeaway is that no matter where I went in the world, regardless of the politics between nations, people were simply trying to get on with their daily lives, feed their families and educate their children so that they may prosper and enjoy a better life. At our local level, community is what matters, and that's something we can all contribute to. It's why I think the generosity of strangers stood out so much: we all have an adventurous spirit deep down, a desire to explore and go beyond our horizon, so we can't help but support those who are venturing beyond theirs.

I realised the value of 'organised spontaneity': though I had to intricately plan the permissions to fly into countries and follow aviation regulations, I kept the rest of the journey loose, so that I could react and engage with the environment around me. I realise it's a similar approach to how the Sun Theatre evolved, and in a world that changes so quickly I think it is how we can best find the path forward in most endeavours.

But whenever I have tried to express my journey in one sentence, I realise it is only for others that I'm seeking some magical summary. After nearly a year of reflection and discussion, I have come to this: *don't overthink it*. I had a dream, and I went and lived it. Sometimes we just need to be okay with going on an adventure because it will be fun and wondrous and fulfilling.

'Communerism', or socially conscious enterprise, is now my focus. It's about being community-focused, with economic sustainability allowing long-term growth and purpose. Every local cinema – whether privately owned or not-for-profit, in cities or in country towns, in changing, developing or underprivileged areas – has a unique and important role to play, and when nurtured they can be the heart of a community. I believe each of them can make their part of the world a better place, somewhere to gather for shared storytelling and rarely shared choc-tops.

Onwards and upwards.

'*Travelling – it leaves you speechless, then makes you a storyteller.*'
IBN BATTUTA, *THE TRAVELS* (CIRCA 1355)

Credit Roll

S pecial thanks to Morry, Chris, Julian, Rebecca and especially Aaron for bringing the *Southern Sun*'s story to print.

To Greg Ure, for his magnificent maps and illustrations, and to Jack Morrison for his Southern Sun postmark. I oh-so-proudly did a few drawings all by myself:

All photos were taken by me on my iPhone, GoPro or Garmin VIRB, except for: flying boat photos: Qantas Historical collection and Qantas Airways Ltd (thanks to David Crotty); departure at Williamstown: Timothy Smith; landing at Shannon: Malcolm Nason; Ireland in-air photos: Andrew Fenton and Adrian Corcoran; with the school kids: Ruth van Sommeren; Longreach photos: David Geers, Nicole Kuttner and Ashley Moore; Rylstone photos: Rob Loneragan and Ian Westlake.

I'd like to thank in Act i: the flying boat history gurus Matthew Holle, David Crotty, Phil Vabre and Cesare Baj; Michael Coates, XCOM Avionics; Michael McNamara, Simon Hooper and Jenna Davies from QBE Insurance; Rob and Kim Skyring from Transaero; Wal the Rotax Whisperer; Captain Jack Peters; Rod and Leonie Gunther; Andrew Thorne; PC David Seaman; David 'Daffy' Wallace; David Allen; Terry O'Hare; Ian Westlake; Chris Smith, Vanderlin Island; Tarmo, King Ash Bay; the guys who lent me their utes in Darwin!; Darwin's patient

341

air-traffic controllers; Angelo and Lou, Cinema Loro sa'e; Alex, Dili Airport; Wachira 'Jee' Chhatrakul na Ayudhya; Prakash Ranjan; Chef Rakesh Guniyal; Ahmed Naazer Minhaj; Pete 'Dingo' Forbes; Shane O'Hare; Yigal Merav; Amir Erez; Joel Pearlman (from Melbourne); Cesare Baj; Luigi Grasselli from Aviare S.R.L.; Francesco Frigerio; Mike Gray from White Rose Aviation; Chloe and Helen at Signature, Southampton; Captain Alistair in the Signature lounge; Deepak Mahajan.

In Act ii: Alan Sutton; members of the Damyns Hall Flying Club; John and Caroline Brennan; Margaret O'Shaughnessy; Andrew Fenton; Adrian Corcoran; Bryan Sheane; Gerry Humphreys; Malcolm Nason; members of the Limerick Flying Club; ILAS, The Patrick Gallagher Wing; Jacob Vadgaard; Ujarneq J. Serensen; Whoever in ATC Narsarsuaq found and posted my cashmere jumper; Thomas Branner Jespersen, president and sole member of the Greenland Flying Boat Club; Mary and Gary from Botwood Taxis; Mayor Jerry Dean; Deputy Mayor Scott Sceviour; Kerry Richter; Russell Brown; Paige Lynette; Angel Rivera; Dan Nickens; Jim Walsh; Adam Yang.

In Act iii: Kristen Messner; Jim, projectionist & organist extraordinaire; Capt. Karen Stemco; Capt. Burke Mees; Walter Fellows; Ross Mahon; Ben Ellison; Mary, Cold Bay Lodge; Lucinda, Chris (the mayor) and Marina from Atka; Julie and Molly; Ruth van Sommeren; Mike and Imelda, Blue Bird Cafe; Vince; Elaine; Peter Steeger; Taco san; the Seahawk crew in the South China Sea for not being trigger-happy; David Geers (from Brisbane, at his computer, I imagine in his PJ's); the residents of Rio Hondo; Skytrans Airways; Rebecca Hyde; Christopher Palmer; Paul Hewitt (Innisfail); Nicole, Shell Aviation; David Geers; Doug Bauer; Nicole Kuttner; Ashley Moore; Rob, Harriet, Phoebe, Toby and Tom Loneragan from Rylstone; John and Lynn Taylor; Helen, Glenn and Danielle from RYCV; and Rod Gunther (double thanks).

Thanks to the team at the Sun Theatre: Krissa Jansson, Lewis Thorne, Trish Tabone, Clare Vanderwarker, Sam McCabe, and and all the staff who just kept working while I kept not coming home.

Blimey, there are more thankyous here than an emotional Oscars speech. Are we there yet? Almost ...

Thank you to *Australian Geographic* for their 2016 Adventurer of the Year award. And to Bremont Watches (www.bremont.com) for their beautiful Supermarine watch, which was presented to me as part of the award.

There was a point in my journey when I wasn't sure I would make it. I came out stronger, though, realising that it's not just what we do, but also how we do it that matters. Thanks to John Price, Stuart Wood, Garry Fitzgerald, Siobhan Ryan, Andrew Taylor, John Geilings, my Anne and especially the Hon. Michelle Gordon.

To those who have inspired me along my 48-year journey thus far: Willy Wonka, Grandma and Grandpa Smith, Robin Lee Graham, Mike and Mal Leyland, Jonathan Livingston Seagull, Sir Winston Churchill, Greg Hunt, John F. Kennedy, Darryl Kerrigan, Sir Francis Chichester, John Bertrand AO, Howard Hughes, Michael Corleone, Alby Mangels, Dick Smith AC, Barry Peak, and Ferris Bueller.

Thanks to the birth-givers: Briony Smith and Geoffrey Smith (1948–2004), and Grandma Jean Smith.

And last but not least, to my family, for their love, patience and unwavering support: Anne Smith, Jack Morrison and Tim Smith.

The book was assembled and written in The Australian Club's library, Melbourne; at my grandfather's desk in my office at The Sun Theatre, Yarraville Village; a farm house in Praiano, Italy; ironically, on board many a Qantas flight; and even in transit in Mongolia (but that's another story).

Aaron worked on the book at home at Willoughby, holidaying at Portsea, and on a Carnival Cruise from Sydney to Sydney via, um, nowhere – but it was ideal for writing!

SOUTHERN SUN WILL RETURN IN *A VILLAGE SOMEWHERE*

Visit www.southernsun.voyage for more photos, information about the film of my journey, *Voyage of the Southern Sun*, and to follow the next adventure ...

Flying High

'*Just the facts, ma'am, just the facts.*'
JOE FRIDAY, *DRAGNET* (1987)

I was pretty chuffed at how well the *Southern Sun* performed on the trip. She really wasn't the ideal plane for a trip such as this, and in many ways I was lucky to make it. But she was the plane I was familiar with, and I did spend a lot of time preparing, so it felt right at the time to fly her. Although she made the journey low and slow, I was never interested in how quickly I could complete the trip.

This post-credits chapter features some of the journey's technical details, which would have slowed down the narrative had they been included in the main story. I've listed the equipment I used, statistics about the flight, and the questions I'm most regularly asked in Q&A sessions after a talk or a screening of *Voyage of the Southern Sun*, the film about my trip.

STATISTICS

Journey duration: 7 months, or 213 days
Countries visited: 25
Cities / towns: 80
Cinemas visited: 70, in 24 countries
Distance travelled: 32,500 nautical miles, or 57,500 kilometres

Days flown on trip: 82

Landed at: 93 airports and / or water bases

Fuel used: 9798 litres, roughly one-third avgas and two-thirds petrol

Flying hours before the trip: 450 over 12 years

Southern Sun hours before the trip: 250

Flying hours during the trip: 480 over 7 months

Records: First solo circumnavigation by flying boat

First solo circumnavigation by amphibious plane

Air Sport Australia Confederation: Melbourne–London, Rose Bay–Southampton, London–New York, Southampton–Port Washington

Awards: *Australian Geographic* Adventurer of the Year 2016

SPAA Ross Vining Exceptional Achievement Award

Royal Aero Club Silver Medal

Acts of Generosity: ∞

EQUIPMENT USED

I had no sponsors on the trip, so I selected and paid for items because I thought they were the best for the job at hand. I list the stand-outs here as a reference for others, and also to say thanks to the makers of such great products.

The *Southern Sun*: www.searey.com

Flight permission management: www.whiteroseaviation.co.uk

Spidertracks satellite tracking: www.spidertracks.com

Portable espresso machine: www.handspresso.com

Merino underwear, thermals: www.merinocountry.com.au

Merino shirts and trousers: www.toorallie.com.au

Fuel bladders (custom-made): www.fleximake.com.au

Barocook cooking system: www.barocook.net

Kangaroo leather boots: www.rmwilliams.com.au

Flying overalls: www.sisleyclothing.com.au

iPad apps and mounting: Avplan: www.avplan-efb.com

Meteo Earth: www.meteoearth.com

Mounts: www.quadlockcase.com.au

Equipment installed in Searey

Rotax 914 engine with Ivoprop IFA (since replaced with Airmaster)

MGL EFIS, Xcom radio, Microair Transponder

Inmarsat Isatphone

Vertical Power VPX circuit breaker system

Spidertracks satellite tracking

Little John flying range prolonging system

FREQUENTLY ASKED QUESTIONS

How did you go to the bathroom?

Carefully. Think hospital bed procedures. Never drink from the red bottle.

How did you prepare for the trip?

I knew I needed to lose some weight. I was on the wrong side of a tenth of a tonne, but rather than 'go on a diet' for a few years before the trip I slowly changed my habits: ate a little less, exercised a bit, did simple things like a hundred sit-ups and fifty-two push-ups a day to improve core strength. I managed to lose 25 kilograms this way. I was 88 kilograms when I left, 80 kilograms when I got home and hover around 83 kilograms today.

I did the fundamentals: ate smaller amounts more often, didn't eat bread (ouch) or pasta, and drank plenty of water. I started drinking a litre of water before breakfast and 2–3 litres through the rest of the day; this really seemed to help. In Scotland I became hooked on porridge, and perfected it when I was with Caroline in Ireland. Porridge still starts my day, every day.

Mentally, I was pretty focused on getting the plane and equipment ready. I trialled longer and longer flights in the plane to make sure the systems were working and that my body and mind were up to trip.

How did you manage fuel?

Getting fuel was one of the tiring parts of the trip. Not awful – just dull. I tried to use petrol whenever I could, as avgas often wasn't available or it was four to eight times the price of car fuel. That adds up! Getting petrol meant taking flexible jerry cans to a local petrol station. This, of course, involved driving there in a crew van or taxi and then transporting 160–180 litres of fuel in wobbly containers. Upon returning to the airport, I'd sometimes have to take the jerry cans through security, including X-ray machines, before returning to the plane. On average the whole task took about three hours – much longer than a truck pulling up and fuelling in, say, ten minutes tops.

Did you have to pay any bribes?

Not one. It was never asked or even hinted at.

How did you take seven months off work?

I think the key here was that I didn't leave with seven months in mind but three months, to get to London. Then I decided to continue to New York, and that would take just another month. Then another month … and, well, it just kept going!

What was the finding of your master's thesis?

I often hear the remark that 'going to the cinema is expensive in Australia', but I don't think that's true compared to other options for a night out. My research looked at the price in different countries of attending the cinema, the quality of the cinemas, and what the minimum and average wages were – so I could evaluate how long someone needs to work to see a movie. What I found is that Australia has some of the most comfortable cinemas in the world, with the personal area per patron at the higher end, and our affordability is one of the best, with the average Australian having to work only thirty minutes to buy a ticket. This is the same length of time as in the US but nearly half that in most European countries. In contrast, in Asia and the Middle East it can take up to 12 hours of work to afford a ticket. Given that the average movie ticket in Australia costs less than a pizza, yet the memory of a great movie lasts a lifetime, I think going to the cinema is great value, not to mention a wonderful way to escape from the world for a couple of hours. But, hey, I could be a tad biased!

Where is the *Southern Sun* now?
Ah ha! You can see where she is at anytime using the satellite tracking map at www.southernsun.voyage/where.

You did a lot of research during your trip. What was the most bizarre thing you discovered?
That more people die each year from taking selfies than from shark attacks!

For more answers to regularly asked questions, please go to the Q&A section on the website: www.southernsun.voyage/QnA. Have a read and feel free to post a question. I'll reply and share for others to see as well. Thanks for reading. Standing by.

Cheerio,
M.

[CURTAIN ELEGANTLY CLOSES]